GOVERNMENT AND POLITICS

JOBS FOR ALL
by Mordecai Ezekiel

THE NEW DEAL IN OLD ROME
by H. J. Haskell

BRASS TACKS
by A. G. Keller

THE COMING VICTORY OF DEMOCRACY
THIS PEACE
by Thomas Mann

DEMOCRACY AND SOCIALISM
by Arthur Rosenberg

These are Borzoi Books, published by
ALFRED A. KNOPF

FOUNDATIONS
OF DEMOCRACY

FOUNDATIONS
OF
DEMOCRACY

A Series of Debates

BY

T. V. SMITH
REPRESENTATIVE FROM ILLINOIS

and

ROBERT A. TAFT
SENATOR FROM OHIO

NEW YORK · ALFRED · A · KNOPF · *LONDON*

1939

NOTE

THIS BOOK is a collection of a series of broadcasts, arranged and produced by the Columbia Broadcasting System under the title *Foundations of Democracy*. The purpose of the series, as set forth by CBS, was to give a practical demonstration of the effectiveness of the democratic method of government and way of life. These eminent speakers, of clearly opposed political views, sought not to generate controversy, but, by commentary on the day-to-day functioning of our government and on our economic and social life, to find a common ground for agreement. Their purpose was to show that the democratic method of public criticism and controversy is, at its best, not destructive but constructive; that it results in continuous self-rectification of excesses in government and economics, and works its way slowly but securely to a condition in which the greatest amounts of personal welfare and of liberty are enjoyed by average citizens.

The thirteen debates in this historic series took place on successive Tuesday evenings, from February 21st to May 16th, 1939.

CONTENTS

CONTENTS

viii

FOUNDATIONS OF
DEMOCRACY

I

THE AMERICAN WAY OF LIFE

REPRESENTATIVE SMITH

KINSMEN in Texas, neighbors in Illinois, friends in Maine; women and men of America: greetings from Washington.

To join for thirteen weeks now in timely discussion with the junior Senator from Ohio, Mr. Taft, is a patriotic privilege for a son of the South and a present citizen of the Middle Border. The calendar of the season is dotted with distinguished symbols of our common concern. Two Sundays ago we celebrated a national martyr of my own state (Mr. Taft spoke at Cincinnati, I at Chicago) — celebrated this man, Lincoln, whose life and death saved the Union. Tomorrow we pause to acknowledge the greatness of one whose faith and

3

steadfastness gave this nation birth — Washington. Only six Sundays away we shall commemorate the name of the great Virginian, Jefferson, who spiritualized our early Revolution with an immortal declaration of faith in mankind and who later as Chief Executive wonderfully widened the boundaries of the Republic which Washington had founded and which Lincoln was to save.

In between, only ten days hence, Mr. Taft and I will join in celebrating here with our fellow-servants of the Republic the hundred and fiftieth anniversary of the national Congress, to the separate branches of which he and I are honored to belong.

I have no doubt that I speak for the Senator as for myself in saying that in the presence of so gracious a cloud of witnesses, living and dead, any narrow partisanship will be lifted from meanness to magnanimity by the patriotism which we share — share with each other and share with you, our fellow-countrymen.

I

The American way, to which we now turn our attention, is a way of life as well as a way of law and government. So much of the public talk of government is done by lawyers that we are tempted to forget — lawyers are, at least — that the American way is a way of life — of life the first and final object of government. Throughout these discussions I shall tax myself to remember this humble thing which citizens are less tempted than lawyers to forget: that in the beginning was life, that life is a living thing, and that life is by all rights a lovely thing.

This humane emphasis upon life, as distinct from law, sets us Americans apart from foreign fanaticisms and sometimes leaves us at odds with one another — not enough at odds with one another, however, to allow a patriot to call a fellow-citizen a communist unless he be a Communist, nor a fascist unless he be a Fascist, nor a fellow-American a Nazi at all. To escape fanaticism we must find names non-fanatical for one another here at home. As a matter of fact, this distinction between life and law is allowed by our Constitution itself. After setting up governmental machinery for the manufacture of law, the construing of law, the execution of law, our fathers turned around and said, as it were, in the Bill of Rights: " But most of life is to be exempted from the reign of law." They exempted, first, what law cannot cover if it would — thoughts and feelings; and then they exempted what law should not cover if it could — speech, assembly, family privacy, religious worship, etc. In this guaranteed oasis of freedom from law, what is the faith by which we Americans live, and what the common characteristics arising from our practice of that faith?

Well, beginning in a wilderness and driven together by loneliness, we Americans have at length built here on this continent a way of life whose faith is that there is a common touch of nature that makes all men kin — all races, all religions, all cultures. Regardless of political party, we Americans believe, for instance, that all

5

children of all the people are entitled equally to both health and education. Or do we — with about one-third of our children growing up in the South on but one-sixth of the nation's school revenues? We believe that all life is equally sacred and must be equally secure under the law. Or do we — with gangsterdom now and then a-shooting in the cities of the North and barbarism then and now a-lynching in the counties of the South? We believe that all questions that cannot be settled otherwise must be settled by the ballot. Or do we — with half the citizens unencouraged to vote in the South and oftentimes a third of them unwilling to vote in the North?

Don't we or do we — believe, I mean, in these ideals of equal opportunity, equal protection, equal participation? We do; we do believe in all these ideals. They represent yet and ever our faith, our way of thought, if you will. But they do not fully represent our way of life. We have still to find out how to take up the slack between our way of thought and our way of life. This disturbing leeway between what we love and the way we live is the penance we pay for being at once more than human and less than human — for being both sky-born and earth-bound.

Forgetting its pathos, we may with some unknown poetaster nail this our common shame to the crucifix of fun:

> There was a dachshund once, so long
> He hadn't any notion
> How long it took to notify

6

His tail of his emotion;
And so it happened, while his eyes
Were filling with woe and sadness,
His little tail went wagging on
Because of previous gladness.

II

But, seriously now, midway between pathos and bathos, Americanism as a way of life is a large faith in, and a smaller practice of, what we of ourselves do so well know: *friendliness, humility, humor.*

Friendly everybody admits us Americans to be. We were a "folksy" people long before the Germans made a barbaric cult of the "*Volk.*" The hardships of the frontier, as I have said, compelled us to be friendly. More than once we've had to hang together to keep from hanging separately. Intolerance is a vice which we Americans cannot afford. We came of different religions even while yet of the same race, and later we added vast differences of race to those of religion. We had to learn friendliness not only with friends but, as it were, with enemies. We had to learn, and did learn, to stomach opposition without suppressing opponents. We Americans have learned, in a word, that men do not have to kiss in order to coöperate. We forgo Americanism when we forget that this, our preference for friendliness, is the secret of our success in subduing a continent to the life of man.

This friendliness it is that renders wholesome rather than morbid the *humility* of the American character.

7

Our glad reliance on one another arises from the clear knowledge that we are not God. Humility is born of helplessness and exists to make us strong where we are weak.

That's what gentility of the ballot means, as contrasted with the coercion of bullies. Whoever knows for certain that he's not God is glad to welcome the aid of other men in determining what's politically right. Voting as such an aid reduces the risks of ignorance and doubles our joy in talk. It's a clever device, this balloting business — and profound. It helps us " to split the difference," as we used to say in Texas, and to achieve on a large national scale the golden mean of compromise. We Americans think it literally more important thus to settle issues between us than it is to settle them absolutely right.

This is so because we admit that God alone knows what's absolutely right. We men do know what's friendly and decent. So in decency to one another we've agreed to call right whatever nobody kicks over the traces about. How profoundly we differ from some others in this regard! Now come fascists to share God's prerogative and communists to monopolize it. This leaves many of us plain American citizens (with only revolutionists and immigrants for ancestors) hardly knowing which way to turn. So we just turn back in all friendliness to one another, and we covenant once more to take stock with ourselves and to abide by whatever we can agree upon, whether any of us are fully satisfied with it or not. That's the democratic principle, and that's the decent thing to do.

But we don't do this with a long face. We've found out that it's really helpful to be humble and downright fun to be friendly. In a century we've turned out more than our share of fine *humorists*. The juice of their laughter has kept us " unlaxed." Moreover, we've all become humorists, knowing well, as the proverb has it, that only he who tickles himself may laugh when he likes. When I see, as last week, a diminutive Senator (Glass) straining out a maximum snarl and see a towering Executive (Roosevelt) contriving a minimum retort to the maximum snarl, I do not despair of my country or turn from Washington in disgust. The rather, I hie me away to the privacy of my citizenship and lave myself luxuriously in the Lethe of life with the cleansing soap of self-forgetful humor, crooning to myself the while these delicious lines from some anonymous poet:

> I sometimes think I'd rather crow
> And be a rooster than to roost
> And be a crow. But I dunno.

> A rooster he can roost also,
> Which don't seem fair when crows can't crow.
> Which may help some. Still I dunno.

> Crows should be glad of one thing, though;
> Nobody thinks of eating crow.
> While roosters they are good enough
> For anyone unless they're tough.

> There are lots of tough old roosters, though
> And anyway a crow can't crow,
> So mebbe roosters stand more show,
> It looks that way. But I dunno.

America is safe for Americanism as long as it retains its sense of humor; for *humor* keeps our *humility* from becoming sticky and makes our *friendliness* function fruitfully. It punctures pomp and purifies pretense. Give us, then, another Mark Twain, who could say, " Do right always; this will gratify some persons and will astonish the rest." Give us another Clarence Darrow, who could so sagely admit that " Calvin Coolidge was the greatest man who ever came out of Plymouth Corner, Vermont." Give us, especially us politicians, another Will Rogers, who like some gawky hill-billy from the heights of humor could toss us right and left tablets of sanity unwrapped in cellophane. Peace to the ashes of these ageless men. Wherever they, or such as they, lie fallen and silent, there is the glimmer of a smile and a fleck of mortal dust that is forever American.

One such humorist glorifies a nation more than a whole crop of strutting dictators — " little men in trousers slightly jagged " on their own braggadocio. I'd rather be an apostle of human merriment and go smilingly down to the " tongueless silence of the dreamless dust " than to be the most pompous pretender to power or claimant of perfection that ever dirtied with pretense his little day on earth.

III

While, then, Germany thumbs her nose at the world, chewing to pieces her own tongue in a fit of epileptic frenzy; while Italy bedecks bravado with the smelly trappings of an empire long deceased; while Russia trades tarnished tyranny for tyranny tarnishing before our very eyes — let us proud Americans pursue the tenor of our democratic ways, compromising conflicts and transforming factual realism into an idealism of hope through the friendly discipline of humility and humor. That's the American way of life under law, and of law for the sake of a larger life.

These precious principles of our way of life are better fastened to effectiveness if we ground them in persons whom we treasure. Take Hamilton and Jefferson. Answer for yourselves this question: Why did Hamilton and Jefferson permit each other to live and be so troublesome? — answer that question and you have the secret of the continuing genius of our common way of life in which everybody's as good as anybody, if not a little better. Each of these giants somehow needed the other, as the nation needed both. What's more, each sensed his need of the other. Theirs was a sportsmanship at the prime not required by the etiquette of the day, and monstrous to totalitarian tyrants of our own time. But it was a sportsmanship on which rested then, and rests today, the only worth-while citizenship. These men had learned the deep lesson of tolerance, of progress through conflict.

The lives and hates of these men remind us that the American Way has been historically a lusty lane, not an extended leafy bower soft with the moonlight of romance. We have known how to pass simple words of sauciness, with now and then a cordial look of hate. The Republic was founded with nobody knowing what kind of Republic it was to be. There was room in America, as some one has suggested, for " an aristocratic republic, or a plutocratic republic, or a democratic republic, and the men who made and fought the Revolution divided upon these ideas. These divisions grew out of the varying faith of men in the capacity of the people to rule themselves." This was a battle that from the beginning waxed and waned. The dashing Patrick Henry of " liberty or death " resolve while the foe was foreign, slipped over to favor the " alien and sedition " infamy when the time came to defend at home the liberty he had helped win from abroad. The ambitious Aaron Burr, with no lasting loyalty save to his own personal star, played from side to side as popularity listed. But on each side stood such stalwarts as Jefferson and Hamilton, so opposed to each other that had the stolid Washington not stood between them like Gibraltar, somebody might have won more than the infant republic could stand and stomach. But a principle early emerged in America that summarizes all principles of humane authority: the principle that persons must be allowed breathing room, even though they, like Hamilton and Jefferson, breathe mostly fire at each other.

The Fathers learned this lesson. It is a lesson which

destiny must re-teach us sons, if we allow our memories to relax. "Some teacher of the kind we all need," as Justice Oliver Wendell Holmes says bitingly, "in order that we may remember all that buffoons forget."

~~~~~~

SENATOR TAFT

It is a pleasure and a privilege for me to join in this series of broadcasts on the Foundations of Democracy with Representative T. V. Smith. In the theoretical field I cannot hope to compete with one who is a full-fledged professor of philosophy at the University of Chicago, and even in the practical field it will not be easy to compete with a professor who has been able to translate his theoretical knowledge into political success in a great state like Illinois. This series is intended to be not so much a debate as a development of two points of view regarding present-day conditions in the United States. Perhaps it is the same point of view with merely a difference in emphasis.

What is the American way of life? To determine that, we must look back over the one hundred and sixty years of this nation's existence. In that period it has grown from a small community of four million people along the Atlantic seaboard to the greatest and most prosperous nation in the world today, with thirty times that population. This success has been achieved under an economic and constitutional system which was unique when established, and formed the basis of an American way of life which has remained, certainly until today, peculiarly American. The basis of the American business and constitutional system is political and economic liberty. The basis of the American way of life has been equal opportunity to improve one's condition by one's own effort. The Declaration of Independence declared that all men are created equal, that they are endowed by their Creator with certain unalienable rights, and that among these are life, liberty, and the pursuit of happiness. It is somewhat significant that the right endowed is not one of happiness but merely of its pursuit.

The rights asserted by the Declaration of Independence and conferred by the Constitution are individual rights. They are conferred on each individual, not on any class of people or on society in general. The whole history of America reveals a system based on individual opportunity, individual initiative, individual freedom to earn one's own living in one's own way, and to conduct manufacture, commerce, agriculture, or other business; on rugged individualism, if you please, which it has become so fashionable to deride.

The American way of life has attempted to reward, by increase in material welfare, those individual qualities of intelligence, ability, industry, genius, and daring which have played such a great part in building up the nation as we see it today. The basis of the system has been opportunity for all. The motive power has been the incentive to effort provided in material reward; that is, a better standard of living, a better education for one's children, a better provision for one's family after death.

I, too, believe that the American way of life is not synonymous with its governmental or constitutional system, but unquestionably Government and Constitution have protected the conditions which make it possible. The American way of life is a flexible, living, breathing philosophy, which is continually adjusting itself to meet the changing needs of a growing nation. The Government was designed to fit that philosophy and be controlled by it, and not to regulate and control that philosophy. Government has been generally conceived to be a keeper of the peace, a referee of controversies, and an adjuster of abuses, not a regulator of the people, or their way of life, or their business and personal activities. Throughout a large part of our history the maxim was accepted that that government is best which governs least. Life has become so complex that we feel today that more positive government action is necessary to preserve the American way of life; but the statement of President Garfield is still true: " It is a safe and wise rule to follow in all legislation, that whatever the people can do without legislation will be better done than by the intervention of the state and nation."

The ideal of opportunity characterizing the American

way of life led very quickly to universal free education. Obviously a child who is not taught to read and write does not have the same opportunity to succeed in life. The public school became the typical American institution. Obviously this does not mean the same education for every child. If it did, we would have to send every boy and girl through college and add perhaps three years of training in some professional or vocational school. It does mean a good foundation in reading, writing, arithmetic, and other fundamentals, and access to the books on which an education can be built. Abraham Lincoln had a most elementary education, and yet that education gave him the opportunity to rise to the greatest position which any American has ever occupied. The American way of life certainly does not guarantee equality in mental power or in character or in energy. It has only guaranteed that a man who had the necessary qualities might rise in public life and acquire a greater influence, a greater fame, a greater power, than his fellows; that he might rise in material wealth and acquire a greater comfort and luxury, if he desires it, for himself and his family; that he might earn a simple living on which he could base the development of true happiness for himself and his family without either wealth or power.

It is no reflection on the present plans for social security to point out that security has not been an important factor in the American way of life. Perhaps it should have been. In a country of great natural resources and the ability to begin life over again in a new field, there has perhaps been too much of the spirit of the gambler in America. But even today, while social security may be a desirable adjunct, it is no American ideal. The slaves of good masters in the South, before the Civil War, enjoyed social security. So did the lotus-eaters. If American progress is to continue, the greater rewards must still be for industry, for intelligence, for ability. Opportunity, and not security, is still the goal of young America, and even of middle-aged and old America. The burden of security for those who cannot work must not be so heavy as to destroy or seriously reduce opportunity for those who can work.

No system is perfect. The American way of life has not proceeded without injustice to some, but in general it has worked. The names of the Presidents of the United States, together with all those who have succeeded in public life, reveal a long list of men who rose from nothing, men who were no better off when they began than millions of their fellow-countrymen. And this is true today. Not long ago I attended a dinner of the Gridiron Club, where were gathered leaders in every field of activity in the United States, politics, journalism, industry, agriculture, the professions. I checked over that list as far as I was able. Four-fifths of those men, even today when the system does not work quite so satisfactorily as in a simpler age, were men who had no privileges when they began, men whose families were not different from four-fifths of the families in the United States. They have succeeded through their own individual efforts, not because they belonged

17

to any class or any family. The system has even worked to permit the success of men handicapped by wealthy and privileged parents; witness the present President of the United States. And that is not intended to be humorous; even the Christian philosophy makes it almost impossible for a rich man to enter the Kingdom of Heaven, but the true American way of life recognizes no distinction of origin.

But it is said today that we are not preserving the American way of life and that we must engage in unlimited Government interference and regulation in order to preserve it. It is said that wealth has acquired privileges, and that it has caused one-third of the people to be underprivileged and has deprived them of the opportunity to improve their position, and therefore we must redistribute wealth. Fundamentally, I do not think that the American way of life has changed, though unquestionably the long depression and particularly the serious unemployment conditions have interfered with opportunity to a very considerable group of families and their children. I would estimate that loss of opportunity as affecting rather one-sixth of the people than one-third, but even then it presents a serious challenge to the American ideal of opportunity. The increase of industrialization makes the problem much greater in urban industrial districts than it is in rural America. Last year I traveled through every county in the State of Ohio, and it is interesting to see that in most of the small towns and country districts the American system is still more popular than in the cities. The people realize that the leaders of their communities, whether they like them or not, have usually succeeded by reason of their own ability, character, and intelligence; that those who have failed have failed because they lack those qualities.

Nevertheless, a condition of poverty in city and country alike does interfere with opportunity. The Government, therefore, must and has undertaken to relieve this condition, to provide a minimum, through relief, old-age pensions, unemployment insurance, or otherwise, which will enable a family to live, and the children to go to school and pursue their education. The Government has undertaken to provide housing for the poorer people.

I doubt whether the condition has been brought about by excessive accumulation of wealth, but certainly the Government should see that wealth is not improperly acquired through monopolistic or other unfair practices. The policies of inheritance taxation are rapidly cutting down the larger fortunes, and I think that in America there is plenty of evidence that the old maxim still prevails, " From shirt-sleeves to shirt-sleeves in three generations." Certainly the arbitrary redistribution of wealth would not assist in restoring the American way of life, because it would absolutely destroy all the incentive and initiative through which our success has been created.

There is one other mistake which economic planners are too likely to make. People cannot be made happy by opportunity and education alone. We cannot legis-

19

late them into leadership and equality. They can only secure happiness through their own individual effort. We cannot make their work pleasant and agreeable, because nine-tenths of all work in this world is drudgery and can only be made agreeable by the person who is doing it teaching himself to enjoy the accomplishment of a task, no matter how uninteresting that task may appear to others.

We cannot accomplish the American ideal by education alone. There has never been a time when people have had so many means of education — public schools, the movies, the radio, libraries with books of every type. We have made it exceedingly easy to acquire knowledge, but we have fallen down in our job of teaching men to think. No man ever succeeded or progressed until he acquired the ability to do his own thinking.

What the Government must do is to provide the conditions under which it is possible for the people to achieve individual progress, and much of the increased Government activity in recent years is justified on that ground. But Government help cannot even produce the increased standard of living which we would all like to see, and there is one danger in it which threatens the very foundation of the American way of life. It must be administered so that the people generally are not taught to lean on the Government and let other people think for them. It must be administered with the determination to retain and not destroy the rewards which heretofore we have always given for industry, thrift, and intelligence. In improving the condition of one-third of the people, we must not drag down the other two-thirds to a lower standard of living and a lower incentive to intelligent, directed effort. In the tendency to rely on Government to cure every ill, we stand in danger of depriving the people of initiative, of thinking power, and ultimately of happiness itself. The Government certainly must assure every family of conditions on which opportunity may be based. It must prevent interference with individual and commercial liberty wherever it is threatened by the power of wealth, but it must be certain that it does not substitute for this threat from the power of wealth the threat from the power of arbitrary government itself. The American way of life is still substantially with us. If we pursue the proper policies, it can be preserved.

THE CONSTITUTION—WRITTEN
AND UNWRITTEN

SENATOR TAFT

WHY have a Constitution? We have heard it denounced as a bar to progress. We have heard the men who wrote it, Washington, Franklin, Madison, Hamilton, Randolph, and others, denounced by Irving Brant and Morris L. Ernst as interested only in protecting their own pocketbooks. President Roosevelt does not seem to like the Constitution unless it is construed just the way he wants it construed. The scoffer says, "What's the Constitution between friends?"

Well, the greatest value of the Constitution is to keep all our public officials from bossing us around. If it were not for the Constitution, the Government could tell us what we could eat for breakfast and how we should comb our hair; the Government could pass laws to take away our property, and even take away our lives. Many governments have just that kind of power when there is no effective constitution, and it is not a prospect that anyone can contemplate today with comfort or pleasure. If the Constitution were repealed, or construed away to have no meaning, it would not be long before our government became more and more arbitrary, and more and more like Germany, Italy, and Russia.

No one who reads history can seriously question the intense and disinterested patriotism which moved the men who drafted the Constitution in their effort to create a nation. For that purpose they made every compromise, and accepted provisions which often differed from their individual opinions and interests. The history of the United States is a testimony to the success of their efforts.

But these men and those who ratified the Constitution deliberately limited the powers of government because they were afraid of arbitrary government. They had had experience with it, and they didn't like it. They knew also that many republics in the past had slipped into despotism even while preserving the forms of a republic. They were students of government, and they knew how the democracies of Greece had developed into tyrannies. They knew that under all the forms of a republic, powers under the Roman state were gradually concentrated in one man until he became in fact the arbitrary emperor of the Roman Empire. They knew that the granting of unlimited power on every subject, even to a popular majority, would lead ultimately to unlimited power in an individual or a class. They knew that if all the powers of government were concentrated in one man or one group of men, it would not be long before the exercise of those powers became arbitrary and dictatorial. They tell a story about old Benjamin Franklin as he came out of the Constitutional Convention. He was asked, " Dr. Franklin, have you given us a monarchy or a republic? " His reply was, " A republic, if you can keep it so."

And so they imposed three great limitations on the power of the national government. First, the national government was made a government with power to deal with only certain national matters, and all powers not granted were reserved to independent states or to the people. We are told that state lines have become artificial and have no meaning, but except for state independence, local matters, like schools, roads, cities, would soon be governed by the arbitrary will of Washington. The founders knew that preservation of local home rule was essential to real liberty. They had seen before the Revolution that government from a distant capital, like London, was bound to be tyrannical. It is impossible for any man or any board, no matter how well-intentioned, to make detailed regulations for all sections of the United States which will really fit more than a very few localities. To the rest of the nation

24

those regulations are tyranny because the people have had no effective voice in their making, and they are not the regulations they desire.

Of course it is true that in the growing complexity of modern life more matters have come to acquire a national interest and have passed beyond the power of the states to control. It is true that more matters have come within the scope of the power to regulate interstate commerce conferred by the Constitution. But laws telling the farmer what he can plant and what he can't plant, and regulating even retail trade, the administration of local work relief by Federal officers, and the proposals to control all local health, welfare, and education through the use of Federal funds, have seriously infringed on the rights of local self-government guaranteed by the Constitution. The real New Dealers would like to abolish the states and give all power of government to Washington. They resent any opinion of the Court which recognizes a limit to the powers given by the interstate commerce clause. Unless there is a limit somewhere, however, there is an end to local self-government, and soon to liberty itself.

In the second place, the founders of the Constitution carefully separated the powers of the national government between the executive, legislature, and judiciary, so that no one branch should be able to exercise all of even the limited powers given to the Federal Government. They knew that if the legislature delegated all powers to the executive, and if the judiciary were made subservient to the executive, it would be but a short time before a dictatorship would put an end to any actual rule of the people.

In the Supreme Court bill of 1937 the President attempted to destroy the independence of the courts. The bill gave him power to appoint six additional judges, and his unquestioned purpose was to appoint men who would decide every case the way he wished to have it decided. The bill was constitutional, but if there is an unwritten part of our Constitution, it is that the fundamental principles embodied in the Constitution shall not be violated even by powers granted in the Constitution itself. The attempt to destroy the Government was so clear that the people rose up in violent protest. The bill was defeated by a Senate of which a vast majority were members of the President's party. The report of the majority of the Judiciary Committee, most of them Democrats, said of the bill:

> It would subjugate the courts to the will of Congress and the President, and thereby destroy the independence of the judiciary, the only certain shield of individual rights. It stands now before the country, acknowledged by its proponents as a plan to force judicial interpretation of the Constitution, a proposal that violates every sacred tradition of American democracy.
>
> Under the form of the Constitution, it seeks to do that which is unconstitutional.
>
> Its ultimate operation would be to make this government one of men rather than one of law, and its practical operation would be to make the Constitution what the executive or legislative branches of the government

choose to say it is — an interpretation to be changed with each change of administration.

It is a measure which should be so emphatically rejected that its parallel will never again be presented to the free representatives of the free people of America.

This attempt to destroy the division of powers was the measure which first shook the people's confidence in the President and led to the extraordinary reversals of public opinion in the elections of 1938.

In the third place, the people of the thirteen states insisted, as a condition of the ratification of the Constitution, on the express limitations of the Bill of Rights contained in the first ten amendments. No limitation on government is more typical of the American system than the Bill of Rights. It provides, in effect, that even the power of the majority of the people shall never be used to tyrannize over any minority, no matter how small that minority. On the coldly formal words of the first ten amendments depend the right to worship according to a man's own religion; the freedom of speech and of the press; the right to assemble; the right to be secure against unreasonable searches and seizures; the right to trial by jury; the right to life, liberty, and property. If these rights were suspended to give arbitrary power to a majority of the people, it would not be long before the arbitrary power so conferred would be usurped by a small group or an individual. It is probably true that in their zeal to protect these rights the courts have given too much effect to the so-called due-process clause. In a complicated modern nation, individual rights must be more curtailed than in the simple American colonies of the eighteenth century. But a complete planned economy under which the Federal Government regulates prices, hours, wages, and every detail of business and agricultural life, is impossible to administer without abandoning many of the protections given by the Bill of Rights. Whether we wish to abandon any of those rights may be debatable, but we can hardly criticize the courts for giving them effect.

Finally, the founders set out their checks and balances in a written Constitution and gave an independent judiciary the right to construe it. Some question the right of the courts to declare laws unconstitutional, but without that power the limitations imposed would have been meaningless, because Congress and the majority it represents are seldom restrained from doing what they wish to do to any minority by the mere words of the Constitution. As Madison and Hamilton said in Volume II of *The Federalist:*

> The complete independence of the courts of justice is peculiarly essential in a limited constitution . . . Limitations of this kind can be preserved in practice no other way than through the medium of courts of justice, whose duty it must be to declare all acts contrary to the manifest tenor of the Constitution void. Without this, all the reservations of particular rights or privileges would amount to nothing.

28

Those who wish to destroy the independence of the courts, those who wish to construe constitutional limitations away until they mean nothing, are in fact desirous of destroying the Constitution itself. Their course, whether intentional or otherwise, is directed towards an all-powerful state.

The Constitution is our bulwark today against both fascism and communism, and against the bitter conflict between them, which is destroying Spain and threatens to destroy Europe. No constitution can be perfect, and it may be highly desirable to make additional changes. As George Washington said in his Farewell Address, "The basis of our political systems is the right of the people to make and to alter their constitution of governments. But the Constitution which at any time exists, until changed by an explicit and authentic act of the whole people, is sacredly obligatory upon all."

The Constitution did not create the American way of life; the character of that life has changed and extended since it was adopted; but it did impose certain restraints on the exercise of governmental power which have prevented democracy from destroying itself. The progress of America has been due to the retention of the spirit of liberty and individual initiative, kept alive by the freedom of the different localities and the freedom of the individual.

All over the world we have seen how easy it is for a temporary majority of the people to turn over all the powers of government to a dictator, and how difficult it is ever to recover those powers once they are delegated. Such a thing cannot happen in this country as long as we revere the Constitution, as long as we retain an independent judiciary with power to interpret it, as long as we refuse to listen to those sirens who would construe away the essential restraints which the founders so wisely imposed.

REPRESENTATIVE SMITH

I'M only an ignorant man and a Congressman at Large from Illinois; but even I can see that the Constitution of the United States, like Caesar's Gaul, is divided into three parts. There's, first, the Bill of Rights, which, admitting the poverty of political power, declares what our Government will not do. We Democrats and Republicans are agreed on that part, for it tells us what our rights are. In the second part, where duties begin, differences begin. (These differences, of last week and this, will presently be given a perspective above the low level of partisan debate.) This second part of the Constitution sets up the three branches of government, describes their duties, and provides for amendments.

Then there's the third part, which isn't in the Constitution at all, but which makes what's written there live and grow. To the Fathers the Constitution was " an opinion and a hope "; they had to write it in words to keep it from being written in water. To us, their sons, it has become so much an institution and a hope fulfilled that we love it as though we had read it. The historic miracle of turning that legal mechanism into this living organism which we love, that is the inner story of our Constitution's life.

I

Prosaic people think the Constitution is just the Constitution — and not another thing. To them the flag would be, I fancy, only " a bit of bunting." But has not an authority no less great than Chief Justice Hughes told us that the Constitution is what the Court says it is, at any given time? We know, too, without his telling us, that there are at least two Supreme Courts; the court of the Justices who construe the Constitution strictly and the court of the Justices who give the Constitution the benefit of the growth that springs from its " implied powers."

These differing points of view are inevitable, and so intelligent men must respect each other's honesty, as do Senator Taft and I, across this age-old line. The view, here as elsewhere, depends upon which point of view we take. And there's the rub; for the point of view that interprets the Constitution is not itself in the written document. This first unwritten article has uses more momentous, too, than to damn legislation which

one admits to be constitutional but happens nevertheless not to like.

The second article of the unwritten portion has to
do with leadership as between the three separated
branches of government. Mr. Taft defends the right of
the Court to the final say. He reads this right from *The
Federalist*. I do not read it in the Constitution. But
both of us can see it firmly planted in history, and
neither of us, I take it, would relish a quarrel with history in fifteen minutes. So let that pass for the moment,
with the simple observation that the Constitution is also
served by a Court that sometimes stoops to conquer.
Constitutions are documents made by history-makers,
and their questions obtrude themselves anew as creak-
ings of the political machinery in every nation's recurring rendezvous with the quickening consciences of
the people.

As between Congress and the President, however,
history is equivocal. The Constitution does *define*
the powers of each, but it does not *confine* the prowess
of either. A strong President will, like the untamed
bridegroom, say to a weak Congress, or a strong Congress to a timorous President, "You and I am one, but
I is de one." But that's been going too long a time to
justify hysteria. The Fathers left, and were glad to
leave, something for their sons to settle. They separated the powers but left inexact the accommodation to
each other of these separated powers. This flexible arrangement as regards initiative is not something to rant
over, I believe, or to shout "dictatorship" or "rubber

stamp " about. A see-saw between Congress and the President saves us from boredom, and we thank the Fathers for that; but merely to go up and down is not really to get ahead. Progress requires leadership. Echoing the Senator's earlier words, I may suggest that no Congress can legislate itself into leadership, any more than any President can fix himself into preëminence by simple fiat. Leadership is imperative if government is to govern rather than to grovel; but *leadership is as leadership does*. That's the second unwritten article of our Constitution.

The third is a sort of hidden prelude to the great Preamble of our national charter. It reads, when written out, " All experience hath shown that mankind are more disposed to suffer while evils are sufferable, than to right themselves by abolishing the forms to which they are accustomed." This article gives us powerful, even if gentle, warning against that conservative rheumatism of the mind that would delay action until the only remedy that's left is revolution. In a check-and-balance system like ours, we need this warning to keep the checks from producing a balance befitting only the graveyard. Inertia has not been, and is not now, a prudent policy for a great state.

II

Let me write down now, in reverse and cumulative order, this unwritten lore: first, *all good things may lapse through lethargy;* second, *prowess remains as the quality which fixes and unfixes constitutional power;*

and, third, *nothing that's written is either great or small but thinking makes it so.* To forget these precious unwritten things is to neglect the one quality which statesmanship requires: Imagination. To forgo imagination is to doom the Constitution to its death by making it a cult. Constitutional*ism,* the cult, then becomes, in the wily words of a contemporary scholar, " the name given to the trust which men repose in the power of words engrossed on parchment to keep a government in order." [1] Wise men will not press the preternatural patience of mankind beyond the power of " sufferance." It is a bad thing for a growing nation to discourage creative constitutional work. The pathos of it is that conservatives do just this with the most stodgy honesty — an honesty that lacks only one thing to make it magnificent, the imagination to see others as others feel themselves to be.

III

This lack of imagination is the error, if I may respectfully suggest it, that leads conservatives, like Mr. Taft, to suggest that the American way of life has not changed since the Constitution's birth. So they say, but it appears otherwise. For one simple thing — and it I emphasize without animus — when the Constitution was written, there were less than two dozen business corporations in America.

Individual rights then belonged to plain individuals; for otherwise there was only the Federal Government,

---

[1] Walton Hamilton in the *Encyclopedia of the Social Sciences,* on " Constitutionalism."

which voluntarily renounced such rights, and then the states, which were later required to renounce them. To-day legion is the number — actually more than half a million — of these constitutionally unexpected entities that occupy the leeway left by the Constitution between individual citizens and their government. These curious half-breeds of the law, soulless always, though sinister only when uncontrolled, have come tripping along with the bloodless machines to make so easy our living but so arduous our modern life. Knowing no good and evil but only profits and losses, corporations have by the grace of lawyers acquired the rights of persons without assuming fully the responsibilities of citizenship. Outside of agriculture today, it is practically impossible to discover the individual citizen save through a network of corporate organizations retailing to him such individual rights as are judged compatible with prior corporate claims.

This single difference was enough to justify the exclamation of Mr. Charles Taft in the Landon campaign of '36. "The truth is," said Mr. Taft, "nothing which concerns this nation of 120,000,000 people can ever be simple again." This single difference was enough to render statesmanlike and conservative the recommendation to Congress by President Taft in 1910 of a voluntary Federal incorporation act involving, as he put it, "complete Federal supervision and control." [1]

This single difference is enough to explain the constitutional crisis witnessed to this day by the amazing

[1] *Messages and Papers of the Presidents*, XVII, 7449-58.

change of popular attitude toward our central government — a change from general enmity in the days of our fathers to genuine friendliness today.

This single difference is enough to explain why security, social and economic, has become an American ideal, whatever conservatives think ought or ought not to be ideal. It is not merely *an* ideal; it has become almost *the* ideal of our time. Nor is the ideal new, but only now conspicuous. Manufacturers called early for security while exploiting their opportunity, and the Government gave them the tariff for their pains. Later, railroads called for security while exploiting their opportunity, and the Government gave them, as it also at the same time gave more luckless men, the western lands for their joint security. Shall we reverse the constitutional trend of a century merely because more people, including more corporations, are now in greater need of security (which corporations and conservatives call "confidence")? Is opportunity to be left unsecured only when men, and machines, are down and out?

We Democrats would not act so if we could, nor could we if we would. We could not, for nobody really sees today in any country of this mad world how to discharge the ancient duties of government — for inner order and outside peace — without undertaking what even the conservative Lippmann has called the "new imperative," the duty of guaranteeing by Government a minimum standard of life for all citizens. It was this necessity, and this danger, that finally brought Mr.

Hoover around grudgingly to what Mr. Roosevelt has continued gladly.

As we Democrats could not turn our backs upon this demand, so we would not, if we could. The greatest success of the Constitution, written and unwritten, is that in a century and a half it has won the people away from an ancient distrust of government to an acceptance of it as their friend. And why not, pray? A democratic government *is* the people themselves incorporated to make corporate competitors useful, to render opportunity equal, and to touch with more secure hope our pathetic enough pursuit of happiness.

A government so constituted and so accepted by its own people cannot ask the most insecure of its citizens to take the major risks of crucial readjustment, when those most in favor of risk and adventure, metaphysically speaking, are least inclined to take either, practically speaking. Why do those who praise risk not accept it as their lot; why do they not quietly proclaim confidence instead of praying for it so loudly? Because they're human — that's why. We're all in a jam together and we ought to pull together like team-mates, with a little lighter oar for mates less lucky than we. To fulfill as best we can this demand for security is the surest way, if indeed it be not the only way, to guarantee the continuity of our dynamic constitutional system.

IV

Men and women of America, if we're a dead nation, come, let's have a grand funeral in Constitution Hall and then go bury ourselves in the mausoleum of the Fathers, leaving the lawyers, who profit from the cults that we provide, to settle our patriotic estate with elegiac " whereases," " whereins," and " whereuntos." But if we're a live nation, let's move on to that rendezvous with destiny which every nation has that works effectively to enfranchise all citizens in the struggle for life, for liberty, for happiness.

Whether we are alive or dead, you would know — not I. For what you are thinking and feeling this very hour, out there in the hamlets of America, with your radio by your side — this determines what as a nation we are today and what our Constitution will be tomorrow. As for me, one of your politicians, driving at the close of day down Constitution Avenue with its opening toward the West, ever toward the West, I frequently hear, or seem to hear, the voice of the venerable old document itself a-calling to us all: " Sons, a Constitution —

> " . . . but in its mindful ones
>   Has immortality;
>   By living, me you keep alive,
>   By dying you slay me.
>
> " In thee resides my single power
>   Of sweet continuance here;
>   On your fidelity I count
>   Through many a coming year."

THOMAS HARDY

CONGRESS—SHOWMANSHIP AND STATESMANSHIP

REPRESENTATIVE SMITH

FRIENDS in Massachusetts, where at last the Bill of Rights is ratified, kinsmen in Texas, neighbors in Illinois; men and women of America: greetings from Washington.

Though I'm only an ignorant man and a politician, I can see that a century and a half is a long, long time. That's the life span thus far of our national Congress, whose birthday we celebrated Saturday. This week we legislators have settled to our 151st year of competitive talk. Thrilled over the week-end as I was by the magnificent ceremony, I came back Monday to my seat in the House to hear a visitor from our gallery exclaim,

" God must be with America for any progress to come from a bedlam like that." Her companion, referring to the vacant seats, replied, " It was more like noise in a vacuum "; adding, " They certainly are frivolous to be engaged on such serious business."

I

Truth to tell, my fellow-countrymen, Congress is and has been both frivolous and serious. It is so frivolous that I myself can hardly practice proper mirth control when I think of it. In the House of Representatives there have been and are lean men and fat men, tall men and short men, bald men and Beaux Brummells, old men and young men, sober men and smiling men, modest men and mere men, rich men and poor men, college men and self-trained — men, indeed, of every sort and condition. Yes, and women, too — with their own color, warmth, and shrewdness.

The Senate, the same, unless my good colleague, Mr. Taft, from over there, wishes to amend my impression.

The men-of-the-Senate-who-will-tell average today 58 years of age; the men of the House, 51. As for the five women in both, I dunno; your guess is as good as mine. Of the 96 Senate members, the Congressional Library tells me, 66 are lawyers (68 per cent), 9 are business men (10 per cent), 8 are journalists (9 per cent), and 5 are listed as farmers (5 per cent). Of the 435 House members, 239 are lawyers (55 per cent), 84 are business men (20 per cent), 20 are journalists (5 per cent), and 10 are medical doctors (2 per cent), with an honorable horse doctor or two thrown in.[1] (Let the figures be a warning to farmers, who send less than 6 per cent of representatives to speak for more than a third of the nation that's agrarian.)

Now I ask you: How could you get such human variety together without a lot of frivolity? It wouldn't be natural, nor, as a matter of fact, wholesome, either. The American way of life is a way of humor, and we are the official representatives of the American way. It's not merely that much horseplay goes on in Congress; it's also that one side of politics is necessarily showmanship. Abraham Lincoln of Illinois, for instance, used during his single term in the House to prance up and down the aisles, waving his ungainly arms while pouring out stories that barely passed the bar of good taste. But he's dead now, and so a statesman. The more ordinary way of exhibiting ourselves is merely

> . . . to set our tongue a-going
> And forget to stop it,
> When our brain has quit
> A-thinking thoughts to furnish it.

If you've ever watched monkeys chattering, you know how funny speech can be from the gallery of any zoo, human or simian. A talk-fest is funny enough even

---

[1] You may be surprised that only about 60 per cent of national lawmakers are lawyers. That's double, too, the proportion of State legislators who are lawyers. If surprised, be also pleased. Lawyers tend to make two laws grow from the spot where only one grew before, and, I suspect, to let the juice of life be lost by attending too closely to the letter of the law. Lawyers are fine, but law to be living must grow from life rather than merely from previous law.

when you know what it's all about. Nobody can talk much without out-talking his information, and to see a grown person doing that, especially if he doesn't know it, is always funny unless you're sympathetic with the person whose show-off it is that's taking up the logical slack. Easy as it is to laugh at the other fellow, however, each of us, you see, is " it " in turn. We'd as well admit it: we all frequently talk not to say something, but to see what it was that we were going to say, if anything. You'll remember, too, that the exhibitionist is only the fellow who tells you all the things about himself that you were going to tell him about yourself, if he'd given you a break.

Let Congress then plead guilty to an over-production of talk, but we represent you — in nothing more than in this. You force us to get elected on the verbal easement of oratory. We swell the flood of wind and word during our terms of talk. And we pass, when pass we must, upon the gentler receding flow of elegiac whisperings, " too full for sound or foam." While we live, however, and represent you we must dignify as best we can the larynx, demonstrating to you daily from the galleries (whether we listen to one another or not) that we also serve who only stand talk! [1]

You really expect it of us, you know; and we succumb to nothing like temptation, especially when it be temptation to talk. We know that you oftentimes think ill of us for our much speaking; but we also know that you'd

[1] See White and Smith, *Politics and Public Service* (Harpers, New York, 1939), pp. 243–44.

not forgive us if we didn't do it. Indeed, this curious quirk in you builds in us defenses that protect us personally but impair the serious work of Congress, to which I must shortly turn.

As long as we out-talk our information you brand us as politicians. You don't like politicians. So we must become statesmen to please you. This consists, while men are still living, in talking big about the same little subjects. Pomposity is a prerequisite for a living statesman. Simplicity and good humor count for statesmanship only after a politician's dead. So we must pass as rapidly as is possible from the despised cocoon of sensible silence to the soaring wings of magniloquence. We must become statesmen or cease to be politicians the next election. All of us, your own kith and kin in Congress, are therefore on the verbal up and up from the first day out. This irresistible temptation you offer us to jump the guns on statesmanship impairs the apprenticeship of those who like myself are ignorant; it hampers the legislative effectiveness of other new members who are already knowing; and it cramps the style of older members, who are of course uniformly sagacious, efficient, and genuinely statesmanlike.

Of course Senator Taft has some advantage in this regard, for over in the Senate where he sits there are only ninety-six talkers to divide the time. Still he has his own problem, for the Senators divide the precious hours as in a marathon rather than a relay race. Effectiveness of action even in the Senate has been known to bog down in laryngeal liquidity of the filibuster. But

I'd better leave his branch of Congress to the Senator, as also to him largely the heavy side of Congress as a whole. (Our sedate Senator Taft is frowning at me already for my own frivolity.)

Having, however, told you the truth about our frivolity, perhaps you'll believe this, my closing tribute to the more serious aspect of our legislative craft.

II

The legislator is of all men the man who knows for certain that he's not God. His personal preferences count for no more than the personal preferences of several hundred others, each responsible to his sovereign constituency with no one in Congress responsible to anyone in Congress. Nor does the legislator's deepest convictions boot him anything unless he can get others to share them. Each representing interests equally legitimate and regions equally precious, each must come to terms with all the others; or nothing's done.

Men who think they're God, caught in such a situation, call their equals devils and depart, like Lucifer, for fairer fields out of preference to rule the roost rather than to serve the nation in Congress. Congressional government crushes weak men, makes cynics of men more proud than patient; but rewards sagacity with an overview of conflicts in which coöperative endeavor can prevail. Those who all too naturally suppress conflict, all too inexorably crucify coöperation. The extremity of

44

individual Congressmen becomes thus the opportunity for Congress itself.

This magnificent institution has ever been and today still stands as the nation's most trustworthy training school for tolerance. Wherever you find our retired graduates, you'll find men who know what man's life together is all about: its pains, its precariousness, its preciousness. A country with Congress at its core creates men, not puppets; builds morale, not terror; fortifies the souls of men against their own baser undertows. Congress socializes the fanatical conscience and turns the raspy will to power toward what our Fathers called " the perfectibility of mankind."

III

You see, I think well of Congress and believe profoundly in the remedial work of Congressmen — in their showmanship no less than in their statesmanship. After all, a simple thought will tell you how central Congress is to our constitutional system: *it makes the laws which the Court interprets and which the President applies.* Where does that leave Congress, last or first? First, if I could have my way. But I've learned from Congress that I cannot have my way. History has given the Court first place by giving it the last say; and the cumulative initiative of our greatest Presidents — Washington, Jefferson, Jackson, Wilson, and the two Roosevelts — has given the executive a strategic advantage over the legislative in the eyes of the country.

Many legislators complain at this. But complaint is not enough. Congress lacks even a congressional council to bring it abreast of progressive states, like Kansas and Illinois, that are attending to this leadership through legislative councils. Republicans in Congress who are set to oppose executive reorganization without doing anything to facilitate legislative efficiency do but advertise to the nation that what they want is inaction, which in dynamic times like these means reaction. If I myself do not complain at executive and judicial dominance in our present constitutional system, it is because I am too much a humorist to quarrel with history about the judiciary, too much a realist weakly to envy in the executive what we cannot produce in the legislative, and too much a patriot to wish my country to drift leaderless in a world attuned to vibrant leadership. I know, alas, that leadership cannot be complained into existence; nor can it be legislated, not even by Congress for Congress. "Leadership is," I repeat, "as leadership does." Moreover, I see work enough left for Congress to do, work that it can actually do and honorably do — and work that it is doing today.

This work is not the finished product which Congress turns out, important as that is in all conscience. Its major work is the finishing process which it applies to its members and dramatizes to the nation. Here, indeed, whatever must be done gets done — and little else, save the continuous "lathering of one another's ego." Though not all wrongs get righted in Congress, all needs do get aired, all subjects debated, all dissident voices heard. To inform the public mind through public debate, to allay private aggressions through public hearings, and to adjust collective tensions through public compromise — this is Congress at work, this the work of Congress. Not less talk but more, more debate and better debate — this is the manner in which the very principle of revolution is peaceably preserved in our American institutions and the spirit of evolution is made the deepest law of our land. Thus Congress saves the Constitution from cultism, and thus it furthers civilization through the high art of continuous consultation and accommodation.

IV

Men and women of America, you may still think Congress " the cave of the wind " where puny men do but mouth their way to eminence. But I tell you that it is a gentle wind; it blows few people ill and it clears of mustiness the vasty corridors of our national life. Touched with mirth and not untouched by greatness, Congress is our people themselves incorporated. We representatives, your own board of directors, are bone of your bone and sinew of your sinews. Combining, as best we may, the ridiculous and the sublime, the comic and the urgent, we labor for a cause that cannot be ever wholly lost nor ever fully won. We work, indeed, to make America the homeland of brave men, of free women, of happy children.

> You may not like the way the cards are shuffled
> But still you like the game and want to play.
> So through the long, long night will we unruffled
> Play what we get until the break of day.

Mr. Taft, I propose a toast to our honorable body: Showmanship and Statesmanship; long may they live — united, as in the Congress of the United States!

〰〰〰〰〰〰〰〰〰〰〰〰〰〰〰〰〰〰〰〰〰〰〰〰〰〰〰〰〰

SENATOR TAFT

CITIZENS of the United States of America: Representative Smith has proposed a toast to the Congress of the United States, and such a proposal is so unique that certainly any member of Congress can only rejoice in the opportunity to join. Representative Smith's proposal was so dramatic that I looked around to see whether the well-known hospitality of the Columbia Broadcasting System was supplying the materials usually considered necessary for a toast, but I assure you that this little broadcasting studio doesn't offer even the acid refreshment of tomato juice. And so, perhaps without offense, I may differ with my colleague on both the showmanship and statesmanship of Congress.

I did not have anything to do with choosing the subject, and frankly I doubt whether Congress has very much of either. My picture of a statesman has always been a large, rather pompous gentleman, with his hand stuck into his coat, insisting on great principles which have little to do with everyday life. Undoubtedly there have been great statesmen, but most of them are dead. I don't mean to say that statesmanship is not a very desirable ideal for Congress, but it is difficult to attain.

As for showmanship, Congress as a body has very little of it. As far as publicity is concerned, a single thoughtful executive, like a governor or President, can overwhelm any legislature or Congress, for the simple reason that publicity coming from a legislative body comes from hundreds of men, expressing every point of view, without system or coördinated effort. I know a good many individual Congressmen who are good showmen on their own account and know how to handle publicity, but usually it is the kind of showmanship which does not do the whole Congress any great amount of good. Congress does give a platform from which individual members and investigating committees may call to the attention of the nation the evils which exist in the body politic. That is a most useful function. But, after all, this can hardly be as important as formulating and adopting the measures actually to deal with the evils so publicized. The qualities which Congress does have, and the qualities which seem to me more important in day-to-day life, are very different from showmanship. Those qualities are common sense and hard work.

After all, what is Congress? Everybody, including the newspapers, refers to it as if it were one man. It is a good Congress or a bad Congress, rubber-stamp or independent, definite or wavering. It is perhaps accused of voting one way one day and reversing itself the next. There is a tendency on the part of the press and the people to personify Congress as if it were a single person. As long as anyone looks at it in that way, he can't understand Congress. It is made up of 531 different people. As Representative Smith has pointed out, they are of every size, shape, appearance, background, and mentality. On any important issue they are hopelessly divided, and of course they should be. If Congress reverses itself on a close issue, it means that one or two men have changed their minds. Congress is not wabbling; just a few men are wabbling.

The public contrasts Congress with the President and treats it as if it were an executive body running the government. As long as people look at Congress from that point of view, they are going to be disappointed, for it is a very poor executive. How can any group of 531 men act like an individual? We frequently see in this country an attempt to delegate executive power to a board of three or five or seven, and it is generally agreed that even a board of five is a much poorer, more uncertain, method of running anything than an individual. I think it was General Goethals who once said that boards were long, narrow, and wooden; and of course a board of 531 would be still longer, narrower, and more wooden if you looked to it for prompt, decisive action.

No, Congress is not an executive; it is a legislature. It represents the people. It is a method of finding out what a majority of the people want. It should move slowly, because it is a deliberative body. It should discuss the matters proposed to it until all points of view are before it, so that it may act more intelligently.

Congress is made up of a group of average men, intended to be representative of the people of the United States. In one respect they are especially qualified for their position. They have all run for office. They have had to campaign and meet all kinds of people in the districts or states from which they come. They cannot have gone through this experience without becoming a little better judges of public opinion than other men, more in touch with the real wishes of the people. Perhaps that experience has made them a little too intensely practical and not quite enough students of the theory of government. But they are men with just a little more experience than the average man. Many election victories can only have resulted from a little better planning and a little harder work than the defeated candidates could offer.

This experience which members of Congress have gone through perhaps qualifies them better than the average man to perform what seems to me the principal function of Congress. For Congress, first of all, is a jury, passing on one proposal after another, prepared by other men or other groups in Congress or out of Congress. Under present conditions, few Congressmen could possibly be experts on the hundreds of important subjects which come before them. Some may be expert on one subject and some on others, but, considering Congress as a whole, it can do no more than apply to particular proposals the basic principles of American government, and the sound, practical sense which most Congressmen have. They aren't statesmen, they aren't showmen; they are just average Americans with a little better preparation than the average.

Of course there is a second function which Senators and Congressmen ought to perform and frequently do. Individually they are workmen, specialists on particular subjects, willing to spend their time making thorough examinations of those subjects and drafting laws for the consideration of the jury.

In the very nature of Congress which I have described lies its essential weakness. Measure after measure is proposed and considered on its own merits, without much attention to the question whether it fits into a larger program. It is hard enough for 531 people to give proper thought to a particular problem, without trying to agree at one time on a whole program of legislation and government policy. The press and some of the people yearn for the development of leaders and criticize Congress for lack of leadership, but to a certain extent the very nature of Congress resists leadership. Most men have been sent there by their constituents to express their own views and not blindly to follow party leaders. Particularly in the Senate, with its smaller numbers and the right to discuss every subject at length, aggressive leadership may defeat its own purposes.

The difficulties of Congress can perhaps be illustrated best by its attempt to deal with the financial problems of the budget. The President is advocating a policy of spending approximately $9,000,000,000 in the year which begins on the first of July, although the already excessive taxes are only going to produce $5,600,000,-000, a deficit of nearly three and one-half billion dollars added to the huge deficits of recent years. I feel quite convinced that Congress and a majority of the people of the United States are opposed to that policy. But what happens? A budget consisting of a thousand pages of fine print is prepared by the Director of the Budget. Many appropriation bills carrying out the President's recommendations are presented one after another in the House of Representatives, and, after consideration there, are sent to the Senate. The different departments are heard from and testify to the tremendous public good resulting from their activities. It is very difficult for Congress to effect reductions in particular departments for the simple reason that they cannot make the thorough investigation required for real knowledge. Possibly in one department twenty per cent could be saved, while in another a reduction of twenty per cent in the budget might force the elimination of work which is absolutely essential. Reduction in the expenses of executive departments ought to be done by or with the coöperation of the executive and his department heads. The problem of saving money against the wishes of the executive cannot be done through the ordinary processes of congressional action.

For instance, look at the reduction of the supplemental appropriation for the W.P.A. Last year $1,425,-000,000 was appropriated for eight months. Largely because of a tremendous increase in W.P.A. expenditures in the months of September and October, just before the election, the money was used up in seven months, and the President requested $875,000,000 more to last until the first of July. Congress felt that the W.P.A. might be more economically administered and that even with $725,000,000 the total appropriations for the year would amount to the huge sum of $2,150,000,-000. They also thought that business conditions were improving and that the increase in agricultural work in the spring ought to relieve the W.P.A. rolls of hundreds of thousands of men. And so they provided that no reduction in excess of five per cent should be made during the winter months of February and March, and suggested that the President ask for additional funds for later months if the reduction did not materialize. A coöperative President, feeling as the President does, would have said to Congress, "I don't think you are giving me enough, but since you have indicated your desire for economy I will do the best I can to cut down expense and will be back later if I need the money."

54

Instead of that, all the propaganda from all the pressure groups benefitting from relief was turned loose on Congress, and the President, with every indication of annoyance at the suggestion of economy, demanded an immediate additional appropriation of $150,000,000. Not only that, he announced his intention to use freely during the months of February and March the money which had been appropriated. This would create a condition to justify his demand for an additional sum in April, May, and June. Under these circumstances, there is little doubt in my mind that because of the lack of coöperation on the part of the President additional millions will have to be appropriated and spent. I hope not as much as $150,000,000.

So, also, Congress in its nature considers each of the new activities of government on its own merits: relief, social security, public works, T.V.A., army, navy, and hundreds of other agencies. But no one has sat down to consider the whole program. The nation is somewhat like an individual. A new automobile is a nice thing to have; a new house is better. Certainly any man would like to give his wife a fur coat and provide his children with the finest possible education, but he knows he can only spend his income or he will end in bankruptcy. The same thing is true of government. Most of the government agencies can be justified, although certainly some are extravagantly administered; but someone must take the burden of saying that we can only afford a certain amount of government, and we must plan our expenditures within our income. What is the use of having a budget at all if it does not balance?

Ordinarily this responsibility of balancing the budget and the responsibility of coördinating the whole program of government activity have been assumed by the executive. Every President, Democrat or Republican, has heretofore felt deeply the moral responsibility of holding government expenses down to its income. But today apparently it is up to Congress to develop a collective responsibility, in spite of the difficulties that I have described. Perhaps it is a good thing, because I believe Congress, if forced to do so, can develop that quality of statesmanship, which is not very natural to it. It is hard to concentrate responsibility in a group of 531 men, but I feel confident it can be done.

Many of the leading members of House and Senate are intensely interested in opposing a spendthrift policy. A small committee might be authorized to survey the whole field of income and appropriations at one time and recommend a plan of expenditure which will balance the budget in the course of the next two or at most three years. Such a committee could say to group after group and to special interest after special interest that seeks government money, " Your project is interesting; it may be sound, it may be justified; but we are so far in debt today and the burden of taxation on the producers and consumers of this country is already so great that we can't afford to spend more until we have caught up with ourselves."

Congress hasn't much showmanship and can't possibly compete with the President even with the assistance of the radio. It is a good sound jury. It is made up of hard workers. It hasn't much statesmanship, but I think it can develop statesmanship if statesmanship disappears from the other departments of government.

IV

THE EXECUTIVE—TRADITION OR INITIATIVE?

SENATOR TAFT

CITIZENS of the United States of America: " The Execu tive power shall be vested in a President of the United States of America. He shall hold his office during the term of four years." So says Article II of the Constitution, after Article I provides for a Congress and defines its powers. To this broad grant of power are added a very limited number of more specific powers, among which principally are the following:

" The President shall be Commander-in-Chief of the Army and Navy of the United States . . . and he shall have power to grant reprieves and pardons for offences against the United States. . . . He shall have power by and with the advice and consent of the Senate to make treaties . . . and . . . by and with the advice and consent of the Senate shall [make appointments]." And then we come to initiative. "He shall from time to time give to the Congress information of the state of the Union, and recommend to their consideration such measures as he shall judge necessary and expedient." Finally, "He shall take care that the laws be faithfully executed."

The powers of the President are granted in such general terms that undoubtedly any President has a wide possible range of policy. As the title to this discussion suggests, he may be guided solely by tradition, and he may confine himself to the simplest possible administration of the laws passed by Congress; or he may display any amount of initiative, adopt many policies through his administrative powers under the Constitution or existing law, and recommend more important changes in policy to Congress.

There can be no doubt that the American people have approved the policy of initiative pursued to a greater or less extent by every President. The presidency was created because under the Articles of Confederation the weakness of a government without an executive head had been revealed. It is clear that the founders of the Constitution expected the Executive to assume the initiative, or they would not have written the clause I have quoted, calling on the Executive to recommend to Congress a legislative program. Of course this does not mean that Congress is in any way bound to follow the recommendations. Much of the criticism directed at the President in recent years, the charge that Congress had become his rubber stamp, was no criticism of the initiative of the President; it was a criticism of Congress itself for adopting his proposals without consideration, and a criticism of the President for his policy of " must " legislation, his insistence that his recommendations represented a mandate directly from the people, which Congress must obey without discussion.

No one can question today the duty of the Executive to propose a definite program. The importance of a presidential program has exceeded the importance of political platforms. The New Deal program of Franklin Roosevelt was developed in defiance of the Democratic party platform of 1932, although he had run on that platform. In fact, the President's power to propose a program has changed the whole nature of the Democratic party and caused it to abandon its tradition of States' rights, local self-government, and the freedom of the average man from Government interference. We may disagree with and criticize the program and initiative of any President, but we cannot doubt that the policy-making power of the Presidents has always been the most dynamic force in American progress.

But, after all, the principal duty of the President is to wield the executive power and execute the laws of the United States. This is a long way from mere tradition. It is a far more complicated task than it once was, and a much more important one. The Government's activities touch the ordinary citizen in ten times as many places as they did in the days of Washington. It has become an elaborate problem of administering an institution costing nine billion dollars a year and of directing a force of more than eight hundred thousand employees. Whereas it is reasonably easy to propose to Congress broad general policies, it is a much more difficult task to administer those policies so that they carry out their purposes without doing more harm than good in constant interference with every man's life and every man's affairs, and with the progress which has always sprung in America from individual enterprise. A failure in administration can do the country an infinite amount of harm. A combination of too much initiative and too little administration may be a good deal worse even than a simple following of tradition.

That, frankly, has been one of the main reasons for the growing criticism of the President. He proposes scheme after scheme intended for the ultimate benefit of the people, but he has no interest in the manner in which each scheme is worked out, no concern to see that it fits in with other schemes carried out by other departments. His interest is always flitting into new fields before the plowing of the old fields is finished. Such is the present proposal to extend Federal activity into health and education, before we have begun solution of the problems of social security and relief. Good administration is still the paramount if humdrum duty of the Executive, but there is hardly a field of New Deal activity today where the administration of a policy is satisfactory. Often there is an overlapping of departments in the same field, each administrator operating in a water-tight compartment of his own. Often their policies are guided by radically opposed theories, and there seems to be no effort or interest on the part of the President to reconcile their views, surely a task for the Chief Executive.

For instance, consider social security, withdrawing from the productive enterprises of this country today, through payroll taxes, a billion and a half dollars a year. No persons are yet being paid from the old age security fund; all those receiving pensions receive them under State laws. Unemployment insurance benefits are still far below the taxes paid in to the Government, and are so inadequate that the recipients must still be given relief or put on W.P.A. Meanwhile the workers and the employers of the nation are building up so-called reserves, sacrificing real purchasing power, and their cash is being used to pay the huge deficits of an extravagant national administration.

The problem of relief and unemployment is wholly unsolved. There are still more than ten million people unemployed, and the administration of W.P.A. became so involved in politics that it has utterly forfeited the confidence of the nation. The administration of relief is intimately connected with social security, but it is administered by numerous independent departments, the W.P.A., the C.C.C., the N.Y.A., the Surplus Commodities Corporation, and various farm security organizations; and now the Department of Agriculture is going to step into the field with a new kind of currency based on orange and green stamps. I believe that the whole relief problem should be turned back to the States and local governments, with a Federal grant and a supervision, probably by the Social Security Board, to see that State administration of relief is free from politics and coördinated with the social security plan.

Take the problem of the control of credit and banking. The banks are supervised by the Federal Reserve Board, the Federal Deposit Insurance Corporation, and the Comptroller of the Currency, all with separate powers of inspection and control. In theory, the Federal Reserve Board is supposed to be a Supreme Court of credit to prevent the recurrence of depressions like that of 1929, and yet those powers may be completely nullified by the powers granted to the Secretary of the Treasury to buy and sell Government bonds, to control a secret stabilization fund, and change the value of the dollar. Surely it is part of the executive function to work out a coördinated plan of control in this field, which is so essential to business stability.

The administration of the Wagner Labor Relations Act has provoked almost universal condemnation, and it is generally agreed that proper administration might have cured the difficulties produced by the law itself. Amendments are sought by business organizations and by the American Federation of Labor, but the President fails to make any recommendation and protects and defends the faulty administration of the law.

The confusion in the administration of farm policies is even more pronounced, and the policy intended to eliminate surpluses and raise the price of crops has resulted in starvation prices and a surplus of eleven million bales of cotton, in effect owned by the Government. The present Farm Act confers on the President and the Secretary of Agriculture power to carry out almost any kind of farm plan, so that the problem is almost entirely one of administration. But no one has heard a word from the President with regard to any change in the administration of the law to solve the growing problems of the farmer.

Housing is another field where a thoughtful, comprehensive administration is impossible because of a confusion of hastily conceived policies. We have the Home Loan Bank Board, financing homes through the building and loan associations, and liquidating the old H.O.L.C. We have the F.H.A., guaranteeing mortgages on new homes up to ninety per cent of their value, and old homes up to eighty per cent of their value. We have the U.S.H.A., eliminating slums and building great housing projects in our cities. We have the Resettlement Administration, liquidating the old Tugwell projects. Only this week representatives of these different organizations have presented to the Banking and Currency Committee of the Senate diametrically opposing views on Government policy. Certainly no one has sat down and thought out the problem of just where the Government is going in its housing program, what its ultimate purposes are, and which line of activity is the most effective to accomplish the ultimate objectives. That is the duty of the Executive.

Some of the problems I have suggested can be met by an improved administration; others can only be met by a reorganization of the government departments. Through such a reorganization, properly done, expense can be reduced, overlapping and conflict eliminated. Everyone agrees on the necessity of reorganization, and it is unfortunate that it has become such a center of political controversy.

Last year the President demanded a reorganization bill which would have greatly increased his powers. It eliminated the office of Comptroller of the Currency, established by Congress to prevent the expenditure of public money by executive departments except in strict accordance with the appropriations made by Congress. It provided for a reorganization of the Civil Service Commission, which would have given the President much greater power in making Civil Service appointments. It subjected many of the semi-legislative and semi-judicial commissions to the power of the President. It was not even claimed that it would reduce the expense of government. Congress objected violently to any increase in the already extraordinary powers granted to the President, and the bill was beaten.

This year reorganization bills have been proposed in both Houses, eliminating the more controversial features. A bill has passed the House, giving the President power to rearrange all of the departments, unless Congress acts adversely on his proposals within sixty days. Anyone who knows the ease with which Congressional action can be delayed will realize that this gives the

President almost unlimited power to rearrange departments as he sees fit. The Byrd bill in the Senate, on the other hand, authorizes the President to submit complete or partial plans of reorganization, to go into effect if approved by Congress, and changes the rules of Congress so that the proposals submitted must be considered, and accepted or rejected, without becoming involved in all kinds of amendments.

The reorganization of Government departments is a legislative matter. It may change the whole character of certain government activities, or combine them, or abolish them altogether. Logically there can be no question that Congress ought to debate and decide on reorganization proposals. Senator Burton Wheeler, the able Democratic Senator from Montana, stated Saturday that these changes involve fundamental principles of government, and that Congress would be abdicating its powers by turning them over to the Executive if it adopts the House bill. If the President will accept the Byrd bill and submit plans for reorganizing the relief, social security, banking, housing, and other activities, he can count on the earnest support of Republicans as well as Democrats, in improving the economy and efficiency of the United States Government.

I do not intend tonight to discuss the wisdom of the objectives of those Government policies I have used for illustration. With some I heartily agree; for others I would substitute a different policy. But there is hardly one in which the administration is accomplishing its objectives. In discussing the character of the office of

President of the United States, I have suggested these examples because they show so clearly how much today, perhaps more than ever before, we need in that office an Executive who is a great administrator. He need not lack initiative, but that initiative must be directed far more to the solution of existing problems than to the suggestion of new kinds of Government activity. It is a tribute to Mr. Roosevelt that he has suggested methods of dealing with the most serious problems of American civilization, but he is not interested in performing that essential constitutional duty of seeing that the laws are properly executed.

~~~~~~

REPRESENTATIVE SMITH

KINSMEN in Texas, neighbors in Illinois, friends in New York, men and women of America: greetings from Washington.

It's easier for a lawyer to " cloakroom " a living President than for an ignorant man to do justice to the office of the presidency itself. In the effort, however, to take just counsel of the harder task, which is our subject this time, two queer matters arrest attention at once. The first is that the presidency has outgrown early popular distrust to become the strongest office in our constitutional system. The second is that the Republicans, who as Federalists wanted it strong (Alexander Hamilton, you remember, preferred a king), today work to make it weak. They will neither themselves produce strong Presidents, nor suffer the strong ones we Democrats produce. Leaving Lincoln aside for the moment, Theodore Roosevelt is their only outstanding exhibit; and he finally had, or thought he had, to bolt the party in order to preserve his own integrity.

I

Why do the Republicans chronically minimize presidential power, while maximizing the power of business executives? Look you, for instance, to the genial late President William Howard Taft, who was certainly a typical Republican. "My judgment," Mr. Taft declared, "is that the view of Mr. Roosevelt, ascribing an undefined residuum of power to the President, is an unsafe doctrine. . . ." Elsewhere he spoke of the matter not so calmly, expressing fear that Theodore Roosevelt was literally "pulling down the pillar of the temple of freedom." Strong words, those — even for a conservative.

Now this difference, temperamental and constitutional, which cost Taft and the first Roosevelt a long and fruitful friendship, has likewise cost the Republican party the presidency in every trying time since Lincoln. Only in the safe days do the American people seem to think it safe to allow a Republican full run of the White House.

Lincoln's attitude — the exception which proves the

rule — was the traditional Democratic one, the wide use of executive power for popular ends. So the Republicans then in Congress appointed a joint committee to see that Lincoln ran the war constitutionally; they tried to reorganize his own Cabinet for him; and they voiced through Senator Wade their noisy conviction that " the country was going to hell, and that the scenes witnessed in the French Revolution were nothing in comparison with what we should see here." All that hysteria, my fellow-countrymen, merely because the simple Lincoln, finding " the Constitution . . . silent on the emergency," proceeded upon the common-sense notion that whatever was " indispensable to the preservation of the Union " was constitutional.

This was the doctrine of Jackson and the doctrine that Jefferson before him had resolutely practised. Jefferson, indeed, frankly admitted that he had gone " beyond the Constitution " in purchasing what is now almost half America for a song. " Strict observance of the written laws," he explained, " doubtless is one of the high duties of a good citizen, but it is not the highest. The laws of necessity, of self-preservation, of saving our country when in danger, are of a higher obligation."

And who says otherwise? The Republicans, that's who — in Lincoln's day and this very day in Congress. Against the Republican view that whatever is not allowed is forbidden, we Democrats set from Jefferson to Franklin Roosevelt the liberating thought that whatever is not forbidden is allowed, when it is needed.

II

That means it's permitted to save the banks, when otherwise they'd fail, and, failing, ruin the country. That means it's permitted to lift the mortgages on homes and farms, when otherwise private debt would impair public morale. That means it's permitted to save the railroads, when otherwise they'd fail, and, failing, sever the arteries of trade. That means it's permitted to re-form the stock and securities market, when the system is ripening its leaders for the penitentiary; to purify foods and drugs when they're poisonous; to correct the utilities, when they're dropsical of stock and rheumati-cal of rates. That means it's permitted to arm for de-fense, when there's no safety without it. That means it's permitted to take the youth off the streets, when otherwise they're going to the dogs, to aid women otherwise stranded, to protect children otherwise stunted in health and outlook. That means, in general, it's permitted to extend public credit to make private debt bearable and to render human life more secure.

The Senator asked last week, What's a budget for if not to balance? Pending our future discussion of that specific subject, let a rhetorical question answer his po-litical question. I ask, What will it gain a nation to balance a budget without balancing what the budget's about? I ask, What's wealth for if not to use when we most need it? It's still permitted calm men to be sen-sible in meeting situations, however hysterical conserv-atives grow in congressional cloakrooms.

Yes, all this is permitted by the Constitution — all this
and more. Permitted whom? Permitted whoever cares.
That means permitted the President, working through
Congress and under the Courts. Make no mistake
about this business of leadership. It belongs to the
President. He is, after all's said and done, our highest
executive, our chief officer in getting things done. It's
all Hoyle, in spite of unbecoming hysteria from every
generation of conservatives. Our highest tribunal has
fully validated these powers which the people have ac-
corded their presidency.

To set Congress against the President, as Republicans
are always trying to do, is to weaken both Congress and
the Executive. For without executive leadership the
legislative branch may prevent but not perform —
that's the voice of American history. Theodore Roosevelt was but echoing our national experience in declaring that by and large " the action of the Executive offers
the only means by which the people can get the legislation they demand and ought to have."

Those who don't want this leadership don't want
popular legislation; and those who don't want this legislation don't want democracy extended in America. Can
democracy be healthy without growing? Why don't
they frankly say here what Anthony Eden said in England not so long ago: " We have not got democratic
government today. We never had it, and I venture to
suggest to Honorable Members opposite that we shall
never have it. What we have done in all the progress
of reform and evolution of politics is to broaden the

71

basis of oligarchy." Aye, there's the rub! A weak Executive in government means strong executives elsewhere having their way with the people. Crying down the powers of the presidency, even opposing the present puny effort to reorganize the executive branch for efficiency, the Republicans may fool conservative Democrats some of the time and fool themselves all the time, but I wonder whether they are fooling the American people any of the time.

Our people trust the President when they trust nobody else. They've had experience with leadership and with its opposite. They rolled Jefferson into office, expecting action for their needs; they rolled Jackson into office, expecting action for their needs; they rolled Franklin Roosevelt into office, expecting action for their needs. And only such Executives as have acted energetically for their needs have they glorified in history. The presidency is clearly the center of our constitutional system when the hour calls for action. Elected by the whole people, responsible to the whole people, appealing to the whole people, the American President it is who can go places, democratically speaking. He can take a popular cause through a debating Congress. He can take a popular cause through a deliberating court.

The people trust this office for cause, though, alas, not always with effect. For when the people grow tired of exertion in their own behalf, then the Republicans take over. Elevating inertia into a public policy, they profit privately until inaction becomes reaction and the

72

people learn once more who are their friends. " The time did not require a first-rater for President," said Senator Brandegee in promoting Harding to the presidency. When they want big men for the big job, the people turn to the Democrats, whose philosophy is, as Woodrow Wilson expressed it, that " the President is at liberty both in law and conscience, to be as big a man as he can. . . . If Congress be overborne by him, it will be no fault of the makers of the Constitution; it will be from no lack of constitutional powers on its part, but only because the President has the nation behind him, and Congress has not." It is a wise Constitution that allows the people this leeway of their own lethargy, but let us not fool ourselves that by playing Congress against the presidency we're strengthening Congress. We're weakening government, that's what we're doing — and there are always those who like it.

The Constitution itself of course invites the President to become the leader of Congress. I refer not to the negative power of the veto but to the positive power " to recommend " to Congress. That neat phrase " to recommend " covers a multitude of opportunities to the energetic leader. Lincoln spoke of it as including " certain indirect influences to affect the action of Congress." In practice this " influence " may mean anything from addressing Congress in person, or even going before its committees, up to or down to the gentle spreading of that sweet pap known to Congressmen and their hungry constituents as patronage.

III

The latter is the lasting pity of all power, when used without imagination. No President has yet been able to use his accumulating powers to bring to perfection the purely administrative aspects of his vast leadership. This is the one most unsolved problem of our government. President Taft began a process which the present President has tried desperately to culminate. But the cry of dictatorship against legitimate leadership, ever raised by those who stand to profit from weak government, diverts attention from his greatest failure. Administrative reform commensurate with our crying modern need awaits a Congress willing to follow where it cannot lead and a citizenship ashamed of favors got by " pull " and of offices fulfilled without the " push " of efficiency.

Pending a President strong enough to do it, and a Congress and country wise enough to permit him genuinely to organize his branch for administrative efficiency, let us citizens keep clear of partisan poison the powers of this great office — " that government of the people, by the people, for the people shall not perish from the earth." We'll be needing these powers before our nation's day is fully done.

IV

But see how big a subject the presidency is for fifteen minutes! If the pathway of our logic now crosses the

74

career line of a living man, perhaps we can suggest to the imaginative what time does not allow us to say to the prosaic — to say of this most powerful, this most lonely, this most alluring job, the presidency of the United States.

Schoolboys of America who hope to become President, hear you this final word and lay to your heart this magnificent example. The pathway to your high goal has run in song and story not mainly through mansions of the mighty but from cabins of the poor. Jackson vivified that story; Lincoln made that song ring true. But those who pass through poverty to glory may distort fond hope in long delay or even bow in middle course to some heathen shrine along the prickly path of pride. Those who start the race from riches may grow short of wind and weak of will, until —

> . . . enterprises of great pith and moment,
> With this regard, their currents turn awry,
> And lose the name of action.

Be you not dismayed by your fate. If poor, know that history is with you. If rich, take heart. Take heart, indeed, whatever be your lot. For of late came one upon our national scene who matched his will against the ways of witless Fate — and won. Summit-born, an only child — one child alone. No chance! And yet . . . but no! — Fate caught him full in flight and hurled him low and grinned to watch him die, alive. He lived! — *how,*

God knows — lived to face fear unafraid and to laugh with men at Fate.

Now Fate, my young friends, when laughed at, slinks away and leaves men free — leaves men free from fear and Fate.

V

THE COURTS—UMPIRE OR GUIDE?

REPRESENTATIVE SMITH

KINSMEN in Texas, neighbors in Illinois, friends in New Jersey (where sonship spells judgeship and smells foul); men and women of America: greetings from Washington.

Though I don't know much, I know that the Supreme Court is our most distinctive Federal institution. Heading as it does our judicial hierarchy, it represents, under God, America's nearest approach to infallibility. Let us focus attention upon it.

Congress can gainsay the President. The President can veto Congress. Congress can override the President's veto. But the Court can veto the President, can veto Congress, can veto both Congress and the President together, without either or both being able directly to unsay this judicial negation. In our distribution of Federal powers, then, the President proposes, Congress disposes; but in the Court reposes power over constitutional policy, no less final because acquired. I say "acquired," for this duty of finality over Federal equals is not categorically provided the Court by the Constitution, nor is this acquired privilege of mortal infallibility judicially claimed in any other great country of the world. The privilege is claimed here; it is exercised here; it is approved here. If, then, the Presidency holds the sword and Congress the purse, as Mr. Chief Justice Hughes so recently reminded us, the honorable Court over which he presides with such dignity may be said to wield the word. And, to echo the biblical phrase, "in the end is the word." Fortunate for the nation when this final say represents the heart as well as the voice of reason!

I

How to the one least powerful agency of government came this power of the final say is a story fascinating in the extreme. I do not know the whole story, nor could I tell it all here if I did. But it is the story of the Court's rise from a traditional umpire to an American guide, negative in nature but conclusive in authority. We can see that the story has ended in a victory which few begrudge the Court, a victory so complete that it was not disputed even during the late unpleasantness over the Court. It is a victory the secret of which it pays to understand; for it reinforces the moral I have been pointing as regards all branches of government: that wherever power is concerned, its distribution is determined by prowess. And it helps to explain why there's ever recurring trouble between the Court and Democratic Presidents like Jefferson, Jackson, and Franklin Roosevelt, not to mention Democratic-minded Republican Presidents like Lincoln and Theodore Roosevelt.

But for the prowess of Marshall, John Marshall of Virginia, the Supreme Court might still be but modest umpire in legal conflicts. It was Marshall — a great statesman even when not impartial as judge [1] — who made an ancient theory into the American practice of judicial supremacy. Marshall found the Court relatively weak, so weak, indeed, that the best men of the time did not jump at its membership as they do today. John Quincy Adams declined membership on it, as did a good many others, after being appointed and confirmed. John Jay resigned to become special Ambassador to England and later declined reappointment as Chief Justice. Oliver Ellsworth resigned to become Ambassador to France. Rutledge preferred to be Chief Justice in South Carolina. Robert Harrison chose the chancellorship of Maryland in preference to the Supreme Court.

Thus Marshall found it, but through the years his

---

[1] It was hardly the judge in Marshall that declared: " Should Jackson be elected, I shall look upon the government as virtually dissolved." He lived, nevertheless, to administer the Presidential oath of office to Jackson, as he had begun by administering it to Jefferson!

History has a gentle even if ironic way with the consternation of conservatives, when democracy's on the march.

sheer prowess made it and left it so strong in power and prestige as to render it second only to the Presidency in attractiveness to talent and ambition. In our day William Howard Taft was proud to step from the Presidency, when it played out on him, to the Chief Justiceship. And Charles Evans Hughes, who resigned to bid for the Presidency, returned unashamed to the Court as Chief Justice, when the people did not accept his bid. (I'm glad Mr. Hughes stayed off the bench long enough to write his delightful book on the Supreme Court! This is a book from which I'm borrowing in this speech.)

Indeed, I see no better way to make appear the fine human thing it is, this magnificent American institution, than to pass on to you the story which Hughes in this book tells of Justice Field, who, " tenacious of the appearance of adequacy," had tarried on the bench well past his powers. His brethren of the Court sought to toll him off to retirement, as it were, by reminding him deftly, they thought, that it was he who had years before tried to get another proud but decrepit patriarch (Justice Grier) to retire for the honor of the Court and the integrity of justice. Made with great difficulty to remember his part in that earlier ordeal of honor against senescence, Justice Field did at last recall it but burst out, " eyes blazing with the old fire of youth ": " Yes! And a dirtier day's work I never did in my life! " [1]

---

[1] *The Supreme Court of the United States* (New York, Columbia University Press, 1928), pp. 75–76.

II

But age cannot wither nor precedent stale our Court's present prestige. Rich in power, holding and having the final say, the Court invites deferential inspection. What are its functions, and in what fulness of faith performed? Its functions appear to be chiefly twofold: (1) to protect individuals under the Bill of Rights from both State and Federal encroachment, and (2) to co-operate at the task of making the Constitution adequate for the governance of a growing nation. The honorable discharge of the first duty by the Court has brought the whole Government into a position very difficult as touching the second responsibility for national policy. A typical if not key difficulty arises from the fact that the Court has elevated to the rights of men a hybrid species of " persons " unknown to the written Constitution. By a series of bold decisions — best represented in the public mind perhaps by the Dartmouth College case — John Marshall and judicial colleagues made the Government the protector of curious legal entities midway between men and machines. Corporations are men, mentally; but they are machines, morally. They are legal devices permitting, if not requiring, decent men to be less decent as officers than they are as men.

The Fourteenth Amendment, written as it was by war and blood to protect the freed but weak slaves, eventually became and has remained the major text to justify protection of these powerful fictitious " persons,"

of their life, of their liberty, of their property.[1]
With business corporations expanded into hundreds

---

[1] How reluctantly it became the text may be seen from these forth-right words of Justice Miller's majority decision in the Slaughterhouse case (1872): "We doubt very much whether any action of a State not directed by way of discrimination against negroes as a class, or on account of their race, will ever be held to come within the purview of this provision. It is so clearly a provision for that race and that emergency, that a strong case would be necessary for its application to any other."

Well, within a few years the "case" had become urgent enough to make our strongest "persons" the standard beneficiaries of a protection intended for our weakest citizens. And so it remains, unless a recent dissent by Mr. Justice Black forecast judicial reconsideration of the rights of corporations as "persons." Hear these clairvoyant sounding words of dissent from Justice Black (Conn. General Co. v. Johnson. P. 85, U. S. Reports, Vol. 303.): ". . . Neither the history nor the language of the Fourteenth Amendment justifies the belief that corporations are included within its protection. . . . The history of the Amendment proves that the people were told that its purpose was to protect weak and helpless human beings and were not told that it was intended to remove corporations in any fashion from the control of state governments. . . . The language of the Amendment itself does not support the theory that it was passed for the benefit of corporations. . . . This Court has expressly held that 'the liberty guaranteed by the Fourteenth Amendment against deprivation without due process of law is the liberty of natural, not artificial person.' Thus, the words 'life' and 'liberty' do not apply to corporations, and of course they could not have been so intended to apply. However, the decisions of this Court which the majority follow hold that corporations are included in this clause insofar as the word 'property' is concerned. . . . This Amendment sought to prevent discrimination by the States against classes or races. We are aware of this from words spoken in this Court within five years after its adoption, when the people and the courts were personally familiar with the historical background of the Amendment. 'We doubt very much whether any action of a State not directed by way of discrimination against the negroes as a class, or on account of their race, will ever be held to come within the purview of this provision.' . . . Yet, of the cases in this Court in which the Fourteenth Amendment was applied during the first fifty years after its adoption, less than one-half of one percent. invokes it in protection of the negro race, and more than fifty percent. asked that its benefits be extended to corporations. . . ."

82

of thousands by States not above mongering after the fees charged for chartering them, the Federal Government at last faced the predicament of having to defend the rights of private persons against corporational legality. (Consult the recent La Follette Committee report on industrial practice, if you doubt the need for protection by mere men in dealing with these artifacts of legality.) Popular liberty came indeed to be more curtailed by corporations than by government; the property of wage-earners more jeopardized by them than by government; and pursuit of happiness much more hampered by them than by government. The Court has been brought into politics because the chief political problems today are the fruits of the Court's previous decisions.

Theodore Roosevelt's " Square Deal," Woodrow Wilson's " New Freedom," and Franklin Roosevelt's " New Deal " are but recent efforts, all popularly approved, to deal politically with pressing problems in no small degree judicially created. Under Marshall's guidance, the Court made the nation to prevail over the states. Is there a second John Marshall to enable the nation during the twentieth century to turn industrial triumph into democratic triumphs, to convert class gains into mass gains? Speaking very generally, we have moved politically in two directions, the Court sometimes marching with us, sometimes moping behind. First, we tried to cut these giants nurtured by judicial decision down to the size of the natural persons they were competing with. So the anti-trust measures, whose reform edge the Court has from time to time tempered with its own "rule of reason." Failing to cut down the power of corporations, we tried to reduce their corpulency: let them make what they can, but then take what Government needs. So the income tax over the Court's veto and later taxes whereby the Government sought and seeks to distribute the financial fruits of monopolistic strength.

Meantime, the Court itself has been driven by events to permit what earlier Courts had forbidden: the organization of natural individuals into labor unions, to equalize in that way the bargaining power between men and legal mechanisms. Finding the labor unions, however, not more able to hold their own as participants than the Government itself had been as umpire, the nation has sought, with other remedies, to build up giants of labor to bargain with the giants of capital. So the Wagner Act, around which the battle grows hot today. It is clear that we are dealing here and now with an unsolved problem. Every question involved is partisan, many questions representing partisanship for or against the people. It is surely not statesmanlike — neither judicious nor judicial — to expect natural individuals to go forth unaided against legal giants, mentally mature but morally adolescent. Yet we need all strength in our national business, all strength democratized.

III

In this continuing struggle for democracy in industrial America, the Court's social distance from the people puts it at a disadvantage as an agency of advance. Its heavy drudgery for the good of the nation is undramatic, and its crucial decisions cannot be understood at once or at large. The Court's not elected by the people; it's not subject to rejection by the people; it's not easily reached by popular praise or blame. Having no direct access to or from the people, it, like the Delphic Oracle, sometimes goes astray. When common men know not what to trust, they trust they know not what. The Court gets its closest contact with the people, whose sovereign will it also serves, when it can coöperate, as touching policy, with a Congress and Executive who are themselves coöperating. Four Presidents, but only four, have been able to guarantee this coöperation by appointing a controlling number of the Justices — Washington, Jackson, Lincoln, Taft.

But whatever be the Court's relation to other arms of sovereignty, in its own domain it is the custodian of the Word, of the word which itself presumes to be the voice of reason. Reason, however — alas, for our peace of mind! — means two different and sometimes warring things. It means what's compatible with precedent, which is the backward look on reason; and what's prescribed by needs, which is the forward look on reason. To the lawyer, the reasonable means the consistent; to the common man and scientist, it means the useful, whatever works out well. In a world where democracy is the youngest child, humble utility must often war with aristocratic consistency. Lincoln fought a terrible war, for instance, to correct the Court's judgment of the reasonable, to show in short that consistency about slavery is not useful to humanity. The Dred Scott decision — which Chief Justice Hughes has called "a public calamity" — was reasonable enough to the brains of the Court, but undesirable to the heart of humanity — and so unreasonable in the annals of history.

I often reflect upon this ambiguity in human reason as I pass the living tomb of the Supreme Court here in Washington and read this inscription raised in marble: " Equal Justice under Law." Now, " justice," my fellow-students, comes from a Latin word itself meaning " law." So the sign really says: " Equal Justice under Justice," or " Equal Law under Law." There are in fact two justices, two laws (one of the head, one of the heart); and the Court, with an aspiration common to us all, peeks through or peers at the curtain of cosmic ambiguity in quest of a more just justice, of a more legal law. In all its mortal peering, may it remember the magnificent line of its so lately retired son: " If we would guide by the light of reason, we must let our minds be bold " (Justice Brandeis).

IV

All honor to our Highest Court, unparalleled in other lands today! But our honor for the institution may well be tinged with pathos for the Justices, men like ourselves in essence, whatever robes they wear. Most of them with Oliver Wendell Holmes, who was greatest among them, know that they are not God. Yet must they stoop to carry the burden of our own deep need for infallibility. We have made of their collective will our legal papacy. When this, our presumption, turns to a dark brown taste the morning after some five-to-four example of infallibility, we will not too much cavil if we be men who through our own travail have come to understand — to understand that man's reach must exceed his grasp, or what's perfection for?

In the Court, handiwork of our success and failure, we may behold man's will to power, which runs wild elsewhere in the world today, united with man's will to perfection, which here strives valiantly to come to birth through law. The Supreme Court is our Oracle of Reason; and its members, well called " Justices," are this nation's secular saints producing from the vast silences of the Constitution the melodious footfalls of men on the march, yea, of pilgrims cautiously climbing the highroad of thought toward the City of Justice.

~~~~~~

SENATOR TAFT

CITIZENS of the United States of America: The Constitution of the United States provides that the judicial power of the United States shall be vested in one Supreme Court and in such inferior courts as the Congress may from time to time ordain and establish. In clearly separating the judicial power from the executive and legislative power, the founders of the Constitution established in this country the principle of the independence of the courts, and their example has led to the incorporation of the same principle in every State Constitution. In establishing three independent branches of government, they were influenced by Montesquieu, who seems to have ascribed to the English courts an independence which they did not really possess. In fact, before the Act of Settlement the courts were often a major instrument of executive tyranny.

Representative Smith has chosen to discuss only one small feature of the Court's functions, namely, the power to declare laws unconstitutional. But the number of cases in which constitutional questions are involved is infinitesimal, and the independence and impartiality of the judiciary in all classes of cases lie at the very base of civilized government. The great bulk of litigation consists of criminal cases or cases between private individuals to settle their disputes. Many lawyers go through a lifetime without trying a constitutional case, and fewer still ever succeed in getting a court to invalidate a law. In fact, in the whole history of the United States to 1937, only sixty-four acts of Congress have been declared unconstitutional, out of a total of approximately fifty-eight thousand.

The independence of the courts is essential to the administration of justice. It lies at the very base of civilized government. As Daniel Webster said, " Justice, sir, is the great interest of man on earth." Justice cannot be left to the arbitrary whim of individual judges, and therefore we have written laws applying equally to all, and the judges' duty is to determine how those laws apply to particular cases. Without " equal justice under law " there can be no democracy, there can be no republican form of government.

The more complicated life becomes, the more necessary it is that the law tell each man definitely what he can do and what he can not do without infringing on the rights of his neighbor. It is easy today to see what utter confusion would result in our streets if traffic laws ceased to exist and automobiles ran on both sides of the street and over crossings at will. But just as great confusion would follow in all the walks of life if we left to some political power the right to decide every case as public opinion might at the moment desire.

As Sydney Smith said, speaking of justice, " Truth is its handmaid, freedom is its child, peace is its companion, safety walks in its steps, victory follows in its train; it is the brightest emanation from the gospel; it is the attribute of God." One of the great principles of a republic is equality, and the most important aspect of equality is equality before the courts.

We are discussing here the foundations of democracy, and the chief of such foundations is the quality of our courts, their honesty, ability, independence, and impartiality. It is desirable also that the judges be good constitutional lawyers, but in the long run the other qualities are more important. They must not only be impartial but the people must believe in their impartiality. Nothing can be more discouraging to well-wishers of America than a few cases like a recent one in New York; nothing can do more to shake the underlying belief of the people in democratic government. The steps which the Administration has taken to prevent the recurrence of cases of this kind can only meet with the approval of good citizens. The honesty and ability of local judges is just as important as that of Federal judges, and the wide study being given today to methods of selection of judges is the most important activity in the whole field of the law.

But Representative Smith is only interested in attacking the Supreme Court because it has sometimes held unconstitutional laws on which the New Deal Administration secured a rubber stamp from Congress. There is a strange similarity between his arguments and those which were presented in behalf of the President's bill to permit him to appoint six new judges and swamp the Court so that its decisions would be neither just nor impartial but exactly what the President might desire. These arguments were repudiated by an overwhelmingly Democratic Congress in 1937. The President set out to purge from the Democratic party those Senators who dared to vote in behalf of the Supreme Court, and in every case their course was approved by the Democratic voters of their States. The elections of 1938 show that the people of this country believe in maintaining the independence and impartiality of the courts.

Because the direct attack on the Court has failed, the

arguments presented tonight are more in the nature of sniping, designed to stir up prejudice without advocating any particular action. They affirm that the Supreme Court "is, under God, America's nearest approach to infallibility." It has power, it is said, over constitutional policy, the only arbitrary court recognized in the world. According to Representative Smith, this power was not given it by the founders but is a power which the Court itself grabbed.

A more complete distortion of the real situation cannot be presented. No more infallibility is claimed for the Court than for the President or Congress. It derives its power from the people of the United States through the Constitution. If it does anything which the people do not like, they can amend the Constitution, and in many cases they have done so. The Court's independence is unique, but the American Constitution is unique, and the American Government is unique. It is a written Constitution, because the people had every intention of limiting the powers of their executive and their legislature and their government, as they had not usually been limited in other countries.

Because the founders knew that democratic governments in the history of the world had nearly always degenerated into autocracies, or tyrannies, or empires, the Constitution imposed three great limitations on the Federal Government: first, that its power should be confined to certain limited subjects of national importance, and that the people should retain within the States the rights of local self-government. The making of laws on local matters from a distant capital had been tyranny before the Revolution and would be tyranny afterward. Second, the Constitution divided even the limited powers of the Federal Government between the executive, legislature, and judiciary. The concentration of power in one man or group of men had destroyed democracy before and would destroy it again. Third, in the Bill of Rights they provided that no majority, no matter how great, could deprive a minority, no matter how small, of certain fundamental individual rights. Surely this is an essential of Americanism, one whose violation in Russia and Germany has destroyed the least semblance of popular government.

When Congress makes a law which violates these, or other, provisions of the Constitution, shall the Supreme Court enforce that law or shall it enforce the Constitution? Article VI of the Constitution says: " This Constitution and the laws of the United States which shall be made in pursuance thereof . . . shall be the supreme law of the land." Shall Congress be the judge of its own powers? Isn't it obvious that Congress is seldom restrained by doubts of the constitutionality of a law, no matter how reasonable those doubts? Haven't we in this very Administration, and even in Representative Smith's remarks, evidence that the New Dealers think that any law is justified which the people at the moment desire, whether it accords with the Constitution or not?

Unless the people change the Constitution, they have indicated their desire to prevent Congress from violating the three great principles which I have outlined.

Surely the question whether Congress has violated those principles should be submitted to judicial examination by men whose duty it is to study in a judicial atmosphere the nature of the principles to be protected and set the terms of the law off against the terms of the Constitution.

Of course the Court may be wrong; judges are men like other men. But they are not likely to override any fundamental principles of democracy. The Court itself can correct mistakes and has done so; the people can correct mistakes by constitutional amendment and have done so.

Some of the principles of the Constitution are entirely definite. Others, like the clause which provides that no man shall be deprived of life, liberty or property without due process of law, are very indefinite; but it is still the duty of the Court to interpret their meaning. The theory that constitutional principles are as weak as water and should yield to every crackpot proposal enacted by a rubber-stamp Congress would utterly destroy the Constitution of the United States. It would destroy democratic government and would permit the establishment of a totalitarian state, whose people would have no rights, whose local communities would have no independence.

The courts did not grab the power they have. It follows inevitably from the words of the Constitution, and no one has ever answered the argument of Chief Justice Marshall for that power in *Marbury v. Madison.*

The Federalist, which was circulated among the people to secure a ratification of the Constitution, made clear the intention of the founders in these effective words: "The complete independence of the courts of justice is peculiarly essential in a limited Constitution. By a limited Constitution, I understand one which contains certain specified exceptions to the legislative authority; such, for instance, as that it shall pass no bills of attainder, no *ex post facto* laws, and the like. Limitations of this kind can be preserved in practice no other way than through the medium of courts of justice, whose duty it must be to declare all acts contrary to the manifest tenor of the Constitution void. Without this, all the reservations of particular rights or privileges would amount to nothing."

I note that Representative Smith does not directly claim that the courts should not have this power. He simply criticizes them for carrying out their constitutional duty. He can't argue against the power because it is obvious that without it there would be no Constitution.

There are several other innuendoes in his talk, notably those which present the Court as a kind of defender of big corporations and a reluctant conceder of the rights of labor. Apparently Mr. Smith would bar corporations from the protection of the Constitution and let the Government confiscate their property without due process of law simply because they are corporations. If an individual has the right to retain his own property without confiscation, why on earth should not three or four persons, gathered together in a business enterprise as a corporation, have the same protection? Corporations are nothing but a number of stockholders banded together in the kind of business enterprise which has built up the United States. There is no argument I know of why they should not have constitutional rights in that enterprise as well as in an enterprise they may undertake as individuals or partners. The question of restraining the power of large corporations or taxing their profits is an entirely different one and one in which the Supreme Court has given every possible power to the Government. The picture of a struggle between the executive and the legislature on the one hand, protecting natural persons from corporations, against the Court allied with the corporations is a fiction of the imagination.

Representative Smith stated that the Court had been driven to permit the organization of labor unions, after other means of restraining large corporations failed. As a matter of fact, labor unions have always been held legal by the United States Supreme Court. The Court has repeatedly reasserted their rights and has now upheld the Wagner Act, which compels the employers to recognize the rights of collective bargaining.

No, the attacks on the Court arise from the intense prejudice of the New Dealers against the Court because the Court found that some of their measures violated the fundamental principles of the Constitution. The New Dealers have not been hampered in any way in any efforts to protect labor or limit the power of corporations. They are indignant because the Court held laws like the N.R.A. and the A.A.A. unconstitutional, laws which would permit the national Government to go down into every community, tell the people what they should produce and what they should not produce, what price they should get for the things they make, and what price they should pay for the things they buy, laws which destroy all right of local self-government and the rights guaranteed by the Bill of Rights. The New Dealers are dissatisfied because the Court has said that Congress cannot delegate its legislative power to the President, and that the President cannot remove men on independent commissions because they don't happen to agree with him. In other words, the Court has insisted that the division of powers prescribed by the Constitution should not be merged in a single all-powerful dictator.

Representative Smith entirely misconceives the functions of the Court, which he says are two-fold: first, to protect individuals under the Bill of Rights from both Federal and State encroachment, with which no one can disagree; but, second, " to coöperate at the task of making the Constitution adequate for the governance of a growing nation." He entirely ignores the Court's duty to protect local self-government and the duty to see that the powers of government are not concentrated in one hand, and does not seem to think it very important for them to take an occasional look at the words of the Constitution itself.

In considering the constitutionality of a law, the duty of the Court is not coöperation; it is justice, usually between some individual and a government trying to take away his constitutional rights. If it finds the law to be in accord with the Constitution (and in this it gives the judgment of Congress every reasonable doubt), it should uphold the law. If the law violates fundamental principles of the Constitution, it should refuse to enforce it.

The Representative seems to think that the Court has a constant struggle to decide between what is compatible with precedent and what is desirable. That may be philosophy, but it is not constitutional law. Woodrow Wilson once said: " Justice has nothing to do with expediency. Justice has nothing to do with any temporary standard whatever. It is rooted and grounded in the fundamental instincts of humanity."

In fact, the whole trouble with the New Dealers is that they believe that whatever they desire the Court should hold to be constitutional. They do not care what happens to the fundamental principles on which this nation was founded. Most of them would be willing to abolish the States and turn over all local government to Federal control. All of them favor the delegation of legislative power to the President and seem to forget that this was the first step in the growth of autocracy in Germany and Italy.

The high-minded Democrats who wrote the report against the President's Court-packing plan, after long study and debate, realized that an independent Court is the very foundation of democracy. Their report said of the plan: " It would subjugate the courts to the will

97

of Congress and the President, and thereby destroy the independence of the judiciary, the only certain shield of individual rights. . . . It stands now before the country, acknowledged by its proponents as a plan to force judicial interpretation of the Constitution, a proposal that violates every sacred tradition of American democracy. . . . Its ultimate operation would be to make this government one of men rather than one of law, and its practical operation would be to make the Constitution what the executive or legislative branches of the Government say it is — an interpretation to be changed with every change of administration."

The patriotism, the ability, the diligence, and the impartiality of the men who have served on the Supreme Court of the United States are not equalled by those of any other group of public servants. The people of the United States know that the power of the Supreme Court is the bulwark of Americanism.

VI

THE STATES—SOVEREIGN OR SUBSIDIARY?

SENATOR TAFT

CITIZENS of the United States of America: The Tenth Amendment to the Constitution of the United States, adopted almost simultaneously with the Constitution itself, says: "The powers not delegated to the United States by the Constitution, nor prohibited by it to the States, are reserved to the States respectively, or to the people." Before the adoption of the Constitution, the states were sovereign states. There is no doubt whatever that the drafters of the Constitution intended that after its adoption they should remain sovereign states. On the other hand, the Constitution was not a contract between the states, and the Federal Government was not the creation of the states. The Preamble of the Constitution made it clear that the Federal Government derived its authority direct from the people, just as the state governments derived their authority direct from the people of the respective states. "We, the people of the United States, in order to form a more perfect union . . . do ordain and establish this Constitution for the United States of America." The Constitution divides the field between the Federal Government and the states, but each one remains sovereign in the field assigned to it and is not subject to any laws of the other in its sovereign field.

This was a unique conception in government, and of course many conflicts have arisen, giving rise to a great volume of law defining the two fields of power. But no one has ever questioned the sovereignty of the states, much as some reformers have questioned the wisdom of the policy.

In colonial days, each colony was independent of every other one, and subordinate only to England. The people regarded themselves more as citizens of the state where they lived than of the united colonies. It would have been impossible to adopt a constitution in which the states did not remain sovereign, and the experience of the colonies with England only made that sovereignty more important to the newly independent states. From actual experience they had learned that government from a distant capital is necessarily tyrannical. The English people of the eighteenth century had democratic ideals. They had no serious intention of trampling on the rights of the colonies, but they were many miles away, and few people in London knew enough about the situation in the colonies to govern correctly even when they desired to do so. The colonists had no intention of substituting a tyrannical government in Washington for a tyrannical government in London, and they did not do so.

On the other hand, they realized that in national affairs their action must be unified or their independence would be destroyed, and, roughly speaking, the principle underlying the drafting of the Constitution was to assign to the Federal Government those matters which were a national concern, and to retain in the states those matters which were a local concern.

Since the days of the Revolution, there has undoubtedly been a tremendous change in the whole nature of the United States. California and Maine are closer together today than Virginia and Massachusetts were in 1789. Our cities are more alike than they were in the eighteenth century. We receive our news and our movies and our radio broadcasts uniformly throughout the United States. The growing complexity of life has removed to the field of national concern many matters which were purely local in the days of Washington. State boundaries have become more artificial. There is not the intense loyalty to states that there once was. But the sovereignty of the states is still essential to democratic government, and local self-government is still the greatest safeguard against the growth of an autocratic state.

Today local self-government for counties and cities and schools is more important than state government itself, but if the sovereignty of the states were abolished, it would be a short time before every city and every school district and every county would be directed by some Washington bureaucrat, with little care for the wishes of the individual district. And yet the independence of state government itself is still of vital importance. There is a wide difference in the methods which the people desire for the selection of their officials. In some states they prefer a direct primary; in other states a convention form. In some states the governor is elected for two years; in others for four. In some states the legislatures are elected every two years; in others the senate is continuous. Nebraska is attempting the interesting experiment of a unicameral legislature. It can be tried out without every state being committed to an experiment that may or may not be successful. In most states they prefer to have their judges elected; in Massachusetts an appointive system has worked where it might not work elsewhere. In some states there are great private universities; in others the state itself supports universities because the private endowments have not covered the field. In one state one tax system fits; in others such a system would be utterly unpopular. The different states have made experiments with new laws in every field. Some states have struck out new lines of prison reform. Successful experiments have gradually spread to other states where conditions were similar. Unsuccessful experiments have died without the expense and unfortunate results which occur from a nation-wide and half-baked experiment, such as we have seen in some national fields in the last five years.

But the greatest advantage is seen in the field of local self-government. Different methods of administration exist in our various cities. Different forms of government are found effective to deal with the particular situation. Experiments with street lighting and street cleaning and hospital administration and park development distinguish this city or that, and have led, particularly in the last twenty years, to a steady improvement in municipal administration, far healthier than one directed from Washington under a great Federal bureaucracy.

There is no field in which the people have more interest than in the administration of their schools. Parent-Teacher Associations are scattered throughout every state. The people want to have a voice in the way their schools are run and the kind of education their children ought to have. We have seen in education various theories, from the simplest form of the three R's to the most extreme of the so-called progressive educations. Surely it is better that those interested in education be compelled to sell the latest theory to the people of each district rather than change over night the system of education throughout the United States by the change of some Commissioner of Education in Washington.

When I started out in politics I was strong for centralization, on the theory that it would produce greater efficiency. The longer I have been in politics, the more

I have come to doubt the premise of this conclusion. I doubt if centralized government is more efficient, certainly when it is centralized on a unit even as large as a state. I doubt whether efficiency is as important as an activity approved by the people who are being governed. The people can have a voice in the way their board of education conducts its affairs; they can have a voice in the way their cities and their city councils run their business. Their protests are listened to with consideration and care, and they have an opportunity within a reasonable time to replace those officials who do not give that consideration.

How different conditions are in Washington! If you have ever come to Washington with a delegation on any subject, you must have felt that you came as suppliants, begging for action as a favor. There are ways to influence the action of the Washington Government through great national associations claiming to represent manufacturers or farmers or laborers, but within these organizations the individual members again have little influence. The officers and secretaries are chosen for long terms and are even more difficult to change than the Federal officers. The people themselves have a difficult time to obtain a hearing in Washington.

The truth is that the United States is so tremendous, the conditions are so varied in different states, that no man can sit in Washington and make laws affecting the activities of the people which will fit the conditions in more than a very limited number of communities. He may come from New England and make laws which fit

New England, but of which the people thoroughly disapprove in Iowa, and have a different reason for disagreement in California. The law which may be accepted in the North is simple tyranny in the South. We see centralized governments in England and France and Sweden, but those countries are not much larger than some of our states, and there is nothing like the variety of conditions which exist here.

The founders of the Constitution insisted on local self-government because they knew also that under a centralized government democracy would never be permanent. In case of violent revolution, of course, it is much easier to overturn a centralized government than a federal government. This may be a remote contingency, but under conditions in the world today, nothing is too remote to be guarded against.

One of the forces making a federal form of government more certain to remain democratic is the fact that through frequent elections the general tenor of the government is kept in accord with the wishes of a majority of the people, whether those wishes are wise or unwise. Most people come in touch more with their local affairs than with national affairs. Their schools and roads and city services affect their everyday life. It is vitally important that they be able to change the administration of their local affairs from year to year as they see fit, and that there be no swelling resentment against the necessarily arbitrary action of Federal bureaus.

On the other hand, the growing complexity of modern life, and particularly of commerce between the states, is such that Federal activity must be constantly expanded. More and more matters have moved into the field beyond the powers of the states and into the field where they must be regulated, if at all, by the Federal Government. Nothing any state can do can affect the prices or control of basic commodities moving in interstate commerce. Nothing the states can do can control business organizations or public utilities operating on an interstate basis throughout the United States. Nothing the states can do can affect the control of money and banking or the distribution and marketing of securities. Much of the opposition to the extension of Federal power comes from people who know that they are beyond the powers of the states and do not wish to be subjected to any government power whatsoever.

Because private organizations were able to monopolize certain markets and destroy competition, the Federal Government was forced to step in, through the Sherman Act, the Clayton Act, and other legislation, to control this field. Because of abuses in the sale of securities, the Federal Government was forced to set up the Securities and Exchange Commission. Interference with interstate commerce produced by labor disputes in this national field led to the enactment of the National Labor Relations Act. The courts have found difficult problems in determining what is properly for national control and what is properly within the state or local field. They have had to steer a careful course. They may have erred this way or that way. Every local matter may have a remote effect on national interests, but the court must be guided in part by a determination to preserve the fundamental right of each locality to run its own business unless it interferes substantially with the welfare of the entire country.

One great field of Federal activity has been recently developed. As Government expands its activities into fields in which no government has previously moved, it has increased the tax burden in proportion to total income. Where individuals used to pay five per cent of their income for government, today they pay twenty per cent of their income for government. Much of this expansion falls properly within the state field, like old age pensions and relief. But the states are very limited in their power of taxation. They cannot reach wealthy persons because such persons can move their residence to states where the taxation is lower. They cannot impose a complete taxation on industry without encouraging the development of industry in other states where taxation may be lower. Consequently, it has been necessary for the Federal Government to finance various local activities.

From some of these fields, like the Public Works Administration, the Federal Government should retire. In others, like old age pensions, mothers' pensions, relief, Federal assistance will probably always be necessary. There is always a tendency, when the Federal Government puts up the money, to tell the cities and school districts and states how they shall run their affairs. If this is permitted to go on, it means the indirect elimination

107

of state sovereignty and local self-government. A stimulation of wise Government activity by states and localities is desirable in some fields, but Federal legislation should always make it definitely clear that the Federal Government has no interest in the method of administration except for certain simple fundamental ideals of honesty and good intention. Possibly it would be a better system to have the Federal Government act simply as a tax collector for the states and turn back to each state a lump sum to supplement its general tax resources, without any further strings on the manner in which those moneys are used.

Local self-government is the key to democracy. In every little community in the United States today, the people take a vital interest in their local elections. They do so because they know that their voice is final. Young men and women in any walk of life are able to run for local office, and when they attain that office they have a feeling of responsibility, not to some high mogul in Washington, not even usually to a party organization, but to the people of their community. There is hardly a man in public life who has not come up from the people through his interest in local government. There is hardly a man who has not served his state before he served his nation. Most people take an intelligent interest in national affairs only after they have been drawn into the field of politics through a vital interest in some local problem. There is everything to be said in favor of career men in Government bureaus, but if the whole Government is to consist of career men, picked

108

out by the national Government from school and college, it will be a short time before the national Government is completely beyond the control of the people back home. A government by bureaucrats and experts may do very well in Germany, but it is a long way from Americanism.

The people would be reduced more and more to the right of deciding by a plebiscite once in four years who is going to be their dictator for the next four years. It is only a step from that position to a dictator for eight years, and twelve years, and for life. Democracy can only succeed if all the people take an intelligent interest in public affairs. If states are mere subsidiaries of the Federal Government, and local governments are directed from Washington, it will be a short time before all public interest vanishes and a small group controls the destinies of the nation. Undoubtedly there will be a gradual expansion of Federal power, but in permitting that expansion Congress and the courts must be inspired with the determination and necessity of preserving local self-government and the sovereignty of the states as great ends in themselves, and bulwarks of the republic.

REPRESENTATIVE SMITH

KINSMEN in Texas, neighbors in Illinois, friends in Alabama; men and women of America: greetings from Washington.

Do you understand the Senator's speech as I do — that sin is a bad thing, especially Democratic sin; but that anybody can have all the sovereignty he wants, especially if Republicans dispense it? Of course, the nation's sovereign. The states are certainly sovereign — " nobody ever questioned it," he says. But he seems particularly interested in local independence. He doesn't seem to have reached the limit of localization yet; but, considering the progress he's making in the direction he tells us he's been going, I think he may yet reach the logical limit of precinct sovereignty before his day is done. (I assure you that the Senator is still almost youngish in years.)

Now this generous distribution of sovereignty is a politically practical thing until it comes time to practice it. Then somebody has to give ground. In that regard a curious thing has happened, which I'm sorry about but which I cannot help. It's this: while the Senator has been going his way, the world has been coming this way. I don't mean the way of dictatorships; but that, too, and today " nothing " — says the Senator looking under the bed — " is too remote to be guarded against." The Democratic world has come to believe that governmental

110

lethargy is the latest and the greatest danger of democracy. I've no doubt that the Senator would be glad to set his judgment against the " Democratic world "; but the matter doesn't stop there. The Senator, who lectured me last week on Constitutional law, will be pained, I suppose, by the fact that the Supreme Court has gone the way of the world. Indeed, while he was writing his speech, our Supreme Court was delivering yesterday a reversal of his lecture and showing him the importance of having a fluid philosophy of government. I do not mean that the Court's sustaining reciprocal rights of taxation was a blow at state independence or at national independence. It showed rather that the day of opposing that to this, this to that, is done, and that the day has arrived for fuller coöperation between governmental units.

It is easy to speak the states fair; any politician can do it on demand. But the time has come, dropping wishy-washy amiability, to re-define the position of the states and to pledge all patriots to their support. On nothing more than on this showing does the present Democratic Administration, in my opinion, deserve well of the states and the nation. It has set itself to save the solvency of the states; to preserve the dignity of the states; and to further the integrity of the states.

I

In our efforts at state solvency we have had as ally Alexander Hamilton, wrong in many things but wise and right in this. Indeed, there was a time, but it was

111

long ago, when the Republican Federalist party tried to be helpful to the states. Hamilton's first program was almost identical, as touching the states, with the position of the Democratic party today. Hamilton found the states so ridden by debt as to face repudiation. Instead of passing by on the other side of the states, as did Hoover in '30 and '31, and instead of passing the buck to the states, as Mr. Taft suggests concerning P.W.A. and insinuates more widely still, Hamilton boldly proposed that the new Federal Government, itself in debt some fifty-five millions, should assume the debt burden of the thirteen states, some twenty-five millions more (millions then looked like billions now). It was ruin, shouted all those who made it their business to fear their own fears.

Hamilton had this thought about it, however, a thought which you'll recognize as utterly up to date when I repeat it. He asked, substantially, whether this was a " two-bit " country or a two-billion-dollar country. If we're no good, he argued, we'll die of the debts we already stagger under. If we are some good, we'll pay for all these debts out of the very prosperity which our confident action itself will produce. Doesn't that argument sound familiar? Well, the nice thing about it was that it worked in Hamilton's time. Patriots stopped complaining, shouldered their debts under Federal leadership, became prosperous, and of course paid off the states' debts out of the rising national prosperity.[1]

---

[1] Two years later Jefferson could write: " In general, our affairs are proceeding in a train of unparalleled prosperity. This arises from the real

What's to keep us from repeating, save the presence of too many partisans and the absence of too many patriots? Meantime we've been carrying burdens necessary for the people but too heavy for the states to bear.

Not only have we Democrats carried on in these trying times that great policy of saving the solvency of the states; we have also been saving their dignity by a firm extension of control over interstate commerce, as was intended by the Constitution but neglected by recent Republican administrations. Even lawyer Taft, who last week over-earnestly, I thought, and certainly disingenuously, defended the corporations as having equal rights with natural men and women, admits that new corporate occasions now involve new Federal duties. Not content to admit it, we Democrats have now through heroic exertions almost caught our functions up with these duties. In doing so, we have raised a friendly ceiling over the states and laid a solid floor under state standards of industrial decency.

And, faith, it was not a day too soon for the dignity of the states. They are, as the Senator tonight admits, quite helpless against great interstate monopolies. The corporations can migrate from state to state like birds of passage, and can even secede from the nation. Moreover, in dealing with these giants the states are at a great disadvantage in being required to maintain a demo-

improvements of our government, from the unbounded confidence reposed in it by the people, their zeal to support it, and their conviction that a solid union is the best rock of their safety. . . . I believe I may say with truth that there is not a nation under the sun enjoying more present prosperity, nor with more in prospect."

cratic form of government. The corporations can be feudalistic or even totalitarian, so far as state power is concerned to prevent it. They can, and do, maintain private police forces and stock their arsenals not only with arms but with gases. If ambitious Republicans in Congress vote against the bill soon to be introduced in the Senate, depriving these giants of their sidearms, we can pin to the name of each one individually the charge left vague today by Mr. Taft, that " much opposition to the extension of Federal power comes from people . . . who do not wish to be subjected to any government power whatsoever."

Who, then, says the states are not important enough to be protected against national monopolies stronger than they and infinitely stronger than the states' natural citizens? Not the Democrats. Who says the states ought not to have emergency debt burdens equalized in and funded by the national Government, when these burdens are incurred because of national conditions? Not the Democrats. Who says that the national Government should not abolish child labor and adult peonage when the states can't; ought not to save the soil and aid those who cultivate the soil when the states can't; ought not indeed to equalize educational opportunity for states that have more than their share of children but less than their share of national income? It's not the Democrats who oppose these. Guess who! That's right! Watch them in the days ahead proceed to break the backs of the states.

II

We Democrats love the states, love them too much not to help save both their solvency and their dignity. I would not myself know what to do without my states: my Illinois, the state of Abraham Lincoln; and my Texas, the Lone Star State of Sam Houston, that mighty Samson of the Southwest! These states are to me, as yours to you, freighted with great memories. I'd simply not be me without them. Would you be you without your background?

A Missouri woman living in the little neck which runs down into Arkansas was told by a humorist that her part of Missouri was to be thrown into Arkansas. She burst out in consternation: " Oh, not that, sir, oh, no! We'd all die of chills and fever if you threw us into Arkansas! " And so Missourians would, I suppose, die of imaginative chills, of emotional fever. The same of Arkansas, but different. Arkansas may be a scrawny state to us ignorant aliens, but you may bet your last dollar that there are those who love her!

> God gave us each all America to love,
>   But since our hearts are small,
> Ordained for each one state
>   Should prove beloved over all.
>   (*Apologies to Kipling*)

Sovereigns at least of our sentiments, the states carry on also in our Union indispensable work of their own. Moreover, they are laboratories for national leadership.

Both the Senator and I had our first public training in state legislatures, as have more than one-third of our colleagues in Congress, one-half the Supreme Court Justices throughout our history, three-fourths of the Speakers of the House of Representatives, and nearly half of all Cabinet members from the beginning of the republic. More than seven thousand of our fellow-citizens learn each year in state legislatures the lesson of tolerance, good sportsmanship and democratic leadership. Several states, including my own Illinois, are doing more than all the Republican complaints in Congress together to restore legislative leadership. Through Legislative Councils with research staffs of their own, they are giving legislative leaders the same scientific help heretofore reserved for the executive branch of government.

I have myself had the good fortune of late to be chairman of the board of the Council of State Governments of America. This Council represents a far reaching voluntary effort on the part of the states to make more efficient certain borderline functions, otherwise and necessarily becoming Federal. There is a limit, you know, beyond which lethargy may not go in a democracy. Next week, indeed, called by the Council, hundreds of state officials — executive, legislative, and even judicial — will meet in Chicago to deal with the growing menace of trade barriers, virtual state tariff systems, which the written Constitution was meant to prevent but which the unwritten Constitution has come to permit. Contrary to Republican insinuations, the present

116

Federal Government does not wish to have its full power invoked by state inefficiency. So it's coöperating heartily with the states to prevent, if possible, extension of its own power. The President will send to Chicago greetings and encouragement, as he has done before. Thus the central Government helps the states to help themselves, and to maintain the full integrity of all their effective powers.

III

Surveying, then, past and present coöperation between the states and the nation, shall we say that the states are sovereign or subsidiary? Neither, on the best showing. How sovereign, for instance, is a state that cannot secede? Certainly here resides only a middle-sized sovereignty. Still they are not properly subsidiary; for, inside the sphere of their own competency, states carry on the most important business without so much as a "by your leave" to the Federal Government. That sounds like at least a middle-sized sovereignty.

Neither fully sovereign nor wholly subsidiary, the states in relation to the nation present, as Woodrow Wilson remarked, not so much a problem of sovereignty as "a question of vitality." In a living thing, can the hand say to the body, I have no need of thee; or the body to the hand, I have no need of thee? Amputated, the hand is but clay; handless, the arm is but a stump. While the Civil War showed that we are not a union of states, it showed how organic to each other are states and nation in our modern Federal system.

The resulting relation is not one of rights to be asserted against each other, but one of duties to be discharged in a spirit of mutual aid. With our minds freed, then, of cult words, like " states' rights " and " Federal encroachment " (used by those who fish best in muddled waters), we can the better apportion duties, as between states and the nation, *on the basis of which is best able to discharge them*, in each period of historic change. The shift of power today as between them is a matter for gratitude, not for conservative alarm. It rests on the ground solidly presented by Madison in *The Federalist* long ago. He gave the proper reasons for the shift before the fact came due. " If . . . the people should in the future," says Madison, " become more partial to the Federal than to the State governments, the change can only result from such manifest and irresistible proofs of better administration, as will overcome all their antecedent propensities, and in that case the people ought not surely to be precluded from giving most of their confidence, where they may discover it most due. . . ." [1]

With this discussion of the states, the Senator and I now finish our joint consideration of the institutions of our Federal system. Next week we turn to pressing problems of governmental policy today. Allow me a word of summary at this turning point in our debates.

---

[1] We may set down here for light upon both the courts and the states the judgment of our greatest Justice, Oliver Wendell Holmes. It was that while the Union does not require that the courts have power to declare Federal law unconstitutional, the Union could not continue without this power over state laws.

IV

Starting with the American Way of Life, we have considered the Constitution, the Congress, the Presidency, the Courts, and now the States. What the Senator, has, in general, meant to show, I admit that I do not clearly understand. But his dislikes are now abundantly manifest. Since I believe, however, that public men ought to present their positive views rather than merely complain from behind their fears and ambitions, I have sought to show in each debate how our Federal check-and-balance system works to prevent the checks from making the resulting balance a dead level of inaction in this swiftly moving world. Believing, with Woodrow Wilson, that " change as well as stability may be conservative," I have gloried in the resiliency which allows now this branch of government, now that, to forge ahead under changing circumstances. I have constantly assumed that for these trying times the business of Government is to govern, not to play checkmate as between three equal Federal branches or between the Federal Government and the states.

For this organic view of our own government I have a name. I cannot speak for the Democratic Party itself and I will not speak for a faction in the Party. But this view of government I call the New Federalism, and rest the cause upon the merits of the case.

This may not offer pleasing constitutional doctrine for a conservative lawyer like Mr. Taft, but it hails from the Constitutional fathers, who left great works for their sons to do — and left leeway enough for the doing. It invites prowess and rewards it with leadership to make the Constitution come alive in action today, as it came to birth through action long ago. It recognizes that while politics may be a professional game for the lawyer, government is a grim game of life and death to millions of our fellow-citizens. It is a view of the Constitution which invites complainers to complete their complaints with good works. It's a free country, you know; but an ounce of betterment is worth a pound of complaining.

VII

UNEMPLOYMENT AND RELIEF—
FEDERAL OR LOCAL RESPONSIBILITY?

REPRESENTATIVE SMITH

KINSMEN in Texas, neighbors in Illinois, friends on W.P.A.; men and women of America: greetings from Washington.

You have no doubt heard of a class of people called the "new rich." There aren't many of them now; but some of you can remember samples from other days. They were people who got wealthy so quickly that they weren't able to develop the set of manners supposed to go along with money. There is another group in our day, uneasy and numerous, which we may call the "new poor."

You'll find this group, the new poor, mostly on the

W.P.A. I propose to confine my discussion largely to them. So quickly have impersonal economic forces deprived them of what they had, that they haven't yet lost the manners of freemen. They dare to believe, for instance, that they have the individual's right to work. They believe that they have the citizen's right to vote. They believe that they have the workman's right to organize and to bargain collectively. You see, they aren't like the ancient poor, whom we've always had with us. They haven't been fully pauperized — yet.

The records of these new poor show, according to the *Fortune* magazine in 1937,[1] that they have been substantial American citizens, rather than ne'er-do-wells, that two-thirds of them indeed held their longest private jobs more than five years. Forget your cruel jokes and relax your prejudices to hear that again: two-thirds of these men on relief held their longest private jobs more than five years. Moreover, only 15 per cent of those now on W.P.A. have been on since 1936. The new poor, though down, are not out;[2] they're poor not from personal fault but through national misfortune. Yesterday, so to say, they were like us. Tomorrow, so to say, we may be like them. So today let's count ourselves all alike as fellow-citizens, Americans all!

Now there are those who don't like the W.P.A. Some, I believe, are more irritated by the independence than by the poverty of these new poor. It's not that these

---

[1] *Fortune*, October, 1937, p. 106. This whole article will reward study by all who wish to be fair.

[2] Of the seven million different persons helped by W.P.A. since 1935, less than 10 per cent appear to have been on the rolls continuously.

critics want men to starve, as melodramatists say. To the contrary, they want these men to go back to private jobs. But how? But where?

Failing that, they want the self-respect of these new poor to quit costing us better-to-do people so much money. These critics are not mere critics, however. They propose a plan for the new poor, a plan that means *giving less relief than the W.P.A. to fewer people at proportionately greater administrative cost.* They not only have a plan; they also have a party. It's called the Republican Party. This party has leaders and has a record on this very matter — but the less said about that record the pleasanter the evening. One of the leaders is Herbert Hoover, who on principle was as President against all Federal aid to the unemployed. Another is Alfred M. Landon, who promised diverse kinds of Federal aid if elected President; but he wasn't elected President. Another leader is the Honorable Robert A. Taft, junior United States Senator from Ohio, who promises — well, why should I tell you what he promises? — he's here to speak for himself.

Meantime, I say to you, however, that the plan variously proposed by the Republicans, of turning relief back to the states, will give less relief to fewer people at proportionately greater administrative cost. I have in mind as I go along to show you why and how that's true.

We ought to admit first that neither of our parties knows for certain how to cure unemployment. If we did, of course we'd cure it. As penance paid, therefore, to our ignorance, we surely ought to pool the experience we've had in trying to help the unfortunate victims of it. Under Hoover and Roosevelt together we've had a decade of experience diverse, costly, and clear in its lessons. I say " diverse " because we've really tried out all major proposals, especially the plan of state and local responsibility. I say " costly " because it cost us enough of morale under Hoover to threaten the peace of the land and enough of money under Roosevelt to double the national debt. The lessons of this experience ought to be the dearer for the cost.

I

The first lesson is indeed very clear. It is that *the Federal government must take major responsibility for relief.* Unemployment is, after all, a national problem. The states could not pay for relief even if they would and should. Why, the bill equalled all state taxes collected last year for all purposes and surpassed all state taxes for every preceding year. Fifteen states require a referendum to increase indebtedness and twenty-three a constitutional amendment. Moreover, states mostly depend upon taxes that are bad for business and worse for justice — regressive, like the sales tax.

Nor is it merely ability to raise the money, and to raise it more justly, that makes relief rightly a Federal matter. It is also and mainly the superior ability of the Federal Government for administration. This triple advantage of a coördinated central government is the heart of the New Federalism which I have been proclaiming to you in each of these debates. Financially, it's certainly cheaper to administer these national things nationally. The cold figures show that present state and local relief for unemployables costs fifteen per cent to administer. Former Federal grants to states cost ten per cent to administer. Present Federal cost under W.P.A. is down almost to three per cent. Doctor these figures as you will, and the lesson still sticks out like a sore thumb that the larger the unit, the less the money to administer relief. The obvious reasons will come to your minds.

There's one reason, however, we politicians try to keep out of your minds. (I'm revealing state secrets which I imagine have worried Mr. Taft in Ohio even more than me in Illinois.) This main reason is patronage. Hard as this evil is to resist Federally, it is impossible to resist locally. With forty-eight state political machines, more than three thousand county machines, and millions hungry for jobs in ten thousand precincts which Mr. Taft all but made sovereign last week, the political waste in store is appalling. Talk of the few mistakes on W.P.A.! Why, " you ain't seen nothing yet," not until you face the political pressure of localities uncautioned by Federal selection of projects and supervision of the work.

The relative immunity which the Federal Government has from the worst patronage grabbing explains in large part why the administrative costs of W.P.A. are only a little over three per cent, while the law allows W.P.A. five per cent. The local communities, at least in Illinois, frequently exceed the legal allowance, whatever it be. Even the *Chicago Tribune* is now complaining in a series of scandal articles about the "pull," favoritism, and unevenness of relief given by supervisors (a great many of them Republicans) to the unemployables in downstate Illinois. (The uneven range goes from $7 to $21 a month!) Our experience with the three types of administration (local-and-state, state-and-Federal, and Federal) ought to close debate on this matter for all save theorists and fanatics. A national matter like relief must, if adequate, be mostly financed by the Federal Government and must, if economical, be centrally controlled. To fear this indicated arrangement is to fear fear, not facts. As Republicans fear to learn this first lesson, so they forfeit the second lesson of our experience.

II

This second lesson is that *work relief is better than direct relief*. It is better, first, because it really "relieves"; it helps the mind, I mean, as well as feeds the body. This might not be important for slaves, but it's of prime importance in dealing with citizens. Work relief is better, second, because it spends to create wealth as well as to relieve man. It justifies itself while it's going and leaves monuments to itself when it's gone. What insane notion of economy could lead us to waste both men and money on the dole, when through W.P.A. and P.W.A. work we can save the men and have these magnificent buildings, bridges, roads, and parks all over the nation, to show for our sanity? Only a pauper na-

126

tion will waste its wealth in pauperizing its helpless people. We are not a pauper nation. Economy means spending to conserve, and any other spending is waste, however large or small it be.

This lesson that relief must be work in order to "relieve," enforces the first lesson that it must be Federally administered. Ignore the first lesson and you leave no basis for the second. Even if states have the will, they lack the wit (the tradition of merit in personnel) to provide and manage public works. States are poorly prepared, and lesser units hardly prepared at all, to set up and to execute work projects other than of purely trivial activities. Only the Federal Government is prepared to follow the wise advice of the National Resources Committee; that is, "to provide a reservoir of selected projects which can be utilized in periods of economic depression." As states lack the scientific resources to lay out the projects, so they lack the political tradition of civil service to administer them without the waste of patronage. Republicans ignore this second lesson in order to avoid the third.

III

The third lesson is that *cheapness is not economy and cannot be made so by any talk about the budget*. Sit down and really think a moment whether the fifty-odd dollars a month averaged on the W.P.A. is too much for your family, for any family, to live on in America today. Are men to count, or are we to go mad about money? Do we know what wealth's for, or don't we?

127

The head and front of our Democratic offending is that we are spending more money on men than the Republicans want spent. We are spending twice as much per man, in fact, on the W.P.A. as together with the states we spent per man through the F.E.R.A. So what?

Well, we Democrats believe in men. We suppose that money exists for men, not men for money. We could go back to the Federal grant system and drop to the twenty-five dollars a month per family. We might even drop the employables to the state and local average for unemployables, of fifteen dollars a month per family. That is, we might do these things if we were not Democrats, who believe in men.

We Democrats know that where selfish wealth accumulates, helpless men decay. We know that children today will be citizens tomorrow, and we don't want them so undernourished and disgruntled that some Hitler can play upon their hate to the everlasting hurt of our republican institutions. (Who does not know that it was our Social Security program that stopped Huey Long in his tracks?) We Democrats know as well as the Republicans that pauperization is cheaper than the relief of citizens; but that doesn't make us Democrats prefer pauperization to patriotism. This is the gist of the Republican position for direct relief by local communities; that it is cheaper than work relief under Federal supervision.

Of course, it is.

As to that issue, I tell you frankly that Mr. Taft or anybody else can win the victory any time he has the heart to do it. I have no heart, nor has the present Democratic Administration, to let men made poor by accident be pauperized by intent. If that be economy, then make the most of Democratic treason. I do not care for the economy of cheapskates nor for a patriotism that sees merely the purse.

Beware the attitude of cheapness that feeds upon its own proud flesh. Citizens who begin in the name of such economy to deny fellow-citizens the right to work can so easily end by denying them the right to vote. I do not charge this as a wholesale intention. But I report honestly what I hear the whisperers whispering when they congregate to " cloakroom " the new poor. Their bitter whisperings remind me of the odious blandness of a British colonial surgeon. He told me that in South Africa he did not ordinarily use anaesthetics in his operations. He long ago discovered, he said, that the natives did not feel pain as Englishmen do. It's not honesty that's lacking here or there; it's imagination. Yet honesty is not enough — not if it be deaf to the suffering of others or dumb to its own squelched sympathies.

IV

Reconstruct now for yourselves the psychology which leads Republicans to skip lesson after lesson that we Democrats have learned from their experience and ours. They want to diminish Federal responsibility for relief so that they may edge out the work relief to which the Federal Government is committed. They want to

129

get rid of work relief because a dole's cheaper. They plump for this sort of cheapness, largely, they say, because they want to force men off relief into private jobs. But where are the private jobs to absorb ten million men? " That's easy," reply the Republican wiseacres; " they're waiting, just around the corner, if we'll only stop this spending for relief."

Well, now, who says that Republicans are not men of faith? Why, that's a faith not only to remove mountains of debt but to build mountains of prosperity and morale. Who's to take the risk, however, of the Republican faith that if we stop relief we won't any longer need it? Echo answers, " Who? " The unemployed, of course; they are to take the risk that this grand faith is more than cruel theory.

Here, then, is the final issue on the matter of relief: Republicans want relief cut so that private jobs will return; Democrats want jobs to return so that relief may be cut. The question is, Who shall take the risk, the weak or the strong? Shall some who hope to become the new rich pauperize the new poor to further their own prospects? We Democrats do not see how the defenseless can be justly asked or expected to become the bulwarks of industrial confidence. Is it really fitting that the giant say to the pygmy, " Buck me up now, and watch me lick the depression "?

v

The very psychology of this situation shows, I think, that the trouble with America is not primarily economic.

The trouble is with our conscience. We know that men are more important than money; we Americans of all people know that; but we haven't yet fully made up our minds to put men before money and thus keep first things first. Hence our terrible sense of guilt, which impairs united effort and seeks insistently for a scapegoat. We must learn this final lesson: that it's creditable to have a guilty conscience, but that it's suicidal to be ruled by it. Let's not invite a Hitler by letting our guilty consciences get us down. We can forearm ourselves by beholding clearly the trinity of our guilt.

First, our Christian conscience hurts us. Why? Hear this text, you Christians; hear and understand: "Whoso hath this world's good, and seeth his brother have need, and shutteth up his bowels of compassion from him, how dwelleth the love of God in him?" Second, our Democratic conscience hurts us. Why? Hear this text, you patriots; hear and understand: "We hold these truths to be self-evident, that all men are created equal, that they are endowed by their Creator with certain unalienable rights, that among these are life, liberty, and the pursuit of happiness." Third, our industrial conscience hurts us. Why? Hear this text, Senator Taft, from the Republican mayor of one of your own hardest hit cities, Mayor Burton of Cleveland (only one of the ninety per cent of American mayors, ladies and gentlemen, who have praised W.P.A.): "The crisis that remains is an industrial and manufacturing crisis. . . . W.P.A. work relief is especially well suited to this need. . . . The working habits of these men are at the foundation of American industry. . . . It would be an industrial tragedy, both from the point of view of the public and of the workers themselves, to throw away their productive time and capacity."

This, my Republican and Democratic friends, is the terrible trinity of our common guilt: guilty discipleship, guilty citizenship, guilty workmanship. And the guilt of neglected workmanship is the greatest among them; for it means holding off the day of plenty, leaving it visible to all, but available to few. On whom, now, shall we take out this our mortal sense of guilt? Shall we soak the fortunate rich? Shall we pauperize the honorable poor? Shall we wait around in the hope that God will give us the easy victory of a 1929 prosperity? Or shall we stomach our own guilt in the larger faith that those who bear one another's burdens double their own joys and cut their griefs in two?

Ten million men are, after all, too many millions to get mean about. Of our guilt, therefore, I ask you, Shall we " give it " and be mean, or can we " take it " and be men?

∾∾∾∾∾∾∾∾∾∾∾∾∾∾∾∾∾∾∾∾∾∾∾∾∾∾∾∾∾∾∾∾

SENATOR TAFT

CITIZENS of the United States of America: I do not quite understand the guilty conscience which Representative

Smith seems to have regarding the present relief situation. Apparently he feels guilty because the W.P.A. is only employing three million men when he wants it to employ six million, and is only spending two and a quarter billion dollars when he wants it to spend four and a half billion dollars. In a ferment of emotion the Government is to employ, at higher wages, every man who chooses to apply. Where the money is to come from is no concern of true New Dealers. As long as a few rich people remain in the United States they will take the money away from them, and when they are gone the millennium will arrive.

The Administration does not share any guilty conscience. The W.P.A. has always planned to reduce the present number on W.P.A. in April, May, and June, even if it received the full appropriation, and plans to dismiss men steadily during the next fiscal year until by July 1, 1940, there will only be one-half the number of men now employed. Today the present Democratic Congress regards even the Administration's program as dangerously expensive.

Before considering the question of Federal and local responsibility, let us see why high relief costs are so dangerous. It is not a question of taking the money away from the rich or the large corporations. The increased relief cost will be paid by rich and poor alike, and will bear most heavily on those average workmen standing today on their own feet and earning a living for their families. Once our tax bill took five per cent of the national income; today it takes twenty per cent. When it took five per cent, the money could be raised from the wealthier people, but if we confiscate today all incomes over five thousand dollars a year, we will not pay the present cost of government for more than six months.

The Federal Government has turned more and more to indirect taxes, excise taxes, payroll taxes. It is not true today that state taxation bears more heavily on the poor than Federal taxation. The soak-the-rich tax bill produced a few hundred million, but when the New Dealers wanted real money they turned to the payroll tax, costing the people one billion and a half dollars a year. Who pays the payroll tax? It either comes right out of the workman's pay envelope or it goes into the cost of every product that labor goes into, and that is every product that the average workman buys. Today the average workman, through the increased price of the things he buys, pays twenty per cent of his earnings to the Government. Do you see what this means? When the cost of government is further increased today, and relief is the heaviest cost, the workman's income buys less; in effect, he has less income. The truth is, the only way people can be supported without working, or working on projects which do not produce a cash return, is by making the people who are working turn over, in taxes and higher prices, part of their earnings to their neighbors who are either less fortunate or less efficient. The more the Government takes away from a man who is working, the less incentive he has to work, the greater the threat of an entire nation on relief.

There is no more serious problem than relief today,

but, for heaven's sake, let's approach it in the spirit of calm consideration of facts, and not in one of guilt and emotion.

Relief is an age-old problem. There have always been unfortunate people, incapacitated by misfortune or age, or unable to obtain work. There have always been orphans to be cared for, aged people without families, widows with children, and many other groups. The responsibility has always been recognized as a strictly local responsibility. First of all, we have recognized an obligation on relatives and family and then on neighbors. Charitable people have established orphan asylums, old people's homes, and general charities which provided relief in the homes of those needing relief. The work of private charities has been supplemented by state and local institutions, and the laws of nearly every state recognize the obligation of the city or the county or the township to see that the poor are taken care of and provided at least with the essentials of food and clothing necessary to preserve life. The administration of relief prior to the depression of 1929 was a strictly local concern, and, because the problem was not of great size, it was entirely possible to handle it by coöperation between private charity and the local government.

The depression of 1929, however, changed the entire picture, and the steady increase of unemployment multiplied the financial burden many times. In the early days of the depression the activities of private and local charity were first expanded. President Hoover created the President's Emergency Relief Organization, which encouraged the development of state and local unemployment relief committees, which by the late spring of 1931 were functioning actively in two hundred and twenty-seven large cities, about two thousand small cities, and in over one thousand counties. By 1932 the committees were forced to turn more and more to the state and local governments to provide relief money from increased taxes and bond issues. Then it became apparent that even local resources were inadequate, and the first Federal aid was extended, at President Hoover's request, in July, 1932, through the Reconstruction Finance Corporation, which arranged to lend $300,000,000 to state and local governments.

The idea that W.P.A. prevented starvation is a complete fallacy. There never was a time under either Hoover or Roosevelt in which any needy people were allowed to starve or freeze. Everyone admitted that the primary responsibility was on the states, and secondarily on the Federal Government. The Democratic platform of 1932 said, " We advocate the extension of Federal credit to the states to provide unemployment relief wherever the diminishing resources of the states make it impossible for them to provide for the needy."

The Federal Government was called in, not on any theory that relief was primarily a Federal problem but because, under the conditions which existed and the tremendous cost of relief, the state and local governments were unable to provide the necessary money. Almost the only tax which the local governments can levy with full effect is the real estate tax, and this had already been pushed to high levels and was completely used up in the support of the ordinary functions of schools, roads, and local government.

Various plans of relief were tried, but the most satisfactory form in Ohio and many other states was that in force about 1934, when relief was administered by boards of public-spirited citizens serving without compensation, with an administrative force largely drawn from the private charitable and community-chest organizations but paid by the state or local government, which derived most of the money used from the Federal Government. These committees administered both direct and work relief, and did so on an efficient basis.

The big mistake was made when the Federal Government took over the management of relief and curtly dismissed the local boards instead of financing the states. The overhead organization is top-heavy and expensive. Out of approximately $900 spent per case, per year, which figure includes the average contributions of local sponsors as well as Federal expenditures, the W.P.A. worker gets only about $600. Rules are issued from Washington without regard for special local conditions. Projects are approved or disapproved on the basis of applications submitted in writing and supported by delegations traveling to Washington. Looking only to the report of the Democratic Sheppard Committee, which conducted investigations in a few states in 1938, the W.P.A. was extensively used for political purposes. The supervisory force was largely appointed, as in Pennsylvania, on a political patronage basis. Men were threatened with loss of their jobs unless they voted right. Even the number on W.P.A. appears to have been dictated by political consideration; otherwise there seems to have been no good reason for the increase in numbers on W.P.A. just before the 1936 election, when business was improving, the decrease in numbers on W.P.A. in the latter part of 1937, when there was no election and business was getting rapidly worse, or for the peak employment of nearly 3,300,000 men for a brief period before the November, 1938, election.

We hear tremendous criticism of the inefficient manner in which W.P.A. work is done. Some of this criticism is exaggerated, but much of it is not, and the reason for it is that responsibility for improvement lies far away in Washington. How can an administrator here hope to know what goes on on thousands of work projects from the Atlantic to the Pacific?

Representative Smith implies that local administration means the end of work relief. Of course this is not true. Work relief was conducted by local administrations before it was conducted by the Federal Government. It is conducted by the city of Cincinnati today. But certainly work relief and direct relief must be conducted by the same authority if they are to be coördinated, and that authority must be closely related to the unemployment compensation office. Undoubtedly work relief may be less demoralizing than direct relief, but if the project is poorly managed, or if it is obviously made work which is doing no good to anybody, work relief itself may be as demoralizing as direct relief. How much moral stamina was preserved when W.P.A. spent $150,000 to count the trees in the city of Cleveland? Local administration is more efficient because it can give work relief to those who will really benefit by it, and only to such people. Local officers respond much more quickly to local public opinion. They are more quickly advised of chiselers. They are more quickly advised of obvious inefficiency on particular projects. They know better what projects are worthwhile, and what are not worthwhile, and what projects fit in better with a program of local improvements.

The solution for the present relief problem, in my opinion, is to return the administration of relief to the state and local governments, somewhat as is proposed in the bill introduced by Senator Barbour of New Jersey. I believe that work relief and direct relief should be consolidated under local administration, and the local people should determine how much work relief is really advantageous. A new section should be added to the Social Security Act, authorizing the Social Security Board to put up two-thirds of the money spent locally for work relief and direct relief, but each locality should be required to put up one-third of the total cost of the entire program. However, a special Federal board should pass on applications for a larger percentage to be supplied by the Federal Government, where conditions of special community poverty or extraordinary unemployment may exist. Such a board should be judicial and not political in nature.

Federal assistance should be conditioned on the adoption by each state of a definite legislative plan for direct relief and work relief. Such a plan should provide for a non-partisan board and the selection of relief administration officials under Civil Service requirements. We must not substitute local politics for Federal politics, and there is no reason why the Federal grant of money should not be used to prevent it. Other conditions should insure that the state plan for direct relief would reach all needy persons and meet certain financial standards.

The system which I have proposed was suggested to the President nearly a year ago by the Associated Community Chest Organizations of the United States, which have had practical experience with relief. It was rejected then by the President and Mr. Hopkins, but today committees of the Senate and House of Representatives are considering the plan.

Representative Smith says that relief is a Federal responsibility, and I am prepared to admit that the Federal Government has a responsibility to assist financially in this emergency situation. But when he says that there is a Federal responsibility for administration because of the superior ability of the Federal Government, he is attacking the entire constitutional system of the United States. The same argument would transfer to the Federal Government the administration of the schools and of every other local activity. As a matter of fact, the Federal Government has not shown that it has

140

any superior ability, except a superior ability to tax and tax and spend and spend.

The independence of the people and the permanence of democracy depend on the administration of local affairs by local governments. In the field of relief it should be more efficient; should provide more value for the money paid out; get relief to the people who really need it, and get it to them without politics or favoritism.

VIII

SOCIAL SECURITY—WHY AND HOW?

SENATOR TAFT

CITIZENS of the United States of America: What is social security? It is a term of which we heard very little before the beginning of the depression in 1929. It was not an American concern before that time, whether the Administration was Republican or Democratic. Neither liberals like Woodrow Wilson nor conservatives like Warren Harding concerned themselves greatly with any national action for social security, although here and there throughout the states experiments were being attempted. Social security is a system designed to give every man and woman assurance that they and their families will not be thrown onto the streets and left without food, clothing, and other necessities, either by reason of old age or physical infirmity or inability to get a job. It was not much discussed before 1929, because we thought we had developed a system in America which would provide social security without Government action. We thought we had developed a system under which every man could secure employment. We thought we had developed a system under which a man who was willing to work during his active years could save enough money to provide for himself in his old age or educate his children so that they could earn enough to take care of him. If we had been right, the United States would have had the best form of social security — one dependent on a man's own efforts instead of the Government's, one providing an American standard of living and not a relief standard of living. And let us remember that social security for most of the people still depends much more on this superior American system of individual effort and reward for thrift and intelligence and hard work, than it does on legislation.

Of course, even in pre-1929 days there was plenty of poverty and misfortune. But they were handled by various private agencies and local government institutions which looked towards assuring social security. Old people's homes, orphan asylums, hospitals organized by private charity, or local government took care of cases of misfortune, and in times of prolonged unemployment, charity work was extended to the homes of the unemployed.

But in 1929 we found that we did not have the economic system we thought we had. Thousands of people lost their life savings. Millions were thrown out of work. The immense financial burden broke down the solvency even of local governments. And so the people turned to the attractive plans for social security, particularly for old age pensions and unemployment insurance, which had been developed in various European countries.

Today every party and every sincere student of social conditions is in favor of relief, adequate old age pensions, mothers' pensions, and unemployment insurance, and all feel that the Federal Government must take the lead and provide the financial resources necessary to make the plan effective. The broad term " social security " embraces work relief and direct relief, but it is more often applied to the forms of assistance provided by the Social Security Act; namely, pensions for the aged, unemployment insurance, and pensions for mothers with dependent children.

When it comes to the Social Security Act itself, and particularly the exact method in which old age pensions shall be paid and the money raised to pay them, there is a substantial difference of opinion in this country today. Most people do not realize that nearly all the old age pensions paid today are still paid under state laws by state governments, and the only assistance from the Federal Government is a grant of half the money required. The states pay the other half out of state taxes. The Federal money comes out of the general fund of the treasury and does not even come from the payroll tax. In Ohio, for instance, our old age pension system, from which 120,000 people are drawing pensions, was enacted by state law, initiated by the Ohio Federation of Labor and the Fraternal Order of Eagles. It was adopted before the New Deal began, and it was a universal plan to reach all of the needy aged, and not contributory or limited to certain groups.

On top of this system, the Federal Social Security Act provides for a reserve plan of old age pensions, each man to build up a reserve from a payroll tax on the wages he receives, paid one-half by the employer and one-half by the employee. This tax is now two per cent and is to increase to six per cent. Unfortunately it will be many years before anyone gets as large an old age pension under this plan as he can get now from the state without making any contribution at all. Incidentally, the reserve plan only reaches certain classes of employees and omits entirely large groups like agricultural laborers, household servants, itinerant workmen, and others. It is extremely complicated to keep lifelong records for everyone who is covered, and there will be countless errors in these records.

One difficulty with the present plan is that it has two systems of old age pensions which overlap, and no provision is made for their ultimate reconciliation. The theory of the plan is that a man accumulates a reserve to pay his own pension in his old age, but for many years he will not get as much of a pension under this plan as the state is paying under the state plan without any contribution from the recipient at all.

145

The present Social Security Act has been tremendously burdensome upon industry. Even now the two per cent payroll tax is raising approximately $600,000,-000 a year from the people of the United States, while paying out only about $12,000,000 in pensions. The unemployment insurance tax of three per cent on payrolls, all paid by the employer, raises about $900,000,-000 a year. Ultimately this tax will all be passed on to the consumer or passed back to the workman, increasing the price of every product that the average workman buys. But in the meantime it puts a heavy premium on cutting down labor, and there is a constant incentive to employers to cut down the number of workmen through the increase in the use of machinery or otherwise. The payroll tax tends to increase unemployment just at a time when unemployment is the most serious menace in the entire country.

The so-called reserve plan in the Social Security Act contemplates the building-up of a huge reserve, amounting to $50,000,000,000, by 1980. In the coming fiscal year the Government will take away from the people in payroll taxes $1,600,000,000. About three-fifths of the unemployment insurance money will be paid out; the rest used to increase the unemployment insurance reserve. More than half the old age tax will be used to increase the reserve, even if the grants to states for pensions are deducted, so that unless some change is made, the Government will take in over $700,000,000 more than it pays out, including railroad payroll taxes, depriving the people of just that much purchasing power at a time when it is vitally needed.

The law provides that this reserve must be invested in Government bonds. That means that when the money comes into the reserve fund it is paid over into the treasury, and the treasury prints and puts into the reserve fund the same amount of Government bonds. In other words, the Government invests its money in its own IOU's. After the money gets into the general treasury, it is used to pay the current deficits of the New Deal Administration. The reserve is supposed to provide pensions in the future, but what happens in 1980, when the Government wants to get money with which to pay the pensions? There is no cash in the reserve fund, so it has to go out and tax the people a second time to pay the interest on the bonds so that there may be money in the fund to pay the pensions. People have to pay taxes a second time, because the first payment of taxes has been used for the payment of deficits.

Of course the truth is the whole reserve plan is unsound. It is sound enough for a private insurance company, dealing with a limited number of policyholders, but an entire people cannot have a reserve. The people cannot live on machinery or buildings or property. They are interested in food and clothing, and no nation ever has had a reserve of more than a year's supply of food and clothing. In substance, the only way we can feed and clothe people who are not working is to tax the people who are working at or about the same time or are receiving a return on past savings at or about the same time — a sufficient part of their earnings to take care of those who are not working. Under a nationwide old age pension system, we might as well recognize that these pensions must be paid substantially out of current taxes. The whole plan should be on a pay-as-you-go basis. If we do that, we can reduce the payroll tax for the present, because one per cent instead of two per cent will take care of all the money now paid out by the Federal Government to assist in the payment of pensions.

After protesting for years that the New Deal social security plan was the last word in perfection, Secretary Morgenthau last month suddenly admitted that it was fundamentally wrong, and that the reserve should be cut down to a much smaller sum, sufficient only to take care of minor variations in probable tax receipts. The Secretary and the President both seem to have finally come around to Senator Vandenberg's proposal that the payroll tax increase, which was supposed to go into effect the first of January, 1940, should be deferred, but no action has yet been proposed by the Democratic leaders in Congress. Even if this preliminary step is taken, however, the Federal Government is still going to tax the people during the next fiscal year $1,600,000,-000, and turn back, in the form of unemployment insurance benefits, aid to states for pensions, and expenses of operation, only about $860,000,000, so that more than $700,000,000 will go into reserves at a time when we need all the purchasing power possible in the United

States. With Secretary Morgenthau's change of front, the whole future of old age pensions is in complete confusion, and a new start must be made.

Personally, I see no sense in a contributory reserve system as long as we are granting pensions anyway to all of the needy old, unless that contributory reserve plan be supplementary and optional. And there can be no doubt in my mind that the American people demand a universal system of pensions regardless of past earnings. If the reserve plan were made optional, so that any man dissatisfied with the amount of the standard pension could build up, with the assistance of his employer, an additional reserve for himself and receive a supplemental pension, the reserve plan could be fitted into a universal pension plan.

The natural method of establishing a universal pension plan is to rely on the present state pensions, with assistance from the Federal Government as at present, or perhaps in a slightly increased percentage, provided through a sales tax or a general transactions tax rather than through a payroll tax. But no additional tax should be adopted unless the payroll tax for old age pensions were repealed.

The unemployment insurance plan is being extended to additional states, and there is reason to hope that it will prove to be satisfactory and acceptable. It is important that the tax be lightened on those industries which provide stable employment, so that there may be a strong incentive to other industries to stabilize their own employment. After all, our main purpose should be to prevent unemployment rather than to provide insurance against it, for unemployment insurance will only take care of comparatively short periods of unemployment, and after it is exhausted the employee again faces the relief rolls.

Unemployment relief and social security are different parts of the same problem. They should be administered by the same department, under the local or state government, with financing and supervision from the Social Security Board in Washington. When a man first loses his job, he will be taken care of for some time through unemployment insurance benefits based on the contributions of his employer. When these are exhausted, if he has not yet been able to find a job, the state can provide direct relief for a certain number of additional weeks. After that, to prevent demoralization and improve his income, he should be put on work relief. When he reaches the age of retirement, if he is still in need, he receives an old age pension.

Today the whole relief and social security field is in complete confusion. Few men understand what they are entitled to receive. All of them are being taught to lean on the Government. The appropriations for relief create a tremendous deficit, while taxes for social security pile up in the treasury. Certainly the time has come to deal with the whole problem of social security as one problem, on simple, logical lines, with as little confusion between different agencies of government as possible.

Of course the principal difficulty in any system of social security is the tremendous cost on the majority of the people who still provide their own social security. No one should be more interested than the recipient of social security payments to see that that cost is reasonable, for if the burden becomes too heavy, the entire system may be destroyed by those who have to bear that burden, namely, the average workman with a steady job. Social security should not deprive any man of incentive to improve his own condition and save his own money for his old age and for his family. Payments made by the Government to millions of men will never be much more than enough to provide food and clothing and other necessities, because the cost is so tremendous that it may destroy the incentive of all others to do the very work which is necessary to provide even that subsistence allowance.

If a man wishes a home to live in in his old age, he must still save the money to own that home. If he wishes an income to enable him to live comfortably, with an occasional winter trip to Florida, he had better save enough money in the bank or building and loan association to provide his own pension. We owe to every man a reasonable allowance to protect him and his family against the inequalities of our economic system. But the scope of any plan to accomplish this purpose is so tremendous, its cost is so great, that we may destroy the whole basis of the very economic system to which we are looking to provide social security itself. No one should have any pride of opinion in his particular pet theories, and certainly I have none in mine, but

151

I am convinced that the system must be more simple, more efficient and better coördinated than the welter of confusion which we see in this country today.

REPRESENTATIVE SMITH

KINSMEN in Texas, neighbors in Illinois, friends in North Carolina; men and women of America: greetings from Washington.

The Senator's speech fits discordantly into our Easter meditations upon the passions and the pilgrimage of mankind. The social security law is probably the greatest single effort yet made in America to bury the fears and to resurrect the hopes of average citizens. Great as it is already, it bids fair to extend and to perfect itself with the years. The legislation was born of a time when desire for work and lack of work were both conspicuous. But the social security movement is much deeper than the work relief program, which the Senator and I discussed last week. Though this Act is made up of ten different programs, we may simplify it thus around the problem of work: it seeks to smooth the path of life for as many as possible of those who are too dependent to work (both children and their mothers), those too old to work (both the indigent and the retired), those too

152

weak to work (both the crippled and the sick), and those temporarily unwanted for work (the unemployed).

This social security program has been non-partisan in idea and in plan. It was proposed by the President months in advance of enactment. It was debated by everybody and worked over by non-political experts. It was not a party matter in Congress. Only 33 voted against it, out of 435 in the House, and only 6 out of 96 in the Senate. The almost superhuman job of organizing the work was put into the hands of a board which, so far as I can learn, has done an unusual job of keeping books for millions and millions of people. For, mark you what has been done in so short a time. Already three and a half million of the aged, the blind, and dependent are receiving Federal-state allowances. Already all the states have unemployment compensation laws and more than twenty-seven and a half million wage earners have earned credits toward out-of-work relief under these laws. Already forty-three million workers have applied for accounts under the Federal old-age insurance plan. This is clearly the most far-reaching thing Americans have ever undertaken co-operatively. It is so far-reaching that critics might have been forgiven the advance thought that it could not be done. I find it more difficult to understand those who now complain at it, after it has been done.

I

It's amazing how many things, however, you can complain at if you just sit down and try. You can make anything look like thirty cents — including yourself. Try it on your lodge, and tell me how your lodge looks after you are through. Try it on your school. Try it on your church. Try it on your friends. Don't try it on yourself. Have you been trying it on the social security program, or have you only been listening to them that try it on the program? Well, what's left? Why, the social security program is left, that's what. With all the tone of complaining tonight, did you catch a single one of the ten distinct aspects of this great Act our critic would repeal? I did not. Did you catch a single benefit Mr. Taft would relinquish? I did not. Did you catch a single included group the Senator would exclude? I did not.

No wonder that we did not catch these fruits of his complaining. He's *for* this security business, you see, lock, stock, and barrel. He's for the idea and even for the Act, since he does not propose to do any repealing. Let's assume that he's for security — he says that he is — and try fairly, then, to see what he's complaining at. They also serve who only stand and criticize. He complains at the payroll taxes. Now he may be right about them, but he proposes in their stead something like a sales tax, which certainly as far as it goes outrages every principle of just taxation by making the poor poorer and leaving the rich richer. I'm certainly not impressed by

154

that complaint. Perhaps what he doesn't like, is any tax at all. Well, most of us are with him there; but it won't help much, since we all agree with him also in wanting the benefits.

He complains at the reserve feature of the old-age insurance. Well, he may be right about that, too. But how much will you bet that, if we had adopted a plan without the reserve, he wouldn't have complained even louder that the plan was not fully financed? The matter is debatable, but complaining gets to be a habit also. I know this matter is debatable, because there have been important experts, not to mention sincere politicians, on both sides. I wonder whether one reason the reserve was kept was not the fear that if chronic complainers came into power they'd repudiate the benefits promised unless there were reserves to pay them. But that danger no longer holds. Mr. Taft, who can speak for the conservatives, assures us that now such benefits ought to be paid out of direct taxation as the benefits come due. If these powerful complainers who want to come back into power really feel that way about the matter, then we can safely drop the reserves or cut them to a small amount.

Such a reduction is exactly what's being proposed now by the Administration, ever alert to improve. Instead of complaining at the Secretary of the Treasury and the President for changing with this change of the conservatives, Mr. Taft ought to congratulate the Administration on having an open mind and on keeping up with the times. Maybe that's the reason the reserves were put in, I now further suggest, to bring substantial conservatives 'round to the reasonable position of lending their confidence to the credit of the nation. At any rate, now that they've done it, we can deal reasonably with the reserves in the light of their change of attitude.

I do not myself profess to know much about these matters, and I certainly do not wish to take one iota of credit from Senator Vandenberg, or Huey Long, or Dr. Townsend, or Mr. Taft, or anybody else for their part in bettering this great legislation. It was unpartisan in conception and ought to be kept so in execution and in improvement. Indeed, all such technical matters are in my opinion best left to cautious students who know the subject and have no political interest in the changes. Such groups correct honest mistakes without heat and can prick the bubble of prejudice without the necessity of face-saving.

The latter's exactly what such a distinguished group has already and recently done in connection with a bogey about as scary as the one last national election, you remember, when they tried to make the social security registration a badge of bondage if not indeed a passport to prison. That bogey only scared voters away from prevaricators. I refer now to the bogey of reserves, empty save as filled with Government IOU's. I hoped the Senator would have been above such innuendoes. If we are to have reserves, they cannot lie idle; they must be invested. Does anybody propose anything better than Government securities guaranteed to yield the fund three per cent? The Senator did not, and I hear no such proposal. A distinguished non-partisan group recently advised the Senate subcommittee studying this question to exactly this effect: ". . . the present provisions regarding the investment of the moneys in the old age reserve account do not involve any misuse of these moneys or endanger the safety of these funds." It may be unwise to have a reserve, as Mr. Taft argues; but as long as we have one, whether it be large or small, we shall and must invest it in this prudent manner.

II

So much for prevailing murmurings. I have touched upon all the Senator's important complaints, I think, save one. In treating such details seriously, I have assumed that the critic is in favor of social security. The Senator says that he is, says so tonight. But I cannot forget another night and what he said then. It was the first night we met before the microphone, and then he said: "While social security may be a desirable adjunct, it is no American ideal." How does an American favor social security who does not favor it as, or believe it to be, an American ideal? Well, he might favor it as a political expediency, as some have favored the Townsend Plan. I do not know that this is Mr. Taft's position with reference to social security, though he has apparently left an impression on the Townsend people that he favors their plan. All for economy as Democratic critic, you see, all for extravagance as Republican friend!

I mention this not to be personal with the Senator, as he will understand; but to illustrate what puzzles me about all such conservatives. I clearly got the impression tonight — didn't you? — that the Senator doesn't want the Government in all this expensive business of security. That's his great and steady underlying complaint. Still tonight he pushes away not a single benefit from a single group. He wants the Government out, but he wants what cannot be had without the Government's being fully in. Just as some say that they are in favor of work relief — page Mr. Taft from last week! — but deny what they say by throwing it back to states that simply cannot provide the work, so many are in favor of security — so they say — but want it provided by individualism that cannot provide it or want it handled by states that cannot handle it. This is an old trick, a trick which I honestly believe conservatives use to fool themselves and allay their sense of guilt at the woe of the world, a guilt which Mr. Taft boasted last week that he did not feel. It is as if to say with Hamlet:

> The time is out of joint: — O cursed spite,
> That ever I was born to set it right!

III

I think I understand this divided personality, partly because of what I, the son of a pioneer, feel in myself about this expansion of governmental machinery and partly because of what I met in Illinois last election. Senator Taft's group in my state not only flirted with the Townsend Plan but they actually promised if elected to office in the state, an old age pension out of state funds that would have bankrupted Illinois, and at the same time they swore they'd reduce taxes. We Democrats had to carry the banner of a balanced budget to save the credit of the state. Napping too long in the sleepy hollow of normalcy, the conservatives now find themselves in a world too much for them. They themselves feel insecure and grab at every passing straw. Anything that they can do of what they must do is so unideal that the worst they can do seems to them hardly more bad than the best they can do — or at least what they promise to do in politics.

Politics can be a moral matter only when what we must do in politics still seems to belong to our ideals. Then we can will both the end and the means. To me, I confess, social security seems not only an American ideal but, as I have said before, *the* American ideal. Mr. Taft has gone out of his way to deny that it is an American ideal. No wonder, then, that his very acceptance of social security as a present necessity is shot through with a constant undercurrent of complaining. He's not going to be happy, whatever we, or even he, may do about it. He accepts the mathematics of it but he rejects the morals of it.

This attitude toward security is understandable for the conservative well-to-do who can get security individually. It might even be understandable for my own group that can provide security for themselves professionally. As a school teacher I have for years paid five per cent of my salary and my school has paid another five per cent, so that I may give all my mind to my work and not have to worry about old age. It makes more difference than one might think.

Mr. Taft, a successful lawyer and business man, can provide this security personally and I, a school teacher, can get it professionally. But the great majority of citizens cannot get it either way. We want them to have it, at least I do, as the deepest demand of the greatest American ideal. We want it not merely as a matter of sympathy for them; we also want it for them as a matter of safety for ourselves. Even the well-to-do cannot maintain their security in a heaving ocean of mass insecurity. But to make this class possession into a mass gain, there's only one way, and that's through government. Indeed, that's exactly what democratic government's for, to enable men to get coöperatively what they need, when they cannot get it either individually or professionally. To see how imperative this security matter is for mankind and to see that governmental coöperation is the only way to get it is to dismiss constitutional cult words against a people's government and is to accept the *democratic centralism* which I have been proclaiming as the New Federalism.

IV

The only other thing necessary to get over the notion that security is not an American ideal is to see that it has always been and is now the driving motivation among us of all classes alike. Now this is so easy for me to see that I think I can even show it to Senator Taft. My earliest memory indeed is that of sitting in the spring seat, as we called it, of a prairie schooner, as you movie-goers call it, with my father driving West, ever West, young man, growing up with the country about a hundred miles further on each year or so. It was toward the end of the long trek of the pioneers — in that last frontier, the Lone Star State.

Now, well-to-do lawyers and comfortable movie-goers may think that the trek was due to restlessness, and it was — the restlessness of the poor. You may think it was due to adventure. And it was — adventure after security. I do not recall, however, that my father thought it adventure, and I am sure that my mother did not. They both, I believe, and all their honest hard-working kind, took it as a risk and hardship — endured, however, in hope of greater security for themselves toward the evening of life and of more secure opportunity for their children through the morning and noonday of life. The romance of adventure woven around the heads of pioneers is largely spun from the inexperience of youth or from the comfortable security of the well-to-do.

So also the illusion that the individualism of the wealthy was a personal virtue and quite independent of governmental aid, as the Senator from Ohio constantly seems to imply. When in the past these individualists ventured to build railroads, they expected the Government to " secure " them with a right-of-way, not to mention the added security of every other section of land along the way. When they chanced new lines of manufacture, they expected the Government to " secure "

161

them with appropriate tariffs against outside competition. They were just like us, only they were seeking security as a privilege because they already owned it as a property right. And today the telltale cry of " confidence " (which is but the name for their security) is directed to what they name derisively " the providential state " (so called because it ministers to the poor). Is rugged individualism to be reserved for ragged individuals alone?

V

To get all this clear is to know at last what Jefferson tried to tell us long ago. Since day after tomorrow is his birthday (April 13), I may invoke his aid and close. Jefferson too, you remember, " deserted his class," said and say those who also say that there is no class society in America. When all the conservatives said the sacred trinity was " life, liberty, and property," Jefferson said " life, liberty, and the pursuit of happiness." He said it in our Declaration and later said it in Paris to Lafayette for the French declaration of the rights of man. He dared to make it the business of government to give to men without property the security which rightly belongs to persons, as well as accidentally belongs to property. By doing so, this Jefferson radical to his day became for our day the patron saint of all conservatives. They appreciate having done what they will not do and what they complain about when we do it. Our social security program today has all the marks of Jefferson upon it: it's bold in conception, conservative in execution, and

162

growing all the while. It guarantees to the many as a right what the few have always had as a privilege.

Who says this practice is not an American ideal? Not the workers. They're even willing to increase their half of the payroll tax next year! Who, then, says it's not an American ideal? And why?

IX

THE WAGNER LABOR RELATIONS ACT
—SIT DOWN OR GET UP?

REPRESENTATIVE SMITH

KINSMEN in Texas, neighbors in Illinois, laboring men and women of America: greetings from Washington.

Let's get at the most delicate thing first. Then perhaps we can be reasonable about the most important things. The most delicate thing in this subject of labor is the sit-down strike. Don't get agitated; for I have good news for you, even if it be a little old. The Supreme Court's "agin" it. Attorney General Murphy, former governor of the most-sat-upon state of Michigan, is "agin" it. Senator Taft is "agin" it, I think. And I know that I'm "agin" it. I'm even "agin" the conditions that caused the sit-down strikes. Everybody's

" agin " the strikes themselves, now that safety has returned and popularity whistles down the wind with the
hunters. Since we're all " agin 'em," as is the Labor
Board, why don't we all be so " agin 'em " as to help the
Board keep them, or something worse, from returning?
If the causes [1] remain, there could be worse effects than
to sit down in strike. These curious strikes weren't violent, you remember — not much. They were in fact
and as a whole puzzlingly peaceful.

I

The real trouble has been, and still somewhat is, that
*American employers had to be forced by law to recog-
nize what they ought to have recognized in conscience,
that is, the practice of collective bargaining.* That's the
meaning of the Wagner labor law. Admitting the principle as an abstract right, employers long defeated it in
practice by insisting that they be both the judge and
jury to administer the right. When a government sympathetic with working men came into power in '33 it

---

[1] Speaking of causes, I wonder if we can't agree that the way to keep
men from sitting down against employers, or otherwise striking, is to help
men stand up on the job — hearts calm in a sense of justice, heads high
with hope? That's exactly what the National Labor Relations Act was
meant to achieve and that's exactly what the Labor Board has been working at under the Wagner Act, through a tirade of abuse. This tirade has
caused citizens to forget that fifteen out of eighteen Supreme Court decisions have favored the Act and its Board. It has caused nearly half the
newspaper editorials on the adverse Fansteel decision (154 out of 352) to
accuse the Board of condoning the sit-down, though the Board itself admitted the sit-down illegal and punishable under the state courts. It has
caused the impression that the Board favors the C.I.O., which the figures
show not to be so.

165

made the right into a privilege by the very Wagner law. Moreover, it provided a public body, the Labor Board, to administer the right. Seeing all this, the employers themselves sat down in pious obstruction.

First the Act was declared unconstitutional. No, I don't mean by the Supreme Court. The Court said otherwise. But before the Court could say anything, the employers got fifty-eight lawyers of the Liberty League to save the Court the trouble by themselves declaring the Act unconstitutional. But when the Act wasn't unconstitutional, after all; and when the Board, whose duty it was to see that the Act *acted*, began to make the law work, it in turn became the victim of savage attack; its membership was rotten, they said; its philosophy was biased, they said; its procedures were wrong, they said.

You've heard the Republican conservative story before, haven't you? First, we don't need improvement, for normalcy's enough. Then we need some improvement, but what's proposed is wrong in principle. Then the principle's all right, but the way of working it out (by boards or otherwise) is all wrong. Then at last everything's all right (in about that tone of voice), but we Republicans can administer it better than you Democrats can — and, besides, we'll see to it that the thing doesn't go any further!

II

Knowing this story of obstruction now by heart, we can exonerate the Labor Board from what happened while employers were running riot under legal immunity of their self-invented unconstitutionality of the Act. After the Court gave the "Go ahead," an amazing record has been written by the Board, a record which will bear the most careful and critical inspection. The story of that record I'll make brief if you'll enable me to do it by listening closely to these figures. Less than one-third as much time was lost by American workmen on strike in 1938 as was lost in 1937 (when the unconstitutionality question paralyzed the Board). Last year, indeed, the Board closed 8,851 cases of complaints against employers. In only two per cent of these cases did the Board have to order employers to quit hindering workers from collective bargaining. Is that what all the hollering's about — the correction of an autocratic two per cent? Forty per cent of the complaints against employers were dismissed by the Board or withdrawn by unions. More than fifty per cent of the cases were settled by agreement between the parties. More than half of all the cases!

Hear that record again and behold a Board that's literally protecting employers as well as employees: of nearly nine thousand complaints filed, forty per cent dismissed or withdrawn, fifty per cent settled by agreement, only two per cent of all cases pushed through with decisions against employers! No wonder strikes have now decreased in number and duration, organizations of workers grown apace, and more working agreements signed than ever before in our industrial history!

III

What, then, of the continuing opposition to the Act, coming now to a head in Congress?

I'm not on the committee to handle the matter in the House, as Mr. Taft is in the Senate; and so I'll content myself chiefly with illustrating the spirit in which current outcries should be heard by liberal men and, I hope, by conservatives also. I do this because I am convinced that unless we children of the radio prove less prejudiced than the children of the press, fiction will continue to outlaw truth and delay industrial justice.

Obviously, the Board itself is in the best position to know what has worked, and what not, in furthering collective bargaining. Any changes, therefore, which the Board proposes will be in keeping with the spirit of the Act. The same for Senator Wagner, the author of the Act, who is willing for the Board to change its rules to help employers out of a jurisdictional predicament for which they are not to blame. As for the many changes otherwise proposed, let us be honest and say that there's hardly one that will not, directly or indirectly, impede collective bargaining. (See *Fortune* magazine, October, 1938, for elaboration on this theme, statistical and otherwise.)

We must assume that we want collective bargaining. The enemies of the present act say they want it and the friends know there's no other way now open toward industrial peace. Wanting it, there's one complaint in particular that neither Senator Wagner nor the Board nor any other friend of the Act is likely to countenance. It is the complaint that the Board is both judge, prosecutor, and jury. Even where the intent of this complaint is not to weaken the Act, the result is nevertheless just that — and other results still more far-reaching.

What would you think if an enemy of our form of government said that our famous system of trial by jury isn't fair because the same system prosecutes and judges the accused? That statement's true, you know. The same system does perform both functions. But in the system one prosecutes, one defends, one judges, and twelve decide. So in large measure with the Labor Board. Like the jury system, the Board as a body handles all the functions necessary to prevent and to settle these special disputes. But the Board is some eight hundred trained people. Of these, some investigate, others prosecute, and still others decide. And don't forget that, in addition, the final decisions of the Board itself become penalties only under the judgment and consent of the regular courts of the land.

Most of the complaints against its present procedures are actually covert attacks upon administrative law. The Labor Board is not essentially different, in the regard criticized, from the now highly respectable Interstate Commerce Commission, which also combines investigative and judicial functions. This form of control has grown up in America, in England, and in other democratic lands because there is no other way so simple, so economical, so effective, and so just to deal with problems requiring control. The courts are not available. They are too few by far, and too cumbersome beyond all doubt. To ask the courts to do it is to ask that it be not done. A commission or a board can cut through red tape, can get at the facts, can reach a decision, and can right wrongs while the parties wronged are still alive.

Employers who mean to be a law unto themselves naturally prefer a control that does not control them. So long as there are employers who do not fully and gladly accept the practice of collective bargaining — and there are a good many left — friends of labor must look for the bug of sabotage under every chip of an amendment. They who want no interference with their power over their men join forces with those who want no interference with normalcy anywhere. It is this combination of the industrial autocrat and the political reactionary which must be ever feared — but now be met and mastered. They represent a conspiracy to have those who don't want public control, controlled by those who don't want to control them.

These efficient boards and commissions, on the other hand, can track injustice down to morasses not entered by the courts and can thus clear the ground for judges the better to function. Not to accept and to perfect this type of control is to embrace political lethargy and to restore economic anarchy. And the oldest trick to cover this infamy is to complain at any control that's effective and to praise only the type of government that does not govern. I have this ancient truth on high living authority, the authority of my distinguished opponent, the

Junior Senator from Ohio. I quote Mr. Taft's own telling words from our sixth debate: " Much of the opposition to the extension of Federal power comes from people who know that they are beyond the power of the states and do not wish to be subjected to any governmental power whatsoever."

I hope that the Senator can recognize his specimens as well as he has described them. If so, he will surely rebuke in the Senate, as I in the House, those who attack the Labor Board with amendments intended to prevent the Board from extending to all workers, under the Wagner Act, collective bargaining through agents freely chosen therefor.

IV

Pardon me if I speak too earnestly in this matter. It lies very near my heart, and that for two main reasons. The first is that this Labor Board is a splendid example of what I have been proclaiming in all these debates as the New Federalism. I mean the doctrine of the coördination, rather than the separation, of governmental powers, and the providing of new forms to meet new demands for control. All these boards illustrate how democratic centralism can operate in fashion decentralized. The necessity which called them forth poses this question: Shall we govern ourselves by agencies that coördinate powers, or shall we crucify ourselves upon the cult of separate powers? That's the choice. I for one don't want it said in the hour of democratic failure that we did not even try to govern ourselves.

171

If what we've done in this labor field be one-sided, as conservatives are shrieking, then Al Capone is right in thinking that the jury system was one-sided against him. When men are violating the elemental rights of other men, you tell them they must stop it. You set up a law with proper machinery to make them stop it. You enforce that law until they do stop it. They always say that you have it in for them, and believe that your process of justice is one-sided against them. If that's what they mean by being one-sided, then in this case they must make the most of it; for it's one-sided only against those who are themselves found off-side of justice.[1] True conservatives like Mr. Taft must make every effort to show that their criticism of this Board is really not a plea to return to that industrial anarchy where the strong did what they would to the weak and did it in the name of freedom of contract — not to mention the Golden Rule.[2]

My second reason for such earnest emphasis tran-

---

[1] You remember how Goliath said it to little David: " Come on out on the field of honor just as you are, and let's fight it out like men "? But when they gave David a slingshot, Goliath howled that he ought to have one, too. Do you recall that Goliath not only lost the fight but also his reputation? David said that the giant was a bully, and history has recorded that he was a poor sport.

[2] Wasn't it Judge Gary of the United States Steel Corporation who the day after refusing to meet his men in conference dedicated a great law school by advising young lawyers that he had always found the Golden Rule an all-sufficient guide in business?

It certainly was Chief Justice William Howard Taft who saw and said in 1921 that " A single employee was helpless in dealing with an employer . . . Union was essential to give laborers opportunity to deal on an equality with their employers."

scends all amendments, goes back of the Board, lies back of the Act. It arises from what this Act has in mind to achieve: industrial peace and democratic justice. Starting with a state of war, we must work ourselves out of it through gradually diminishing forms of warfare. In our jury system, a murder trial is, I admit, a rough way of getting at justice. It's a kind of mutual bickering climaxed by a sort of ordeal of oratory. Rough, yes; but a great improvement over the feud. We're just passing out of the feud stage of labor and capital. Our justice may be rough, but it's directed against only malefactors of economic power. This Wagner Act constitutes the first step, and a long one, toward making political democracy at last " democ " in the industrial field. Are there those who actually believe that we can preserve political democracy as only a green oasis in a desert of industrial autocracy? I cannot think that Mr. Taft believes so; and I know that I could never believe so.

Then here's democracy for a fact.

In the elections held by this Labor Board under the Wagner Act, there has been an average vote of ninety-six per cent of all those eligible to vote. Now, that's democracy for you! Compare it with the probable average of ten per cent, or at most twenty-five per cent, of eligibles voting in ordinary elections the country over. Talk about local responsibility; here it is under Federal safeguards of fair play! Talk about faith in self-government; here it's demonstrated that when we provide men a way to express themselves on the things that count for most, rather than those that count for least, men are alert and dependable.

How can one feel lightly about this Wagner Act? *It represents the greatest extension of democracy since manhood suffrage.* All honor to its fair and courageous Board that has in two hard years converted the hitherto empty rights of labor into the daily practice of genuine collective bargaining. That's the New Federalism for you, at work in the factories of our land and triumphant in the hearts of those who man the machines of our great industrial nation.

∾∾∾∾∾∾∾∾∾∾∾∾∾∾∾∾∾∾∾∾∾∾∾∾∾∾∾∾∾∾∾∾∾∾∾∾

SENATOR TAFT

CITIZENS of the United States of America: The argument against amendment of the Wagner Act presented by Representative Smith is so typical of New Deal methods that I cannot help commenting on those methods. The argument is that no one was ever really interested in the laboring man before 1932, when the New Dealers became his champions. Everyone who suggested the slightest criticism of a New Deal policy is a hidebound tory, conservative and reactionary, who always did oppose progress, and whose motives now must be inspired by a desire to grind down the faces of

174

the poor. Since the critics are people of this character, it is argued, their arguments are not entitled to the slightest consideration.

This position certainly has no strength in the field of labor. Neither the Republican party nor myself can be accused of conservatism in labor matters. There were many more labor leaders who were Republicans prior to the war than there were labor leaders who were Democrats. The Republican party was the party which insisted on adequate protection for American labor against low wages abroad, and labor leaders were insistent upon this protective policy. The high wages of American labor were largely created by an adequate tariff against low wages paid in Japan and Europe and other countries. The Republican party was the friend of labor in putting through the restriction of immigration, whereas the New Dealers today are exceedingly doubtful whether they want to continue the strict policy of immigration restriction which the Republican party inaugurated.

The Republican party adopted the first workmen's compensation acts in the United States. It has always recognized the right of collective bargaining. I do not know that before 1932 any labor leader or anyone else proposed a measure guaranteeing the right of collective bargaining by law. I give full credit to Senator Wagner, who developed this idea of making collective bargaining more effective than it was before. It was not opposed by the Republicans, and it is fair to say that its basic principle is accepted by all, and certainly will not be impaired by any amendment which Congress is likely to approve. As for myself, I voted for the Child Labor Amendment, and minimum wage laws for women, and workmen's compensation laws, and the law outlawing yellow-dog contracts, before Representative Smith ever got into politics at all.

Whether the Wagner Act is the panacea which Representative Smith describes is exceedingly doubtful. There are still more than ten million men unemployed in the United States today, and, while wage rates may be higher, the total income received by each workman is lower, because industry has been so completely discouraged by New Deal policies. Contrast this to the record before 1929. The purchasing power of the average laboring man steadily increased in the United States from an index number of 41 in 1820 to 59 in 1850, to 103 in 1920, and to 132 in 1928. In other words, the position of the average workman improved three hundred per cent in a hundred years without any Wagner Act.

Whether the Wagner Act has increased the democratic process in industry is not at all clear. The adoption of the sit-down strike throws doubt on this proposition, because a sit-down strike is the means by which a small minority of the men in a plant may throw all the rest out of work. There is not much democracy about that.

As for creating labor peace, the Board's argument is that there were fewer strikes in 1938 than in 1937. This is true, but there were more strikes in 1938 than in any one of the twelve years before 1937. There were 3,000 strikes in 1938, compared to 2,000 in 1934, before the act went into effect. It was natural that strikes should fall off in 1938 from 1937, because industrial activity suffered a large decrease.

The question before Congress is not one to be determined by emotion. There are very definite criticisms of the complicated provisions of the act, and particularly of its administration by the present Labor Relations Board. In fact, I think the basic difficulty is the bias and prejudice of the present Board, and if it were not for that, amendments might not now even be proposed. The general impression throughout the United States today is that the administration of the present Board is biased, and that many hearings under the Act are a travesty on justice. I have known of enough cases myself to feel that this is probably true, and when I heard this morning the statement made before the Committee on Education and Labor by J. Warren Madden, chairman of the Board, I was more inclined to believe the charge. He reflected upon the motives of every critic of the Board, including the officers of the American Federation of Labor, Senator Walsh of Massachusetts, and Senator Burke of Nebraska, whose public spirit and disinterestedness are beyond all question to those who know them. I can only conclude that impartiality is an unknown quality to the present members of the Board. They do not regard themselves as judges,

177

but as men with a mission to organize all employees in the United States, whether they wish to be organized or not.

Mr. Edwin S. Smith is frankly an advocate of the C.I.O. and against craft unions. Another member, Mr. Donald Wakefield Smith, has been so notoriously biased that Mr. William Green himself protested against his reappointment to the Board, and the President has withheld the sending of his appointment to the Senate.

It is said that the Supreme Court has upheld the Labor Board and that therefore the charges of partiality are unsound. It is true that the Supreme Court upheld the Labor Board in all of the earlier cases. This was due to the fact, however, that in those cases the defendants relied largely on the claim that the Labor Act could not apply to an industry in one state because the Constitution only permits a regulation of interstate commerce. The Supreme Court has taken a much broader view of interstate commerce than existed before and held that almost any industry receiving goods from outside the state or shipping goods outside the state is interstate in character. Relying on the constitutional point, few employers even presented the evidence favorable to them. Since the Supreme Court's earlier decisions, facts have been presented and in many cases the courts have held that the Labor Board's interpretation of the facts was grossly contrary to the evidence presented. This is the effect of the recent sit-down cases and others.

The C.I.O. and the National Labor Relations Board did the best they could to prevent even hearings being held on amendments to the Act, although they were demanded by the A.F. of L. and every business man in the United States. Why should the defenders of the Wagner Act be afraid of public hearings if their cause is so just?

The most important thing, therefore, is to change the method of administration of the Act so that employer and employee alike, A.F. of L. and C.I.O. alike, can be certain of impartial treatment. It is not only important that they receive it but that all are satisfied that they are receiving justice and fair dealing. Only thus can we eliminate the unprecedented bitterness, distrust, and suspicion which exist today among worker and employer alike.

I think the most important step required is to separate the prosecuting function from the judicial function. Today the Board files the charges, hears the evidence, and decides the cases. No human being exists who can be completely impartial in deciding a case on which he himself has already taken a public position. Representative Smith says that is the same thing as any criminal trial. Of course he is wrong. The public prosecutor has no connection whatever with the judge. The judge has never filed any charges or taken any position until he has heard the evidence. The Labor Board's position reminds me of Alice in Wonderland: "'I'll be judge, I'll be jury,' said cunning old Fury; 'I'll try the whole cause and condemn you to death.'"

It is true that various administrative boards combine the prosecuting function and the judicial function, but it is always dangerous. The Interstate Commerce Commission is essentially different because its work is rather legislative than judicial, and it seldom does any prosecuting except in a few technical fields. I think the Federal Trade Commission would be very much better if it did not both prosecute and judge. The Board of Tax Appeals in the Treasury Department provides a precedent in tax cases, where functions are successfully separated so that the taxpayer feels he is receiving justice. But the combination of these functions in the labor field, where prejudice and violent feeling are so prevalent, threatens to destroy the whole purpose of the Act — to produce harmony in industrial relations.

Senator Burke's bill provides that the Board shall be the prosecutor, but that cases may be removed by the defendant to the Federal District Court. Senator Holman's bill provides for the establishment of a prosecuting division in the Department of Labor, the cases to be heard before an independent Labor Appeals Board of nine, responsible directly to the President. Senator Burke's bill also provides for the appointment of a new board, one member to represent the employees, one the employers, and one the public. I should be inclined to favor a prosecuting division in the Department of Labor or the Department of Justice, and an independent board to hear the cases, as proposed by Senator Holman.

Of course one essential of the Act is that employers shall not interfere with the formation of unions. The existence of company unions, financed by employers, and therefore indirectly controlled by the employers, was one of the abuses the Act sought to remove. The Board, however, has interpreted this to prevent an employer from expressing any opinion whatever to his employees. The Board has gone so far as practically to destroy freedom of speech on the part of employers because of some imaginary coercion involved in any statement made by an employer to an employee. Both the A.F. of L. and the Burke amendments, therefore, provide that it shall not be considered an unfair labor practice for an employer to confer with an employee or to counsel and advise employees, orally or in writing, about any matter within the scope of the Act.

Senator Burke's amendments further define certain unfair labor practices on the part of labor organizations as well as employers. Such practices are not to result in any criminal action, but if illegal practices like sit-down strikes are engaged in by labor unions, they cannot take advantage of the Act. I think some of Senator Burke's amendments go too far, but certainly we should make clear, as the Supreme Court has already made clear, that men who violate the law themselves cannot demand reinstatement with back pay, as the Board has tried to decree in a number of cases.

One of the most difficult matters under the act arises from the rule that the employer shall only bargain collectively with representatives chosen by a majority of the employees. This rule is supposed to carry out the principles of industrial democracy. At first blush, it violates our American ideals to say that any group of employees, less than a majority, who join together and wish to bargain with their employer, shall not be allowed to do so, but perhaps it is true that the presence of the various conflicting committees might impair the whole process of collective bargaining.

The application of this rule is very difficult. The Board has deliberately postponed elections to give union organizers a chance to organize the men into unions, even to the extent of taking them away from their older unions, and even though they may be entirely contented with existing conditions in the plant. One of the great complaints has been this delay, which has prevented employers from finding out who the agents are with whom they must bargain collectively, and often required them to determine this question at the peril of expensive back payments if they guessed wrong. All of the amendments propose that the employer be given the right to ask the Board for a prompt election, so that they may know with whom to bargain.

Of course, in determining who is the majority the question arises, majority of what? Of the employees of a particular plant, or of a particular craft, or a particular employer, or of an entire industry? The present Act gives the Board wide discretion to decide this question, and the charge is made that the Board has exercised its power so as to favor the C.I.O. unions. The A.F. of L. unions were largely built up on the craft basis, and their amendments provide for the protection of craft unions already existing, with the right to be represented by their own officers. Certainly it is desirable that more definite rules be made, determining what the units for bargaining shall be; that less discretion be given to the Board; and that no right be given to recognize an entire industry as a unit. If the employees of any particular employer desire to deal with him, they should certainly have the right to do so without being forced into a union with employees of other employers in the same industry with whom they do not wish to join. Peaceful relations will surely be assisted if an employer and his own employees can work out their own particular problems.

There are various other proposed amendments, and it is quite possible that some of them go too far. As far as I am concerned, and I believe as far as any member of Congress is concerned, there will be no amendments adopted modifying the fundamental principle that collective bargaining shall be guaranteed by law, unimpaired by any influence of the employer over his employees. I am concerned, however, that every employer and every employee shall receive, and shall feel that he is receiving, impartiality in the hearing of his cases. The labor peace which we are seeking must be founded upon justice and fair dealing between all parties to the labor relationship.

X

FOREIGN RELATIONS—CONGRESS OR THE PRESIDENT?

SENATOR TAFT

CITIZENS of the United States of America: The express powers given by the Constitution of the United States to the President in respect to foreign relations are quite limited: " He shall have power, by and with the advice and consent of the Senate, to make treaties, provided two-thirds of the Senators present concur; and he shall nominate, and, by and with the advice and consent of the Senate, shall appoint ambassadors, other public ministers and consuls." But from the nature of foreign relations, and from the beginning of the Government, the courts and the Congress have held that the President's power over foreign relations is predominant. The nation cannot speak with a multitude of voices, and the President must be the person who conducts all negotiations with foreign nations. The Supreme Court has said: " In this vast external realm, with its important, complicated, delicate, and manifold problems, the President alone has the power to speak or listen as a representative of the nation. He *makes* treaties with the advice and consent of the Senate; but he alone negotiates. Into the field of negotiation the Senate cannot intrude; and Congress itself is powerless to invade it."

On the other hand, Congress, and particularly the Senate, is given extensive powers and duties with reference to any Government action other than negotiation in the foreign field. Only Congress may regulate commerce with foreign nations. Only Congress may declare war. Only Congress may raise and support armies and provide and maintain a navy, although the President is commander in chief when they are raised or provided. Only Congress, therefore, has power to act in the field covered by the Neutrality Act, involving the embargo of shipments abroad, restraint on American ships, restraint on the loaning of money, or credit to foreign nations.

The President is responsible for what this nation says to foreign nations, but he must be very careful in his statements as to what this nation will or will not do, because, unlike most executives in European countries, he has not the final power to put his foreign policy into effect.

The position sometimes taken that Congress should

keep entirely out of foreign policy is wholly contrary to the Constitution. Congress has no business to interfere in negotiations with foreign governments, but it has not only the right, but the duty, to consider the policies which involve specific legislation like the Neutrality Act.

There is another careless statement made that no American, in Congress or out, should criticize anything the President does or says in his relations with foreign nations, because politics should stop at the water's edge. I quite agree that foreign policy is not a partisan issue, and, as a matter of fact, there is just as much difference on the Republican side today as on the Democratic side. But if in time of peace any citizen feels that the President's handling of foreign policy is wrong, or likely to lead to a war which he thinks unnecessary, it seems to me his right and duty to state that fact clearly and do whatever he can to change a policy which he thinks likely to result in war. The essence of democratic government is that men shall be free to express their opinions on any subject, certainly on a subject as vital as foreign relations. No President should be permitted to lead the country gradually into a situation where a declaration of war is almost forced on Congress, without full opportunity for criticism. The people whose very existence may be terminated by war should hear both sides and approve or disapprove the preliminary steps of any policy; and so it is entirely proper that Congress, and Representative Smith and myself, as junior members of it, should discuss our foreign policy, whether or not that discussion involves criticism of the President.

Everybody in the United States today asserts that he is for peace, though some of the weapons to secure it seem to me rather warlike. The basic purpose of the Neutrality Act and the amendments now being considered is to keep the United States out of war. I believe that most of the provisions of that Act tend to accomplish that purpose. The cash and carry provisions, providing that credit may not be given to governments engaged in war, certainly prevent our acquiring a financial interest which may lead to our support of one country against another. The provisions prohibiting loans directly to such governments have the same effect. The prohibition against American vessels carrying arms to belligerents should prevent incidents of the kind which led to our joining in the World War. The prohibition against American citizens traveling on vessels of nations involved in war is likely to remove a cause of war if such a vessel is sunk by an enemy.

The only provision in the Neutrality Act which seems ineffective to me to aid peace is that which prohibits the shipment of arms, ammunition, and implements of war to belligerent states. Since we are selling on a cash and carry basis the materials from which such munitions may be manufactured, there does not seem any great difference in principle in the shipment of munitions. Nor do I see that any nation can object to other nations buying arms in this country if the same market is open to every nation which can approach it, and so we give them no cause for war. I cannot believe that inability to get arms from us will prevent any large nation going to war, for it can build its own munition plants and buy the raw materials from us. But the refusal to sell arms discriminates against small nations which have no arms plants of their own. I should be inclined to favor an amendment of this section of the Act to permit the sale of arms to any nation on a cash and carry basis.

But I should be very much opposed to the Thomas amendment and to any other amendments which give the President power to discriminate between different nations according to his idea as to which may be the aggressor in a particular war. If we begin to take sides in foreign disputes, we will almost certainly become involved in such disputes. From George Washington to Woodrow Wilson, a policy of neutrality has always been considered as likely to keep us out of war and benefit this country. George Washington said: "Europe has a set of primary interests which to us have none or a very remote relation. Hence she must be engaged in frequent controversies the causes of which are essentially foreign to our concerns. Hence, therefore, it must be unwise in us to complicate ourselves by artificial ties in the ordinary vicissitudes of her politics or the ordinary combinations and collisions of her friendships or enmities." Woodrow Wilson insisted on a complete neutrality for two years, until direct interference by Germany with our own citizens and rights compelled us to war.

If a war occurs in Europe, and our Government deliberately sides with one nation or group of nations, and assists that nation by embargoing exports to its enemies, it will not be long before our people identify their interests completely with one side. In these days of propaganda, all of the propaganda would come from that side. The Government itself, having taken sides, would tend more and more towards war until we find ourselves first financing and then supporting with troops the favored nation. The slightest incident with the nation against which we discriminated would arouse, both in the people of that nation and in our own people, the intense bitterness which leads inevitably to war. I am pleased that even Senator Pittman, in his amendments of the Neutrality Act, proposes no power to the President to discriminate. Should a situation ever arise, after a war has begun, in which our interests seem to be directly involved in the result, Congress can determine at that time whether or not to declare war.

The President's position seems to me much too warlike. A year ago in Chicago he declared his belief that we should " quarantine the aggressor nations." In his opening speech to Congress he said: " The defense of religion, of democracy, and of good faith among nations is all the same fight. To save one, we must now make up our mind to save all." It is somewhat difficult to see how we can save democracy and good faith among nations by a policy of mere defense of the United States. The President said further, in that address, that we cannot safely be indifferent to international lawlessness anywhere in the world and cannot let pass, without effective protest, acts of aggression against sister nations. The word "effective" suggests armed intervention. The President, however, says that he does not mean armed intervention: "There are many methods short of war, but stronger and more effective than mere words, of bringing home to aggressor governments the aggregate sentiments of our own people." This must mean economic sanctions or embargoes against foreign nations, which in my opinion would abandon our whole historical policy of neutrality and lead directly to war.

The President seems to me to accept too easily the assumption that we will become involved in a European war. In leaving Warm Springs two weeks ago, he said, " I'll be back in the fall if we don't have a war." Finally, after his return, he endorsed wholeheartedly an editorial in the Washington *Post* which interpreted his Georgia remark as a threat to Germany and Italy that we would join England and France in case of war. That editorial said: " Nothing less than the show of preponderant force will stop them, for force is the only language which they understand."

There are plenty of other people in the United States who believe that we should threaten to join in a European war. Some of them would frankly be in favor of taking, immediately, an active part in behalf of England and France if war occurred. Others argue that if there is a European war, we are bound to become involved sooner or later, and if we threaten to join England and France, we will decrease the chances of war. I do not accept this argument. I do not see any reason why we must necessarily become involved in a European war if the people do not wish it. If we are determined to stay out of such a war, we can stay out of it. It is a question of our determination to do so. Those who argue that we can not keep out are really in favor of going in. I believe we should stay out of it and can.

The argument is that we should join England and France first, in order to save democracy in Europe, and then to prevent Hitler and Mussolini from overrunning the United States. I do not believe that a war in Europe, no matter what its result, would ultimately assist democracy in the world. As a result of the last war, half the democracies became dictatorships.

The line-up in Europe today is more one between nations, as in 1917, than between forms of government. Already we see lined up on the English and French side the autocracies of Poland, Roumania, Greece, and Communist Russia. A practical dictatorship has been established in France. Before such a war were over, we might find communism or fascism in control in England and France, even if the war were successful from their standpoint. We are primarily interested in the preservation of a republican form of government in the United States, not in Europe. If we join in another world war, I doubt if we could maintain such a government in this country. There would be an immediate demand for arbitrary power, unlimited control of wages, prices, and agriculture, and complete confiscation of private property. We would be bound to go far towards totalitarianism. It is doubtful whether we would ever return. War is the enemy of democracy. Our best service to the cause of democracy is to keep it alive in the United States and provide a standard to which the world may in time return.

Nor do I believe that we face any danger from Germany or Italy. We can defend our position in North America and the Caribbean against the world if we have to do so, and that very fact means that we will never have to do so. There is some selfish reason for each of Hitler's and Mussolini's acts of military aggression up to now, outrageous as those acts have been. But it is hard to see any reason for a military attack on the United States. Germany and Italy will never be released from the complications of the European situation to such an extent as to become a threat to the United States.

Those who desire the repeal of the Neutrality Act, those who favor the President's apparent position, may talk of their affection for peace, but they have already accepted in their minds the thought that we should take an active part in a European war if it occurs. They have developed the same callousness to war which has existed in the past, and they do not even admit to themselves that it involves the suffering and death of millions of Americans under the most horrible circumstances. Modern war is more terrible than any past war. It involves the unlimited slaughter of civilians as well as soldiers. If we had been in the last war from the beginning, as these people would have advocated, we would have lost millions of men instead of hundreds of thousands. Almost any solution is better than war, and certainly we should not admit that the welter of different races in Europe, and the inevitable conflicts which constantly result, should drag us into a maelstrom of destruction.

I hope the President does not mean what he seems to say. Perhaps he is only threatening Germany and Italy without intending to carry out that threat. But such a course is dangerous, for it may lead England and France into taking a position they cannot maintain without our active assistance. It might even encourage a too aggressive attitude, which the French, at least, have often adopted in the past. Let us not threaten anything unless we intend to carry out the threat. Our bluff might be called. Finally, the President should be exceptionally careful about promising support in war, which he cannot give without action of Congress, for Congress accurately reflects today the determination of the American people that they shall not become involved in European war.

REPRESENTATIVE SMITH

IN some lands differences between patriots end at the boundaries in trying times like these. And I think they would in America. But are these trying times? I could not escape the impression from the Senator's speech that because he's secure he thinks everybody's secure, and, therefore, that anybody who talks of war is " warlike," trying to create war. Particularly he seemed to suggest that any American who tries to prevent war is endangering the peace of the world. Bickering along, the Senator has jockeyed himself into a threefold error. He is as obviously wrong in dramatizing a cleavage between Congress and the President in foreign affairs as he is, after the cleavage is made, in taking sides against the President's honest efforts to keep us out of war by helping prevent horrors of war for the whole world. With war and peace at stake, I cannot believe my fellow-citizens primarily interested in a jurisdictional dispute over the dogma of separation of Federal powers, and I will not believe them indifferent to the problem of prevention.

I know, indeed, from my mail that you are immeasurably more interested today in what is done than in who does it. You are justly impatient with bickering as to who shall lead when the world's smouldering with passion and is blazing here and there into flame. I shall return to the minor issue of who is to lead only therefore after getting back into strong focus our common desire for peace and our deep faith in the possibility of worldwide prevention. This desperate desire for peace — I know it as much from my heart as from my mail — is the one fullest thought in America today. I do not know of a single Congressman who does not share with the President and with you this concern over war and this common will to peace. Our differences have to do with ways and means, not the end of peace. That said, and solemnly said, let's look at the Senator's bickering against the President, our strong leader for peace.

I

The Senator is brought around by the bold words of the Supreme Court into admitting that "the President alone has the power to speak or listen as a representative of the nation." He is even brought to admit that "into the field of negotiation the Senate cannot intrude; and Congress itself is powerless to invade it."

But still he bickers at the present President's magnificent use of this exclusive constitutional initiative, accusing the President of being warlike and even of contemplating lightheartedly our embroilment in Europe. Such easy imputations against the Chief Executive of this nation, any Chief Executive of this nation, is to me downright saddening. I will not be so caught up in the spirit of debate, however, as to reply in kind. Walter Lippmann has replied appropriately.[1] Arthur Krock has replied appropriately.[2] I imagine the Senator's conscience will in time reply appropriately to this abuse rather than right use of our splendid heritage of free speech and open criticism.

I am moved, the rather, as a student of American life, to inquire into the causes of such intemperate speech on the part of a conservative. Partly, I suppose, it is merely the tactics of the "outs" who want in. We all do this more than's to my liking. But more importantly, the

[1] Daily column as of April 22, 1939.
[2] New York *Times* as of April 23, 1939, p. 3, Sec. 4.

Senator is guilty of this indiscretion because he sees the fact without seeing the reason for the fact of the executive leadership declared so forcibly by the Court. And yet he might have learned the reason as well as the fact from the Court itself. In the same decision [1] from which he quotes, the reason follows what he quoted. Let me give you the reason in the language of the Court: The President, says conservative Mr. Justice Butler for the Court, " not Congress, has the better opportunity of knowing the conditions which prevail in foreign countries, and especially is this true in time of war. He has his confidential sources of information. He has his agents in the form of diplomatic, consular, and other officials. Secrecy in respect of information gathered by them may be highly necessary, and the premature disclosure of it productive of harmful results. . . ."

Thus the Supreme Court (1936) on the reasons for executive leadership in foreign affairs. The trouble with Senator Taft — if I may speak as frankly of him as of myself — is that he doesn't know what he's talking about. I'm convinced that though he's a Senator he knows as little about foreign affairs as I admit that I know. Indeed, I believe he knows less; for, like old Socrates who knew that he didn't know, I know at least that others know more than I do and that it is knowledge that counts here more than all our prejudices put together. Mr. Taft and I are both Mid-Westerners with the prejudices of our region around us and the igno-

---

[1] U. S. v. Curtiss-Wright Corp. U. S. Reports, 299 (1936), pp. 319–321.

rance of our offices about us. We appropriate several hundred thousand dollars a year, however, so that somebody may know more than we know and may give us guidance for our ignorance before we begin to give you guidance in your ignorance of foreign affairs.

Think a moment concretely of what the Court gave as reason for trusting the President: "He has his confidential sources of information. He has his agents in the form of diplomatic, consular, and other officials." Yes, indeed! He has at this moment 57 ambassadors and ministers and 722 consular officials stationed in listening posts throughout the complex web of this whole troubled world. A half-hundred trained diplomatic officers, I repeat, and more than seven hundred trade specialists out there listening and reporting daily upon everything from a closing market for hairpins to an opening avenue for a new plea for peace.

Daily, did I say? Why, Mr. Stimson, our former Republican Secretary of State, quoted to the Senate Committee the other day a remark of his predecessor "that nothing could happen in this world of any importance that did not come over his desk within two hours." Mr. Stimson added: "Now, certainly, that does not happen to the members of Congress." It does happen every day, however, to the Secretary of State and it happens even faster to the President of the United States. The world is today literally at the other end of the telephone. The President knows what there is to be known; and yet he must tell little that he knows, lest indiscretion further inflame the world. He must sit by with heavy heart while Senators accuse him of fingering lightly the threads of fate, and he must wear his heart out for peace to the tune of senatorial criticism that he is warlike. If he drops at Warm Springs a cautious word (interpreted most incautiously by the Senator) to let the dictators know that he knows what they're up to and that we don't like it (which they ought to know before they plunge), he becomes to dictators and to some Senators alike one engaged in foreign ballyhoo to save his face at home.

II

Let no Senator have the comfort of self-pity to shield him from the consequences of such irresponsible criticism as this. Nobody wants or means to stop free criticism, but we all join in hoping that Senators will progressively learn to talk like statesmen rather than like street urchins engaged in free name-calling to see who can do it the loudest and the naughtiest. The Gallup poll shows that the American people are not partners in this perpetration against the President as our leader. They overwhelmingly share his feeling that we are hit when our religion, our democracy, and our moral faith are attacked. They share the fear that war threatens the world. They share, too, the hope that a conference of nations can help us all more than a mere do-nothing policy.

It was, I admit, the absence of this latter faith in the Senator's speech that disturbs me most of all. He seems to think that Europe is not on the brink of war. I don't know who Senator Taft's private ambassadors are. Is there a Cliveden Set operating behind the scenes to provide us with an American Munich by telling us to be merely neutral until we cannot be neutral at all? Whatever the grounds of Senator Taft's complacency, our President, who has a half-hundred diplomatic and seven hundred trade ambassadors abroad, thinks that war, terrible war, is imminent if things are allowed to drift. Mr. Taft may be right and the President wrong. But Chamberlain since Europe's Munich has lost his face and his courage for nothing, unless there's daily danger of doom impending from the air. If there's not daily danger of war in Europe, what does the Senator make of the apparent extremity that drives Britain to conscription, an extreme measure heretofore faced only in the heat of war itself?

III

It may be that Senator Taft thinks so too but has no faith at all in efforts to prevent war. Yet he has great faith, he says, that neutrality can keep us out of whatever comes, if only we will neutrality strongly enough. The very best way to keep out of war is to keep war out. Who doubts it? Those who surrender to fate in Europe may later have to meet fate face to face with one more reserve lost. We *might* stay out of a raging war; we're *certain* to stay out of a non-existent war. Prevention is so infinitely the better bet for us to avoid war that nobody who cares will spare any effort at prevention. Not to do all we can to prevent war is to me the final callousness.

I emphasize this because every criticism made against the President's use of his constitutional power is directed at his efforts to prevent war. And not a critic has proposed a single thing to do, so far as I can recall, to prevent war. They want us to stay out, as you and I want to stay out. But they seem resigned to let war come and then hope that we can stay out. Only that hope is realistic which uses all peaceable prowess to prevent war at all, anywhere.

All honor to the President who is straining might and main to keep us out of war by keeping war from coming to anybody. He has suggested a just approach to raw materials as well as a gracious respite from the groaning tension of awful armaments. He might have done more but for critics that want nothing done. But how could he have done less, knowing what he knows, seeing what he sees, feeling what he feels? It is too early to say that he may not be successful in his latest bid against otherwise almost certain war in Europe. If those in whose hands our future fate is, since it is no longer wholly in our own hands, can listen to reason, they have been given the most compelling reasons of our generation to leave off coercion and to come to conference with guns parked outside the door.

IV

If this heroic effort fail, God grant it fail not through irresponsible criticism of the President here at home during these days of waiting and hoping for a reasonable reply from Germany. If this effort at prevention fail, then we shall unite ourselves in a drive for the wisest possible neutrality. I join Mr. Taft at that point in a hope as firm as it is desperate. There is no fate that foredooms us to war, even if war comes to Europe. Our best chance seized and lost — the chance to prevent — then we'll hug our last chance, the chance to avoid.

But that chance will prove the less if we make neutrality mean isolation. As a Mid-Westerner I'd personally prefer complete isolation. Why not let the Old World go its old way of war and the New World keep the peace it has? Well, prejudice apart, we cannot possibly isolate ourselves from the fear of airplanes and the insistence of ideas. Even if the airplanes elect to stay away — there's nothing else to keep them away — the ideas undo us, especially when our ideals get completely outraged by those who boast over the radio their outrages and threaten more and more of the very same. The trouble with us Americans is that we aren't used to having to choose between two evils. We don't want war. But we also don't like to see peaceful China crucified. We don't want war. But we also get all fussed up at the thought of death rained from the air on women and children, of cities razed and cruelty enthroned. There is no isolation of ideas. Our sympathies undo us.

Moreover, economic isolation would so dislocate our whole national life that nobody, I fear, but a philosopher who lives on humor and high thinking would stand the gaff. Jefferson tried the embargo until the people decided the cure of isolation worse than the disease — so the war of 1812. We must say, in general, with an ancient sage, that isolation is for gods and brutes alone. Alas, we Americans are not gods, and God grant that we be not brutes.

Our neutrality cannot mean isolation. It must mean self-defense. But it must mean a very spacious self-defense. The Monroe Doctrine involves us in defense to the south of us, and in defense to the north of us. That's a big order — two continents, you know, and some scattered islands. What kinds of neutrality can a country have that has already undertaken to defend two whole continents, in an age of radios and airplanes? We have accepted a man's job, and we must go at it in a man's way.

It must be a bold neutrality. Only that kind is open to us. Such a neutrality may not "name the aggressors," but it will mark who they are when they boastfully name themselves by short wave and through ugly deed. It will not purport to sympathize with crime nor stoop to recognize pillage. It will not be bullied into restricting its trade; but will do so only out of prudence and from a sense of caution. It will arm itself adequately and will keep its powder dry. A bold neutrality will harm friends as little as possible and will help its friends' enemies as little as possible. But most of all and best of all, it will leave inaction to the reactionaries and will push for prevention while yet there's time. It will not lie down on peace just because tyrants ,shout for war. A bold neutrality will be what indeed our neutrality has already become under our dynamic leader — a strenuous struggle for peace through every peaceful means that's humanly possible.

XI

THE AMERICAN FARMER—CITIZEN OR PEASANT?

REPRESENTATIVE SMITH

THE AMERICAN farmer is a citizen at last. He is now a citizen, even though he be a tenant and a sharecropper. Full citizenship for the farmer is one of the proudest achievements of the Democratic party. We did not in 1932 promise the farmer a "full dinner pail." But we did promise that we'd try to end the long-standing discrimination against him. We promised honest efforts in his behalf. We've done all that we promised — and something even better than we promised.

We've made democracy at last "democ" for those who till the soil as well as for those who work in factories. Through the Wagner Labor Act, as I have said before, we have made collective bargaining a reality at last. This industrial extension of democratic machinery was overdue.

Long overdue also was agrarian democracy. We have actually now put the farmer's fate in his own hands, politically. We have made the machinery of representation work where it had long ceased to work, if indeed it had ever worked there at all. We have given the farmer something more important to vote upon than which city slicker shall represent, or alas, more often misrepresent, him. Specifically, the farmer can now decide for himself whether he will join others to conserve the fertility of his soil and to save the soil itself from erosion. He can determine whether he will accept limitation upon the amount of this or that crop to be produced. He can and does, through the democratic machinery of a referendum, determine whether the Secretary of Agriculture shall invoke marketing quotas to hold up the prices of basic crops in spite of the farmer's friendly enemy, the surplus. Literally millions of farmers go to their own voting booths in these various ways each year now, and, without noise or undue friction, plow the democratic spirit right into the soil of their daily lives. The birth of this new spirit is more dramatic to students of the democratic process than is many a manifestation more lurid. It is a tale worth the telling in a perspective that's historic and hardly short of romantic.

I

It's not too much to say that the farmer has chronically got the worst of it in every culture as civilization passed from the rural to the urban stage. From of old, indeed, the farmer has known and felt the worst; but nature's worst is somehow bearable, having no mercy but lacking also in malice. So when the farmer suffers only at the hands of the weather, he does not complain.

> What is it molds the life of man? The weather.
> What makes some black and others tan? The
>   weather.
> What makes the Zulu live in trees
> And Congo natives dress in leaves,
> While others go in furs and freeze?
> The weather. THE WEATHER!

But when the weather provided by nature conspires with the climate provided by man, the combination often proves too much for the farmer's pocket and at last too much for even his patience to stand.

I am told that the third motto of the ancient Oracle at Delphi was born of agricultural distress in even that distant day. You remember the wisdom of the first — *Know thyself* — and the prudence of the second — *Nothing overmuch*. But do you recall the pathos of the third — *Go bail and see ruin?* These three mottoes were cut in stone for all to see and know. The tragic third one — *Go bail and see ruin* — marked a religious effort to halt the foreclosure of mortgages and to stop the peonage resulting from sale of self. These ills, it is said, came about upon the introduction of money into Greece. Before that the farmer bartered what he grew for that whose worth he understood. And all went fairly well with his work.

But when he sold what he raised for something he knew not what, and then bought what he needed with something he knew not what, the farmer sank from citizen to peasant to peon to slave. As a Greek historian put it, the farmer sold his produce for what was offered him and paid what was asked for what he needed to buy. Such double dealing soon did the Greek farmer to the death. Indeed, what farmer can stand to sell for what's offered and buy for what's asked?

II

Well, that's a story too close to the plight of the American farmer in '32 to be comfortable even in the telling. Encouraged by those who knew the value of money and interest, he raised so much of everything that he had to take whatever price was offered him for the surplus. But he had to pay whatever was asked by those who held their own prices high through controlled production protected by high tariffs. The American farmer was on his way to join the Greek farmer in the limbo of urban finance.

All through the decade of the twenties, while Republican administrations heeded the voice of big business, the American farmer was indeed being rapidly turned into an American peasant. The cities felt the throb of a feverish though all too short-lived prosperity, but many thousands of farmers were losing their farms and thousands of country banks were closing their doors. The precious fertility of the soil was rapidly going to ruin.

At last the farm depression overtook the cities. Factory workers, office workers, business men, and professional people found themselves in trouble, too. Farmers went from bad to worse, until millions of them were forced to the very lowest and most primitive level of subsistence. They would have considered themselves lucky if they had had even the dignity and the security of peasants. Actually, they were becoming economic outcasts.

Then came one who cared, choosing as Secretary of Agriculture one who knew. Sympathy and knowledge make an unbeatable team. In our agricultural administration, science has saved us from sentimentalism and sympathy from bureaucracy.

Seeing the farmer victimized by the tariff and by monopoly in general, the farmer's Administration set out to raise agricultural prices unless and until industrial prices could be brought down to the democratic level of something near parity. This process is an established policy of the present Democratic Administration. Much remains, I admit, between the farmer and parity. But the process has produced results, including this magnificent by-product of rural democracy. In this by-product Secretary Wallace has worked out the second greatest extension of democracy since manhood suffrage. He has matched industrial democracy with agrarian democracy.

These are blessings that it takes more than politicians

to produce. Secretary Wallace has the mind of a statesman informed with the spirit of science and led by a
sympathy that's realistic to the end. Such advances in
democratic forms are permanent contributions to the
life of America. Administrations may come to power
that would never have thought of thus extending the
machinery of democracy, but they will not think of
abolishing the machinery — not more than once at
least. For privileges like this gained, men have a new
hold on self-respect. They have become citizens not
peasants, children rather than step-children of Uncle
Sam. We have through this Democratic Administration given the farmer, as indeed we have given the industrial laboring man, a Magna Charta of freedom, a
genuinely national policy for the first time since this
nation's birth; but more important than the given policy
is the machinery whereby the farmer can make his own
politics hereafter. This is what it means to be a citizen:
not to get all that you want but to know that what you
do get is a result of participation with others as equals in
a process informed of justice. That is to coöperate with
the inevitable in the full discipline of responsible citizenship.

III

This is the first part of our answer to those who never
have showed anything but lethargy for the economic
plight of the farmer and now have little but criticism
for our farm program. We have made the farmer a citi-

zen. He does not now live by bread alone. The gift of democracy itself is the greatest possible fruit of democracy. But there are other concrete fruits of our policy for agriculture.

To begin with, the A.A.A. has now been declared constitutional. Agriculture is not a mere local concern, as the Court first tried to tell; but it is a national enterprise with all the power which accrues therefrom. Its problems can be faced on the scale where they actually exist. Its evils can be attacked wholesale now as well as piecemeal. Research laboratories can be established, and are being established, to seek new uses for farm products. The land grant colleges can be further encouraged, and are being further encouraged, to conserve the soil through judicious crop rotation and to increase the yield through improved breeds of plants and animals. Rural electricity can be provided, and is being provided, through a vast and growing national network. Loans can be had, and are being had, on terms heretofore reserved for city dwellers. Schools are being bettered for the farmer's children. Discussion groups can be led, and are being led, to inform the farmer's choices with the best that's thought and felt by students everywhere. Poor lands can be, and are being, withdrawn in a national policy to conserve both the soil and the sons of the soil. These are new services or greatly vitalized services to the farmer, America's oldest inhabitant but newest citizen.

IV

But there are Democratic fruits still more concrete, fruits the mellower as they are contrasted with Republican neglect of the farmer.

In 1932, farm cash income had fallen to $4,300,000,-000, the lowest on record as far back as comparable figures exist. As the farmer began to attain full citizenship, his income steadily rose to $5,100,000,000 in 1933, to $6,300,000,000 in 1934, to $7,000,000,000 in 1935, to $7,900,000,000 in 1936, to $8,600,000,000 in 1937. In 1938, farm income fell back to approximately the level of 1936, but the outlook is for resumption of the income gains this year.

The per capita purchasing power available for family living is 127 per cent greater than in 1932. The farm mortgage debt burden of agriculture has been reduced from about nine and a half billion dollars in 1928 to $7,100,000,000 in 1938. Among the most disadvantaged farm groups assisted by the Farm Security Administration, the average gain in net worth has been $265 per family, or an increase of 37 per cent.

Eighty-five per cent of all the farm families in the United States — totaling nearly 6,000,000 families and more than 25,000,000 people — are taking part voluntarily in the national farm program this year.

Balanced farming and soil conservation are being practiced on 80 per cent of the farm land and 70 per cent of the range land of the United States.

V

Both this democracy and these fruits of democracy have come to the American farmer at a price which the farmer is easily able to pay. It is true that the responsibilities of citizenship are world wide. The farmer now becomes a participant in foreign policy as well as in domestic policy. It is indeed those who hope to profit politically from agrarian unrest that have raised louder voices against our reciprocal trade agreements than have the American farmers. These treaties carry some farm debits without a doubt. What good comes to farmers or others in form unalloyed? But they carry great assets to balance the debits. They work for peace, which the farmer wants. They work against tariffs, which have historically victimized the farmer. They facilitate the flow of both goods and ideas. In all these the farmer as citizen is interested.

Nor has the farmer been regimented, as enemies of agrarian democracy charge. If we were God, we'd make it otherwise; and so, no doubt, would the farmer. We'd make it so the farmer could raise all that he wanted to of anything and everything and still get the prices that he wanted. But the farmer is not God — nor we. If the saving of our soil is a national asset, then we can afford to subsidize that saving. If the farmer is a public servant, then we must see to it that he does not sink below a minimum standard of living, education, and opportunity. But if the farmer is to be safely subsidized, it must be done opportunely, not recklessly. He cannot grow all that he wants to and still get the price that he wants to name. An ideal world would have an unrestricted abundance, but the farmer was born into an industrial world in which the principle of scarcity is at the very foundation.

Until the principle of fixing prices through controlling production be abolished in industry, it must be imitated on the farm. Indeed the farmer must imitate it up to a point in order to demonstrate the need for its abolition. What would be regimentation if imposed becomes democracy when self-perpetrated. The farmers themselves have been the moving spirits back of every plan that has been called regimentation by enemies. They have been driven to self-control through self-defense. Of course there are some farmers that do not like to abide by majority votes, just as there are some people everywhere who want the fruits of democracy without practicing democracy itself. What is called regimenting the farmer turns out in every single case that I know of to be a protest against the application of the majority principle to concrete problems on the farm. In the marketing quota provisions we have indeed required a majority of two-thirds before control is invoked. There is no price here required of the farmer that has not already been paid by every other group on its way to participate in power. The Republicans who promised in 1936 to make two farm subsidies grow where we had grown but one before will not dare to propose to subsidize an unrestricted farm surplus.

No; critics to the contrary, the American farmer is

paying only the standard price for his new power of citizenship. He is paying the price willingly for a policy which he has undertaken with eyes open. It is a new day for him, a day of democratic participation with the responsibilities and the rewards that go with self-government. There's life enough along the farm front once more to support vigorous discussion and not a little discontent. It takes life to provide these signs. But, best of all, there's the responsible recognition that comes from citizenship, and that of at least three precious sorts: first, recognition that mistakes that have been made were made with the consent of farmers themselves; second, recognition that the farmer now has the means at hand to remedy whatever can be remedied politically; and third, recognition that politics cannot remedy as much as seems easily possible from the pedestal of political innocence and impotence.

These are the recognitions of the wise who have become our new agrarian citizens.

SENATOR TAFT

FARMERS of America: In spite of the fact that Representative Smith and I come from the city, we represent farm states. In fact, from the point of view of the value of agricultural products, Illinois and Ohio stand fourth and fifth among the states of the nation, exceeded only by California, Texas, and Iowa. There is only this difference between us: that the electoral majority which I had last November in Ohio came from the farmers, whereas Representative Smith would never have been in Washington if he had had to rely on the farmers of Illinois.

I have listened with interest to all the benefits which Mr. Smith says the New Deal Administration has conferred upon the farmer. In fact, Mr. Smith would have us believe that before 1932 no one ever realized there was a farmer or that he was rapidly sinking into the position of a mere peasant. Yet, strange to say, when we look at the gross farm income during the days of the twenties, when the farmer was supposed to have been sinking into peasantry, we find that every year from 1924 to 1929 the gross income from agricultural production was between eleven and twelve billion dollars, whereas after six years of New Deal nursing it was only eight billion, four hundred million dollars in 1938, about three-fourths of what it was in the twenties, although there were ten million more people in the United States. Of course, the total farm income is more than it was in 1932. 1932 represented the bottom of a world-wide depression, which, incidentally, could not have been produced by Republican policy, because it occurred just as severely in Europe and Asia and Africa, where they never heard of Republicans, and it hit the city workman as hard as the farmer.

Of course, both political parties have always tried to help the farmer, and after the war Republicans adopted a whole series of forward-looking, permanent measures in the interest of the farmer, including the Stockyards Act of 1921, the Capper-Volstead Coöperative Marketing Act of 1922, the Grain Futures Act of 1922, extensive farm credit legislation, and numerous acts dealing with specific commodities. It is quite true that the Republicans did not adopt any panacea or trick device to raise farm prices, for the simple reason that they did not think such devices would raise farm prices, and they knew that in the long run Government price control would be against the best interest of the farmer. Our experience with six years of New Deal experimentation with currency inflation, production control, domestic allotment plans, processing taxes, and the like, is hardly sufficient to convince us that the Republicans of the twenties were wrong. In fact, back in 1920, the present Secretary of Agriculture himself said: "Farmers have been the victims of exploitation. There are too many people in public office who seem to think they ought to exercise some sort of guidance or guardianship over the farmer."

Statistics don't mean a great deal, and I am quite willing to leave it to every farmer to decide whether he has really benefited by the New Deal policy. He certainly cannot regard his present situation as any solution of his problems. He knows that he is selling corn anywhere from thirty to forty-five cents, twenty per cent less than a year ago. He knows that hogs are down from nine and three-tenths cents to seven and three-quarters cents in less than a year; wheat from ninety cents to seventy cents. The index price of all grains was 130 in 1926, 1927, and 1928, and now it is down to 63, or less than half what it was before the depression. It is slightly higher than it was at the very bottom of the depression, but no higher than the average in 1933, bank holiday and all. The drop in the price of cotton and cotton seed is almost as bad. Incidentally, the drop has been a good deal worse in these products which have been regulated than it has been in meat and dairy products, poultry and eggs, which have been more or less free to respond to the laws of supply and demand.

I have referred to the tremendous drop in farm income since the twenties, and there again the drop is greater in the case of corn and wheat and cotton than in the general average. Furthermore, the cotton situation is even worse than the price indicates, because the Government, through its loan policy, has practically acquired the ownership of eleven million bales of cotton, in which it has invested five hundred and fifty million dollars. There was plenty of criticism when the Hoover Farm Board acquired three million bales to stem the drop in price during the depression, and it was pointed out what a disastrous effect that tremendous surplus had hanging over the market, but the Hoover Farm Board was a mere piker compared to the Surplus Commodities Corporation. The same dangerous New Deal policy has been pursued with wheat and corn, in which the Government now has invested several hundred million dollars. The public debt has been increased by twenty billion dollars, equal to a mortgage of $667 on every farm family and city family in the United States.

Furthermore, the policy of limiting production, killing pigs, and plowing up cotton ruined American markets abroad and brought a flood of foreign imports into the United States. In 1937 we imported two billion dollars' worth of agricultural products instead of the one million which we must usually import of products not raised in the United States. The country was flooded with Argentine corn, Polish meat, and other foreign products which never competed with the American farmer under pre-New Deal conditions. We imported more peanut oil than we produced, while Southern acres lay idle. By artificial controls in cotton, restriction of production, Government loans, we have made it difficult to ship American cotton abroad and have so stimulated the production of cotton in Egypt, Brazil, and elsewhere that probably we will never recover our foreign markets. Such a loss is disastrous for the South. President Roosevelt has said that the South is the nation's economic problem number one. I agree; the New Deal cotton policy has made it so.

I listened with interest to Representative Smith's boast that the New Dealers have conferred democracy on the farmer. I spent ten months last year traveling through rural Ohio. If American rural sections aren't the most typical examples of democratic communities in the world, I don't know where they can be found. The farmers of the United States know more about democracy when they graduate from high school than any New

Dealer will ever know before he dies. I suppose Representative Smith is referring to the agricultural referendums. Those referendums are about as democratic as Hitler's plebiscites. The Department of Agriculture proposes a program, thought out by experts who never saw a farm. The voters are flooded with propaganda in favor of the program, and no one could get a list of voters to send any opposing propaganda to even if there were reason to organize opposition. As a rule, the Government announces that there will be special benefits from the Government for all those who join in the program, a proposal which would be called bribery in any ordinary democratic election. I have talked to a lot of farmers who say frankly they are against the whole program but that under present conditions they vote " yes " because no alternative is offered. Either way they get Government regulation, and if they vote " yes " they may get some payments. Of course, they aren't given any alternative program to vote for on their ballot.

But they vote against the program when they go to the real polls in November. As a matter of fact, I feel very confident that the farmers in Ohio today would prefer no program at all to the present New Deal program. They deeply resent the orders from the Government to restrict their acreage. They don't like to have Government agents out measuring their fields. They don't like to have Government airplanes flying overhead, taking pictures to find out what crops they are raising and to what use they are putting their own fields. They don't even like the idea of taking Government checks, but they can't see any reason why they should not when everybody else takes them and they need them to help pay the taxes. They don't want to have a marketing quota applied and have a Federal padlock on their corn crib, so that they can't even use their own corn to feed their own stock on their own farms. The present New Deal farm policy rests on a basis of regimentation and bureaucracy, enforced by hundreds of thousands of Government agencies. It is as far away from democracy as anything which exists in the United States today.

The extraordinary thing to anyone in Congress is that the New Deal Administration hasn't the faintest idea what to do about it today. They have not advanced any proposal that will make the farmer's plight the least bit better next year than it is this year. They are hopelessly divided over the question how to deal with the present cotton surplus. They are hopelessly divided over the proposal to increase the cash payments to the farmers, although they seem to be willing to subsidize the sale of wheat and cotton even to Germany to get rid of them. The guiding spirit in the Department of Agriculture seems to be a stubborn obstinacy to go on with all their present policies, including the reciprocal trade treaties, and hope that something may happen. We don't even hear anything about the Ever *Ab*normal Granary.

Representative Smith says the farmer was victimized by the tariff and by monopoly in general. But certainly the farmer has not been victimized by the tariff as much as he has been by the lowering of the tariff on many agricultural products through the reciprocal trade treaties; and he hasn't been protected much against monopoly, because where the Republican Administrations from 1921 to 1933 prosecuted an average of thirteen anti-trust cases a year, the New Deal, up to January, 1938, had prosecuted an average of only nine cases a year. For a long time they favored the N.R.A. policy of virtually encouraging monopoly under Government protection.

There isn't very much doubt about the farmer's present condition. Last year I attacked the New Deal farm policy in every rural county in Ohio and carried all but a few of those counties by overwhelming majorities. We can't cure the farmer's difficulties by fancy economic remedies and planned economy, but we can work steadily and soundly to improve conditions. America looks to its farm population for new blood, new ideas, and the preservation of sound American principles. Nothing is more important than to make life on the family-type farm as attractive as that of the average city dweller. Unless the farm people are prosperous, city production is steadily reduced. On the other hand, it is useless to hope for good farm prices while the entire country is in the midst of a depression. We must encourage private industry to go ahead, so that it may put back to work some of the eleven million unemployed so they can buy more farm products. We must reduce the burden of Government regulation, taxation, and control of business, so that men again may start new enterprises and enlarge old enterprises. The best single remedy for farm prices is a condition of general prosperity. The Government can stimulate business and leave more money available for investment in private industry if it will reduce the tremendous Government expense, and, incidentally, give up the alliance with the C.I.O.

The basis of any American farm policy under present world conditions must be to secure the American market for the American farmer and build up that market. The Government should deliberately stimulate the domestic market for agricultural products and should assist in finding new uses for them. A start has been made, and the Chemurgic Council is doing a good work in developing that field. Rather against the will of the Administration, laboratories have finally been provided to find new uses for all the products of which there is a surplus. This policy should be energetically and sympathetically pursued.

, The reciprocal trade treaty policy should be amended so that no tariff shall be reduced on any product below the difference in cost of production here and abroad as certified by the Tariff Commission. In the process of a progressive policy of conservation, the Government should buy or lease a great deal of the marginal land and take much of it out of immediate production by the planting of trees, which in time will enable the United States to produce more of its own paper and pulp.

I think the New Deal agricultural policy was less subject to criticism before the passage of the 1938 Act, when reasonable benefits were paid for soil conservation. The farmer has to pay a higher price for some of the things he buys because of our tariff policy, whereas those farmers producing crops with an exportable surplus, like wheat and cotton, must sell at the world price. This condition justifies a reasonable subsidy in the form of benefits for soil conservation, but such payments should not be used as an indirect method of limiting production and controlling price.

There should be a further intelligent promotion of coöperative marketing, so that the farmer is not at the mercy of the buyer. Much may be done to reduce the cost of distribution, particularly through marketing in cities. The progressive work of Fellowes Morgan, Commissioner of Markets in New York, has so reduced the margin between the farmer and consumer that the farmer has received higher prices while the consumer has bought at lower prices and therefore been able to buy more food.

The various farm credit agencies can be coördinated and much red tape eliminated. In spite of the Government lending policy, most farmers find it very difficult indeed to borrow money conveniently at low rates of interest from Government agencies. All these things can be done without Government dictation or the creation of a vast corps of bureaucratic inspectors overrunning the farms like a plague of grasshoppers. If they are carefully planned and consistently carried through, they can bring back the American farmer to the independent and respected position he occupied before the New Deal.

XII

THE PATH TO RECOVERY—THRIFT OR SPENDING?

SENATOR TAFT

CITIZENS and taxpayers of the United States of America:
The Roosevelt Administration has adopted the theory
that this nation can spend itself into prosperity. It is the
first administration in the history of the United States,
and probably the first responsible government in the
world, to be dominated by the spending philosophy. In
1932 the President advocated economy in government.
From time to time thereafter he has promised a balancing of the budget, but it is a long time now since he has
even fixed a date, no matter how distant, for such a return to normal financial policy. Mr. Hopkins this morning expressly endorsed the spending policy for at least

another year. In spite of feeble protests from Mr. Morgenthau, the spending philosophy dominates both executive and legislative departments. Those who believe in it see little reason for ever reducing an appropriation, because, if Government spending leads to prosperity, obviously the larger and more wasteful every appropriation can be made the more prosperous the people will become. To some extent the American people themselves were swept away by this philosophy. It was too easy to swallow the attractive theory advanced by plausible economic quacks that spending, rather than saving, is the new way to the abundant life.

But the continued acceptance of the spending philosophy by responsible officials of government is unique and extraordinary. If any theory was ever completely disproved by results, this one has been disproved. We have spent twice as much money in the last six years as in any other six previous years. The public debt since 1933 has increased by twenty billion dollars, and we have spent that much more money than we have received even from heavy, increased taxation. The Government expenditures today are still increasing. And yet after all that spending and borrowing we fell into another depression in 1937, from which we have not recovered. To cure that depression, the New Deal has found but one panacea — to spend still more money. The deficit deliberately planned by the President for the fiscal year which will end June 30th, will be about four billion dollars. The budget for the year which begins on July 1, 1939, will probably create a deficit of at least four billion dollars more. The deficit spending at this rate has been going on steadily now for a year, and yet the country is substantially in the same condition it was in a year ago. I read only yesterday that the optimistic estimates for a large national income in 1939 had been abandoned. The national income is to be less than seventy billion dollars, far under what it was ten years ago in 1928, when there were ten million fewer people. If twenty billion dollars of borrowed money produced another depression instead of prosperity, if a large additional monthly deficit during 1938 and 1939 has not improved national income, what possible hope is there that any improvement can be obtained from more spending?

As a matter of fact, the huge spending tends to deter recovery. Lack of financial restraint encourages the Government into all kinds of activities where private enterprise can no longer operate in competition. It justifies vast Government bureaus to regulate every industry, regulations which nearly always discourage individuals from going into that kind of business. It leads to increased taxation, which makes profitable operations in private industry almost impossible. Spending feeds on itself. If one pressure group obtains a subsidy, it is almost impossible to turn down another pressure group whose arguments and interests are just as powerful. Spending builds up activities, and, whether those activities are wise or not, their sudden abandonment would throw many men out of work and perhaps start a downward spiral of further unemployment and business depression. Spending, once undertaken, cannot be suddenly abandoned but must be tapered off gradually.

So long as the spending program continues, there always looms ahead the threat of national bankruptcy, and while that threat exists men are not encouraged to risk their money in enterprises which may be wiped out in the general breakdown involved in such a result. No nation ever has continued indefinitely an unbalanced budget without ultimate collapse. Already our annual charge for interest amounts to a billion dollars. A slight increase in the rate of interest might easily make it a billion and a half dollars a year. Sooner or later this interest bill will become a tremendous burden, and already we hear proposals that the debt be paid off in irredeemable paper money. Inflation of the currency is the means which governments use to repudiate their debts, but inflation of the currency always leads to a tremendous rise in prices, which finally breaks down all business activity. It bears particularly hard on the poor and the people with fixed salaries. The savings of a lifetime and all life insurance policies are destroyed by inflation, because dollars are depreciated until they will buy nothing. If we ever have real inflation, it is doubtful if we could reinstate the American system of individual freedom and initiative until we had wasted many years under state socialism. The spending philosophy not only has failed to bring recovery but it contains the seeds of hardship and poverty, and even civil war.

Of course it is true that the prosperity of the country increased from 1933 to 1937, but there has always been a recovery as the inevitable reaction from every depression, and it has always occurred before without substantial Government deficits. As a matter of fact, recovery from 1933 to 1937 was more rapid in England, where the budget was balanced throughout that period; and it was more rapid in many other countries of the world.

To support the spending theory, every New Dealer asserts without argument that the 1937 depression in the United States was due to the fact that the Government stopped spending. This proves too much. If the Government can never stop spending without producing a depression, it would be far better never to begin, for on this hypothesis we must go on spending indefinitely and constantly piling up the debt until we reach the inevitable collapse. But, as a matter of fact, there never was any cessation of Government spending. The 1937 depression began about the end of the fiscal year which ended on July 1, 1937. In that year the Government expenditures reached a new all-time high (excluding the soldiers' bonus payments), and the deficit amounted to approximately three billion dollars, not as large as the super-deficits of 1934, 1935, 1936, and 1939, but still a very respectable deficit. Certainly the depression was not caused because the deficit was reduced one billion dollars through an increase in tax receipts. Nor does a study of what happened in 1937 justify the claim that the 1937 depression was caused by any reduction in the deficit. It resulted rather from Government interference, the lack of saving, and the unwillingness of individuals to invest in permanent things.

The depression first appeared in the capital goods industries. The steel industry fell from one hundred per cent of capacity to twenty per cent of capacity in six months. Hardly a domestic order was given for machinery. The demand for all the goods which go into permanent construction disappeared overnight. Gradually the unemployment in these industries which make things that go into permanent structures reduced buying power until the same condition was reflected in all of the other industries in the United States. The fall in business activity in the last six months of 1937 was greater than in any six months of the previous depression. What happened is quite clear. The railroads buy one-fifth of all the steel produced in the United States. Their taxes, wages, and other costs increased so fast under Government stimulation that no margin was left between their income and their increased expenses to provide for replacements or even ordinary maintenance. The costs of the utilities were increased, while their rates must remain the same, and they faced also the threat of Government competition, so that naturally they could not spend for permanent expansion. Other industries which could legally increase their prices were afraid to manufacture many goods at increased costs for fear they could not sell them at the increased prices they were obliged to charge. There were no new models in the automobile industry in 1938. The immediate cause of the depression, therefore, was Government interference to increase too rapidly wages, taxes, and other costs — so rapidly that prices could not keep up.

But there would not have been such a complete collapse in these industries except for the fact that there had been less saving in the United States and even less willingness to invest savings in permanent improvements. In the twenties we saved in the neighborhood of ten billion dollars a year and put this money back into buildings and machinery expansion. By 1937 savings had dropped to around three billion dollars a year, and most of these savings went into Government and municipal bonds.

America has been built up by thrift and the investment of savings, through life insurance, building and loan associations, banks, and corporate securities, in permanent improvements which would earn a return for their owners. In the United States today we have a tremendous plant, thousands of cities with buildings from small residences up to giant skyscrapers, thousands of factories, a great railroad and utility system, all constructed by private enterprise, with the idea that a return could be earned so that the man who saved his money would have some income during the rest of his life to take care of himself and of his family after his death. This process has largely come to an end. No one is willing to put his money into anything permanent, because, with Government regulation, taxation, and competition staring him in the face, he cannot feel confident of any return. But a resumption of that process is the only way to put men back to work.

This condition was the underlying cause of the sudden collapse of 1937, a collapse which did not occur in any other important country in the world. Far from checking the depression, Government spending only aggravated it. The Government's activities made a return on private investment much less promising. That activity should have been devoted not to public spending but to the stimulation of private spending. An excellent example of how this can be done is found in the Federal Housing Administration, where the Government, without cost to itself, has stimulated the building of houses by private industry and afforded almost the only real stimulation to business which the present Administration has provided. Neither in practice nor in theory is there the slightest basis for the claim that Government spending can produce prosperity.

The New Dealers, I believe, embrace the spending philosophy with ease and eagerness because they want to expand Government activity and regulation in every field and yet don't dare to levy the taxes which are necessary to meet the expense. If they did levy more taxes, they would almost certainly discourage all that is left of private industry and incidentally put an end to their own political power.

How far can Government expense go, assuming you could increase taxes to eliminate the deficit? Today the taxes are taking 22 per cent of the national income, but total expenditures, local, state, and national, amount to 30 per cent of the national income. That means that if the budget were balanced by more taxes, 70 per cent of a man's time would be used in working for himself, the other 30 per cent in working for the Government. Perhaps what the Government gave him might be worth the 30 per cent, but he at any rate has nothing to say about how that 30 per cent is spent, and the chances are that most of it does him very little good. In any heavy tax bill, the inclination is to levy the taxes first on profits, so that the incentive to expand industry and develop new industry is tremendously reduced, because most of the earnings must be turned over to the Government. If we ever get to the point at which 50 per cent of the national income is taken by the Government, I doubt very much if we can keep the other 50 per cent in the hands of private industry. The burden on the private activities remaining would be so great that probably we would soon develop a hundred per cent socialized state. Up to date no one has devised a system of taxation which can get more than 22 per cent of the national income, and even that seems to be a tremendous handicap to growth.

Many of the Government activities are most attractive. Taken one by one, there is the utmost justification to continue them, but the truth is that the people at the present time cannot afford everything they are getting, and someone must decide what is essential and what is not. The average workman knows that there are many expenditures he would like to make. Probably there are few who would not like a new and better house, a new

232

automobile, more and better clothes; but the individual knows that he only has a certain income and can afford only a certain number of pleasant things each year. That is the condition the Government is in today. Dams and canals and slum clearance projects, farm benefits, and P.W.A. may all be attractive and justifiable, but if we try to buy them all, we are only fooling ourselves. Sooner or later we will have to pay our notes in national dishonor, weakness, poverty.

It is not easy to stop the present spending. Friday I cast the only vote in the committee against the $1,300,-000,000 farm bill. Our committees are considering another billion for the Federal Housing Authority, eight hundred million for the slum clearance projects. A general education bill would add two hundred million a year, and a general health bill four hundred million a year to the annual charges of the Federal Government. Everyone is interested in spending. No one ever appears against an appropriation. No advocate of any of these spending proposals feels the slightest responsibility for suggesting where the money is coming from to pay for his proposal. A conservative Democratic Senator said to me last week that in his opinion spending could never be stopped until we went on and on to the final inevitable collapse. I don't agree with him. I believe that if the Executive accepts the responsibilities cast upon him by Congress under the budget law, he can work out a plan which will give us all the essentials of the present program within a figure which the nation can pay in taxes. I believe those taxes can be adjusted to interfere less with the industrious business man and the industrious workman. If the President will not do it, I believe that Congress should create a committee to work out the policy, and that a great public opinion can be created behind that policy to compel its acceptance. I have a determined confidence in the sound judgment of the American people.

REPRESENTATIVE SMITH

KINSMEN in Texas, neighbors in Illinois, friends in Ohio, men and women of America: greetings from Washington! That was a very sobering picture which the Senator has just painted for you of our national predicament. You note, however, that he knows the cure — just get the right President, or failing that, a congressional committee! Simple as the cure is, the picture of the predicament is of course extreme, extreme in color and extreme in urgency. It illustrates very well the common presumption that it is the business of those out of power to oppose those in public office. The chief conservative method of opposing is to view liberal achievements with alarm. So Mr. Taft's lifted voice and lowered brow. Why, to listen to the Senator, you'd think that debt itself was something unclean and national debt a public disaster. Such a view, I repeat, reflects the alarm of extremists. But we have extremists on our side also who leave the impression on many that debt is something delightful and national debt a peculiar delight.

Now, extremists are good — but chiefly good to balance other extremists. (A pessimist, you remember, is a person who has to live with an optimist.) Another good about extremists is that they make necessary a middle course. Leaving both sets of extremists, then — to hold each other in check — I invite you to seek with me a middle ground, some Golden Mean between the over-thrifty and the over-extravagant. And I ask you to take with me the strictly realistic view, that in such matters only those who sleep on the floor will not fall out of bed.

I

The Senator voted against the farm bill last Friday, he says — he alone of the whole Senate committee. But he did not some days before vote against some 6,000 war planes at a cost of some $300,000,000. That time, indeed, he did his part to spend on one roll call approximately as much money as through the centuries Harvard, Yale, and Columbia have accumulated in total endowments for educational purposes. Why, the best of these planes will cost $175,000 each. For one such bomber your whole high school graduating class, up to fifty boys and girls, could be sent through four years of one of these colleges to be turned out as happy, useful citizens. Such price the Senator pays for folly, and borrowed money it is, too. Borrowed money for instruments of destruction, $175,000 per unit. The cost of the bomber is terrible, its work is horrible, its life is short.

Has Senator Taft gone crazy to worse than waste money like that, and borrowed money to boot? You might think so. But I tell you otherwise. I know, because I voted for the planes also. You must believe by this time that what the Senator and I both vote for is likely to represent the lowest common denominator of sanity.[1]

Though voting against the agricultural bill, why did Mr. Taft vote for these evil things, and that on borrowed money? I imagine for much the same reason that I did. He chose between two great evils, hoping and believing that he'd chosen the least. Confronted not by a theory but by a stern condition which he had not created, he had to do the best he could. So the air bombers, and that on borrowed money.

So also, my fellow-countrymen, our peace spending program and the resulting national debt. We Democrats, whom the Senator derides, came to responsibility

---

[1] An ounce of preventive cost is worth a pound of war cost: " The World War, all told, cost, apart from 30,000,000 lives, $400,000,000,000. With that money we could have built a $2,500 house, furnished it with $1,000 worth of furniture, placed it on five acres of land worth $100 an acre, and given this home to each and every family in the United States, Canada, Australia, England, Wales, Ireland, Scotland, France, Belgium, Germany, and Russia. We could have given to each city of 200,000 inhabitants and over, in each country named, a five-million-dollar library, a five-million-dollar hospital, and a ten-million-dollar university. Out of what was left we could have set aside a sum at five per cent that would provide a yearly salary for an army of 125,000 teachers and a like salary for another army of 125,000 nurses." — Nicholas Murray Butler.

in '33 to learn that office holding is not a paradise of power but a predicament that tries the souls of honest men. Recall how it was in '32. Rebellion on the farms was ugly. Insolvency in the banks was terrifying. Prospects of starvation stalked the city streets. Fear was the steady food of more millions than it takes to make a majority of our fellow-citizens.

We Democrats didn't make that situation; we found it full blown and not disposed to wait on our convenience. I do not say the Republicans outright caused the great depression of '29 (any more than we single-handed caused the recession of '37); but the Republicans were themselves in power, long and strong in power, when the great depression happened. That's a funny place to be if later you expect to affect injured innocence about the whole matter — injured innocence in a carping voice. Certainly we Democrats did not make the conditions, though we must take our share of the blame for '37. Indeed we did not understand how serious things were then. We underestimated '29 as the Senator overestimates '37, seeing we're already pulling out of the recession. From '29 to '32 we'd heard it so often as to have our hope raised that prosperity wasn't dead, that it was only waiting around the corner. In our innocence we promised to reduce spending, and once in power proceeded to do what we'd promised, inflicting a ten per cent cut right down the line. Well, the joke was on us, but we didn't see any Republicans around who could laugh other than sheepishly.

To grumble is cheap indeed when you're grumbling

at what you yourself would have done had you been the one that had to do it. We have doubled the country's debt, yes; but for the same kind of reason Mr. Taft and I voted for the airplanes the other day and for a purpose infinitely more constructive than bombers. A good deal of our spending represents permanent improvements, capital investments, as it were. You have but to look around you, wherever in America you are, to see examples of this type of spending. A good deal more of our spending represents repayable loans to almost every group of citizens from big business to little home owners. And the remainder of the spending represents fortification against hunger and insurance against civil strife.

Allowing ten per cent — I doubt if Mr. Taft would charge more — to that louse, the chiseler, the remainder of our national debt represented when not the greatest good the least of evils. Mr. Taft will hardly dare say that he would not have run the Government heavily in debt. He is not irresponsible, and he is not cruel. Don't choose what you want, said a wise man, but stand by the choices you thought wise to make when you had to make them. Knowing why we contracted the debt, we Democrats are not privileged now, as some Republicans think themselves to be, to go back on the noble though hard choice of our manhood in power. We cannot renege like spoiled children; we must face our responsibility like men. The " push " of our spending has been fear, and you know it as well as I. But there was also a " pull " to the spending, and that pull was hope — hope of scotching the wheels against disaster, yes; but hope also of rolling the old wagon on ahead.

II

Now the spending has, by and large, relieved our fears, but it has not yet fulfilled our hopes. It has not yet brought us back to such a level of national income as to balance the budget and to begin paying off the debt. Indeed, it has not yet brought us to where we dare safely stop the spending itself. Mr. Taft has given you a grand Republican explanation of our Democratic recession of '37. I dare say that there is some truth in it. I'm not an economist, nor is Mr. Taft. But I dare say that there's some truth in what he says, as there's some truth in our partisan Democratic explanation. I know only this: that we worked to save the lives, the property, and the morale of the American people until substantial recovery had returned. In '37 we thought it safe to move for a balanced budget. We cut down rather steeply on spending, a recession set in, and the conservatives were among the first to demand resumption of the spending program that had saved them from disaster and had seemed to be promoting general recovery.

Everybody was in favor of Government spending in '33, even Mr. Hoover, I believe. Everybody knows that it's a delicate job, this job of tapering off. Mr. Taft is right about that, and Mr. Taft, I believe, is not in favor of the risk of stopping spending all at once. It's a delicate job. We have no adequate precedents to go by,

239

unless '37 really tells us to go but to go slow on reducing aids to business, agriculture, and unemployed consumers. The economists are not agreed on how to proceed, and the conservatives are, as usual, hysterical. It's a good time for men in power to keep their heads.

"But this spending cannot go on forever," yell the hysterical. "Who said it could?" we calmly reply. "Not we. We know that it cannot go on forever. We're doing our utmost to keep it from going on forever; for we're doing all we can to save the profit system. If you let that system go down through your obstruction and to the tune of your hysteria, you'll see that the spending can go on and on. That's what's happening in Italy and in Germany, and in no small degree because the chambers of commerce, so to say, were not willing to keep their heads and to coöperate themselves out of the jam into which our capitalistic system has got itself the world over."

We Democrats propose to keep our heads. We know that the budget must be balanced, but we also know that it must be approached cautiously. Leave it to conservative extremists to say "today." Leave it to radical extremists to say "never." We propose, exactly as Alexander Hamilton proposed when he put the young nation $80,000,000 in debt, to balance the budget as soon as we can out of rising income and to pay the debt from a stabilized prosperity. But isn't that playing for the breaks? Yes. Isn't that gambling on the future? Yes. The same future of this same great country upon which we all must stake both our hopes and our lives.

240

III

The debt is disturbing but not alarming. In so far as the proposal is not personal and political, I wish Senator Taft's congressional committee well, if he does not get the President he wants. But the committee, if it gets beyond the microphone stage, will face not merely the Senator's beautiful theory dated from days of Republican lethargy; it will also face the hard facts which we Democrats have been facing since the heavy economic hangover from the Republican spree of '27 and '28. I like the leeway between us and disaster which Mr. Taft himself seems to leave his favorite President or, that failing, his congressional committee, if I understand properly his distinction between bad taxes of 22 per cent and disastrous taxes of 50 per cent of our national income. If the Republicans will but be as generous and patient with us Democrats as Mr. Taft is with himself, I think we'll make it all right. That's a lot of leeway he allows.

Meantime, treasuring that suggested leeway, conditions are not without hope today. Everybody not running for office admits, I believe, that times are getting better, though not as rapidly as any of us wish. The hungry are mostly being fed, and many of the able-bodied are being given work. Labor is enjoying collective bargaining, and farmers have democratic power to help themselves, if it can be done politically. More business men are making profits than like to admit it. The health of the nation is at last honestly recognized as a problem, and the morale of our people is by no means shot.

241

IV

" But all of this is on borrowed money," is the constant refrain of the conservative hysterical. Mr. Taft has during these debates hardly been able to give his undivided attention to any other problem than borrowed money. " Yes, on borrowed money," reply the calm, " just as the doctor and the hospital bills we all run up for our sick children are for most of us borrowed money." But there are few things more worth borrowing money for than boys and girls, than men and women, than private credit and a nation's morale. It *is* borrowed money; but it is money borrowed on credit that's good and that remains good even in the face of all the conservative hysteria. Our national debt is something that we can perfectly well and easily carry until we begin paying it back, for the interest rates are very reasonable today.

Mr. Taft admits the bearing of this upon the ease of carrying our debt, but his fear returns, this time fear that the interest rates may go up. Well, now they could go up a long way before the carrying charges would be comparable with those paid by Republicans on their national debt. With or without the Senator's fear, the truth is that interest rates have steadily gone down as the debt has gone up, keeping thus the carrying charge remarkably reasonable. Indeed, while our national debt was increasing some ninety per cent between '32 and '38, our interest charges increased only about forty per cent. This means that instead of some twenty billions of debt at three and a half per cent we have now some forty billions of debt at two and six-tenths per cent.

V

Nor does this tell more than half the hopeful truth about our national soundness. The nation's total debt, private and public, appears no larger than it was in the twenties. Our national debt itself is as large as it is in part because the Government has saved the credit of others by taking on its broader shoulders debts they simply could not bear. We know this is true of farmers, who otherwise would have lost their farms; of home owners, who otherwise would have lost their homes; of business men, big and little; of banks and of railroads. But equally deserving of recognition is the fact that the governmental units of cities, states, and counties have in untold cases been able to pull through solely because of the national Government's willingness to keep them solvent.

Count this as the simple explanation of what the Senator explained in a way that sounded downright cynical. Let us give him the benefit of the doubt, however, and count as a slip of the tongue his notion that we have spent money because we wanted to expand governmental activity for its own sake. It will take more charity, however, to overlook his left-handed slap at both the power of the people and the integrity of their representatives when he suggests that the citizen has nothing to say about how the taxes are spent and that the chances are that most of it does him very little good.

I'm always amazed when conservatives talk with the unrestraint which one associates with loose-tongued radicals alone. To the irresponsible such reckless talk!

When the budget is balanced by a prosperity which Republicans and Democrats alike must depend upon, but which neither of us knows how to cause, the national debt can and will be repaid out of the normal tax returns of a prosperous nation. To pay the debt out of a proper national income will not be hard; to carry it meantime is easy. To have saved the nation by courage and honesty meantime is reward enough for the Democratic party. Once on the highroad again, we will present to the nation as unearned increment of these trying years a new governmental efficiency for this new and dynamic age.

Our New Federalism represents the orderly liquidation of provincial lethargy along the whole front and the creation of public equities in fields previously reserved for private exploitation. As a humanitarian, I do not apologize for relief debt; as a farmer's son, I'm proud of what we've done for both agriculture and labor; as a city-dweller and state patriot I'm proud of the debt-shifting from narrow to broad shoulders; but as a student of government and a believer in the democratic way of life, I'm proudest of our peaceful passage from a government of lethargy to this New Federalism for our speedy and heady age.

XIII

FORWARD AMERICA—WHICH WAY AND WHAT SPEED?

REPRESENTATIVE SMITH

MY fellow-countrymen: This marks the end of these friendly debates with my legislative colleague, Mr. Taft, junior United States Senator from Ohio. In spite of frank talk and hard blows from each of us — never personal, however, from either of us — I am happy to recall at the end our joint hope expressed at the beginning that we would raise partisanship a notch in the direction of patriotism.

Underneath our earnest differences we are both Americans, belonging to great parties both of which are American, and engaging in a type of sportsmanship that is truly and deeply American. I wish particularly to express my pleasure at having drawn an opponent in these debates who is both literate and articulate, who is both honest and courageous. All conservatives I willingly believe to be as honest as other men, but how few conservatives have, like Mr. Taft, the out-loud courage of their inner thoughts! It will be a safer day, politically speaking, when more conservatives out with it — as Mr. Taft has here done — on both our basic national institutions (the Constitution, the Executive, the Congress, the judiciary, and the states) and the major national problems now engaging attention (unemployment, security, war and peace, labor, agriculture, and the debt). I'd like, indeed, to register before my fellow-countrymen my appreciation of Mr. Taft and my admiration for his example. He's one of the very few conspicuous and ambitious conservatives who do not prefer silence to speech, one of the rarest of the rare who show themselves willing to go up or down with their own honest convictions boldly expressed before the country.

I salute the Columbia Broadcasting System for the courtesy of its network, and I thank the many of you who have written in and the millions of you who have not written in. I thank Mr. Taft again for helping me help him demonstrate that one of the foundations of democracy is to accept opposition as also a standard form of coöperation. I salute you, I salute him; but I warn you that he's trying to lead America backwards, whereas our concluding subject is " Forward America! "

I

But what is " forwards," what " backwards," for America? Let me remind you of some simple truths. We live in a highly organized world, and few of us like the way organizations cramp our individual style. Why, in many cities even citizenship itself is hard to enjoy because of the bossism which encrusts it. Some of my friends who belong to labor unions have talked to me frankly at times about how little voice they have in their own unions. They feel squeezed by the very organizations they joined to protect their freedom.

What these labor union men tell me, Senator Taft says the farmers of Ohio have been telling him. The farmers have organized to aid themselves and now feel regimented, he says, by what you and I know to be the program of farm organizations. You remember the Senator in a previous debate hazarded the bold statement that his Ohio farmers resented so strongly what he called regimentation that they'd rather have no program at all than this one they've already worked out for themselves. Though many Illinois farmers tell me otherwise and though some of Senator Taft's Ohio farmers have written me protesting his statement, I dare say that the farmers find, and will find, organizations as galling as do labor union members.

In this discontent at the loss of individuality, I believe that the farmer and the industrial laboring man are but typical of modern men in general. Listen for the same complaint from the retailers, meeting in Washington next week. Moreover, the rest of us see that the labor unions have grown so strong that they can, almost upon the order of a single man, arrest the flow of coal, or electric current, or even of milk for our children. We see that the farmer can now limit his acreage or reduce his marketing quota and thus hoist the prices we pay for what we eat or wear. We see and resent the social danger of such organized power. It touches us as consumers. But it touches the worker as producer and consumer and narrows his rights as a man.

This epidemic abroad in the world deserves a name. Let us call it Organization-itis. When it strikes, it limits our freedom and hurts our dignity as men and women. Echoing in advance one complaint of the retailers, it's chains everywhere — not only chain stores but chain unions, chain farm federations, chain schools, and even chain churches. In our heart of hearts we all know that the spirit of the chain gang has broken out of prison and roams at large, making the whole world a sort of prison house for free spirits. A new feudalism is upon us, in which each of us becomes, as the old word was, a masterless man unless we join something and let our organization try to master other organizations with which we have to bargain for a living — and then, alas, end (our own organizations end) by mastering us. The universality of this feeling makes appropriate Lincoln Steffens's attribution of the secret of it to the devil — the secret that the way to ruin any and every good cause is *to tempt men to organize it.*[1]

---

[1] With apologies to Steffens, I tell his story my own way:

The devil and I were walking down Michigan Avenue and talking, at least I was talking. The devil was listening. I questioned him, and my question was simple enough.

"How did you defeat the great prophets and balk the religions so?"

This feeling is so prevalent, not only in totalitarian lands but even in our own democratic country, that my unknown verse-maker has hardly exaggerated the home-

---

He looked at me with a curiously quizzical expression, as if he didn't understand what I meant or doubted that I did. I illustrated, therefore.

" The founders of the great religions: Moses, Jesus, Mohammed. They had the truth or parts of it. Enough to show that they could grasp more. How did you keep them from going on and getting it all? "

He didn't answer; he looked as if he wished me to explain further. I did.

" But what they saw, they announced. They gave their visions to the people, and the people heard them, gladly, and believed. And then . . ."

He was looking across the street, idly. I could not make out that he had even heard what I was saying. It was very unpleasant, the silence and all. I went on:

" Jesus, for example; Christianity took hold of men. Rome trembled for a while, fought the Christians, persecuted them, drove them under-ground — in vain. Christianity conquered Rome; the emperors bowed to it and believed; and Rome was the world then. And yet, just when the Christian religion had gained the whole world, it lost something. It be-came — what it is today."

No answer.

" What did you do? " I persisted. " And how did you do it? "

My question was almost a plea. I really wanted to know. And still he did not answer; he only smiled faintly. He seemed to be interested in the great crowds of workingmen who were out for the air in Grant Park. Maybe he was thinking of labor. I tried that.

" And then there's the great labor movement, which has shaken the world again and again. The workers rose, became aware of their wrongs, of their rights, of their might. And Rome trembled again, just as the modern world trembles, and then, in Rome, nothing happened. What did you do? And now, here. What's the matter with organized labor today? What are you doing to its leaders, for example? "

Silence. He was still looking across the street, but not as before, not idly. His attention seemed to be fixed upon a spot. I looked where he looked and I saw . . .

What I saw startled me. I saw a man reach up into the sunshine and grasp a piece of truth. It was a little bit of a piece, but it was truth. No wonder the devil was interested.

I looked at him, expecting to see alarm on his countenance. There was

sickness that comes over the veneered pioneer in each of us when the romantic hour of springtime strikes in us the far from lost chord:

> I want to be off to the edge of the world,
>   Away from the realm of law,
> To the land where never a flag's unfurled,
>   And the life is rough and raw.
>
> I want to be off where the roads are new,
>   Or there's never a road to see;
> For ever and ever the long years through
>   The wilderness calls to me.
>
> I play my part in the business scheme
>   Of barter and trade and sale,
> But deep in my secret soul I dream
>   Of the joys of the open trail.
>
> I think of the pungent campfire swirled
>   On the breath of the winds that blow,
> And I want to be off to the edge of the world —
>   But I haven't the nerve to go!

---

none. He was so utterly untroubled that I couldn't be sure he had either seen or understood what had happened. I sounded him.

" Did you see that man get that piece of truth? " I asked.

He nodded, but made no other reply.

" You don't seem to be disturbed by it."

" No," he answered absently.

" But you see how it would hurt business, don't you! " I urged.

" Yes," he said and smiled. " It would ruin mine."

" Well, then," I persisted impatiently, "why do you take it so easily? "

" Because," he answered patiently, " I know what to do about it."

" What will you do? " I asked breathlessly, only to receive this breath-taking answer: " Why," he said, " *why, I shall tempt him to organize it.*"

II

I speak feelingly about this, and even quote poetry about it, because it hits me hard. It hits me hard as one born in a log-cabin where self-help was the only help; it hits me hard as a Democrat, who with his party distrusts organization; it hits me hard as an independent politician, who un-joined all organizations possible before standing for public office. Yet Mr. Taft has throughout these debates blamed my party for too much government, especially for what he calls regimentation of the farmer. I admit that we have enabled the farmers the better to organize. I have even tried to claim Democratic credit for making organized democracy work in the factories also, through the Wagner Act and the National Labor Board. Indeed, I remind you now that the major promise of the Democratic platform of '32 was to try to equalize upward the bargaining and purchasing power of both agriculture and labor. But—I hear a voice from the northwest corner of conscience! —"Don't I know that Thomas Jefferson foresaw that when America got organized in cities and collectivized in spirit, America would become like Europe and individualism would be dead or dying?" Yes, I know it; and I frankly admit that I'm sad about it.

What Mr. Taft ought to be sadder about, however, and isn't is this: Under Republican influence America was so *one-sidedly* organized by '32 that the old free competition called capitalism had actually become a financial feudalism. The Republican folklore of capitalism had entrenched itself behind a folklore of fatalism which made voluntary change impossible because it held change itself unnecessary. Weren't the " right men " secure, even when not prosperous? When the "right men" are secure, they worry little about the rights of men.

There's little doubt that these conservatives were, and are, honest in the aristocratic belief that a moral receivership is better than democracy for the American people. They hold honestly to the " seepage " theory of welfare. Make wise and good men — that is, themselves — secure at the top and whatever welfare is possible for the people will seep through.

They may be right about their own superiority. But no Democrat could believe it and still be democratic. Nevertheless, their organized strength was too great to be directly disbanded. Such drastic action would have required revolution in the depths of Republican depression. That was the predicament when it came our time to go forward for America in '33. Let me illustrate it with a story.

A countryman was asked by a tourist downstate how to get to the capital.

" Start here," said the countryman. " Go straight ahead for two miles, then turn left one mile, then right. . . . No, that won't do. . . . Let's come back and start over. . . . Beginning here go straight ahead two miles, as I said. Then don't turn left, but right for one mile . . . then left. No, that's not right either."

Thoughtfully he paused a puzzled moment and then looked up at the tourist to confess: " Say, Mister, if I wuz you and wanted to go to the capital, I'd not start here! "

That was, I repeat, exactly our predicament in '33. Revolutionists might have started some more romantic place than the hole where the Republicans left the country. But we Democrats had to start where we were. Communists would have started elsewhere by drumming up class hatred that did not exist in America, not even in the hardest times. Nazis would have found a scapegoat to conceal their taking over the financial power and then would have used the power against farmers, laborers, and the capitalists themselves. But we were Democrats who had to start where we were, with vast corporate interests over-organized against the American people.

The Republicans see this evil of over-organization but see it only by halves. They really don't want labor to organize, nor the farmers either, though they bear such ills as best they may in hope of 1940 and beyond. But they do want the present corporate structure to remain and the predominant influence of business to continue (two hundred corporations, if not the sixty families, controlling America). Their own self-interest organized as conscience prevents their clearly seeing that if finance and business are thus over-organized, workers must over-organize or suffer eclipse of their rights as human beings. And if both these sides of the industrial process are over-organized, farmers must over-organize. And if both great producers, industrial and agrarian, are thus over-organized to protect their interests, consumers must eventually over-organize to protect their rights. And so Organization-itis spreads from this single Republican source of group selfishness and rages throughout the body politic. We Democrats, not being revolutionists, have had to treat the disease homeopathically, appearing to make it worse as the only peaceful means of making it better. So much for the disease, its cause in corporate centralism, and its development arrested by the counter-claims of farmers and industrial workers.

III

What, now, about the future? And is there realistic ground for choosing one party rather than another to hold the disease in check and to go forward to a cure? Yes, there is ground for this choice, though the situation is chronic and confused. Ground for choice there is, however, and room for hope as long as the liberal spirit of the Democratic party endures, in whatever form. Contrary to prevailing pessimism, I'm convinced that it's not later than we think, if we'll only think.

Neither party, of course, knows what to do about unemployment; and neither can balance the budget save by a prosperity which both will woo but which neither knows how to win. But the Democratic party will keep the nation balanced meantime by doing its duty to the unemployed gladly rather than glumly with Herbert Hoover. As regards social security for the employed, it's the Democratic party overwhelmingly; for we not only caused social security, but we believe in it. The Republican party does not believe in it as an ideal — at least Mr. Taft has said that he doesn't — and so it tolerates social security as political expediency, flirting the while with wild and strange innuendoes of two hundred dollars a month dispensed according to the political rather than the financial calendar. All checks are equally good, you know, until you have to cash them.

As regards a more lasting remedy, moreover, for Organization-itis, the Republican party is clearly at a disadvantage. It cannot renounce its old allegiance to the corporate one-sided organization of life which it has fostered. Nor can it rob itself of the fruits of its corporate organizations by suffering agriculture and labor to become as strongly organized as it has organized industry. So the best we could hope through it would be a return to financial feudalism, labor and agriculture knuckling under to a dishonorable peace. That would involve such a loss of purchasing power as again to undercut the financial feudalism as in '29. That's the best to hope, however, from the Republican party, a chronically recurring spiral of disaster.

The worst to fear from it is that, agriculture and labor fighting back through the organization we've given them, the corporate power will again lay hold of the government as under Coolidge, roughly pushing labor toward serfdom and agriculture toward peasantry. Even if the so-called Grand Old Party then escapes the corruption of the old Ohio gang and the honest lethargy of Hoover, it will become a sort of Republican fascism. I here use the term not abusively but descriptively. Fascism arises, you know, from having all great interests organized and incorporated. Then the State finds it easy, if not indeed necessary, to become the *incorporation of the corporations*. Organizing thus the organizations, the State proceeds to work upon the many the will of the few incorporators, now turned conspirators. Mussolini, let us remember, more frankly than Republicans, calls his form of government the Corporate State. And any government that arises from strident competition among corporations is likely to become itself the corporate holding company of all the other organizations incorporated under it. If that's the road ahead, let Republicans lead. They'll find it more natural.

If, with the Republicans at their worst, we are to move backwards to this corporate fascism, or, at their best, to an older feudalism of wealth, let us pray that our retreat be not in the winter time and that the speed be slow.

IV

I, for one, am convinced that the American people do not want that ending and so do not want to journey down that road. Indeed we do not want to live in the shadow of such pressure groups as already make our politics closely akin to war, whether the group pressing be labor, agriculture, or business. The only road of safety is to keep these organized pressures equal and balanced against each other *until their fierce competition can be subdued together* into a more coöperative order. It's certainly not safe to let any one of them run away with the show, as Republicans have let the com-

256

mercial interests. I refuse myself to believe that the middle way of practical democracy, already operative in small countries like Sweden, cannot be attained in this great republic, through our traditional spirit of equality and friendliness. Pending the return to coöperative individualism, the least modification of capitalism which the times permit is to equalize between these great organized bodies the competition which capitalism presupposes between natural individuals equal before the law.

But there's no way to maintain this modification or to return toward the coöperative democracy of competing individuals save through the machinery of representative government. Public power is the only possible antidote to private power. And I may add that public taxes are much better than the private taxes of prices controlled from behind the scenes.

Knowing all this, it is the genius of the Democratic party to accept, therefore, a paradox that terrifies honest Republicans and enrages selfish Republicans. It is the paradox that *more government is required to get more freedom for the most people.* The only power we Democrats finally recognize is the power of the whole people, which is government. Today we have used that power to curb corporations of business. Tomorrow we may have to curb corporate labor. And who knows that day after tomorrow we may not need it to curb farmers grown too fiercely strong through organization? This common power of democratic government is our only reliance against corporate greed, however organized and wherever found.

Let us be quite frank about it: to deal with economic monopolies in the modern world there is required monopoly of another sort. A monopoly of the legal force of the whole community used to be called democratic government. The Republicans would now have you think of it as "regimentation" so long as they do not control it. But it remains just what it is, democratic government, and the people's only reliance against corporate encroachment. I am not now speaking of "trust-busting," which has swelled many a political throat and has as yet "busted" very few "trusts." We Democrats have the patience to find out what needs doing before we sally forth to do it. Our present monopoly investigation is trying to find out what monopolies injure, what help the country. This determined, we can move resolutely in the direction indicated by the findings. Nobody else will move any direction save backwards.

To break the old bottle-necks of control once they're located and then to prevent new bottle-necks from forming, we are streamlining our Democratic government. I have in these debates thought it useful to give a new and unexciting name to a government adequate for the tasks before us. This philosophy of government I have called the New Federalism. I call it Federalism because, like Alexander Hamilton, the great old Federalist, I believe that where government is required, it ought to be made efficient through coördinating powers long left inefficient by separation. I call it New because, unlike Hamilton, I do not believe " the people a beast, sir," but the source of all power and the only rightful beneficiaries of their own power efficiently organized as representative government.

Such democratic centralism is giving us cheap electric power. This ought to enable us to decentralize industry. That done, we may democratize finance by a generous policy of credit extension. Both these done, farming and labor could again become, as work should be, a way of life instead of, as now, an individual struggle for existence and an organized competition against corporations for power and place. Democratic centralism of government thus points to a decentralization of every privileged form of collective power and promises a slow cure for the worst form of that social disease, Organizationitis.

I say "slow" advisedly; for, as the White Queen remarked to Alice, " Here, you see, it takes all the running you can do to keep in the same place. If you want to get somewhere, you must run at least twice as fast as that."

v

Whether we shall actually move forwards in this Democratic direction toward individual freedom or backwards with Republicans to feudalism or fascism, it is for the people themselves to say. As for me, I am grateful that tonight we can still enjoy in humility the American way of friendliness and humor. Such a happy way of life enables a Smith to look at a Taft and counsels a Taft to argue with a Smith. Thus the American way unites in tolerance a mellowed tradition and family pride, on the one side, with a joy in skill and a feel for the multitude, on the other.

Long may it remain so!

Now, as the Senator and I, contentedly alone or happily together, stroll from this studio down the grassy Mall, we'll pass from Washington's lofty monument in sight of Lincoln's majestic home, on down by the new shrine rising to Thomas Jefferson. Beyond Jefferson's place, the river, which just keeps a-rolling along — this quiet Potomac, lazily coursing its way to the sea since before Washington was — will become tonight for me a silver symbol of national unity across the gulf of years, softening the landscape of all present political differences. It is fitting that in " Ole Man Ribber's " presence we thus celebrate at the end of controversy our common devotion to a beloved fatherland: in our eyes its beauties of nature and in our souls the legacies of its great sons.

Triumphing over the palsy of fear felt elsewhere in the world tonight, the glory of such a nation as this we'll feel in the high beating of our common pulse of gratitude. And as our eyes wander from lights of city streets and sheen of river to the evening skies above, we'll commune for you all with a vast " universe not measured by our fears," until — as the great Justice Holmes further said — " after the sunset and above the electric lights there shine the stars."

SENATOR TAFT

CITIZENS of the United States of America: In this closing debate I wish to thank Representative Smith for his kind words regarding myself, and even more for the spirit of tolerance and friendship which has governed our differences of opinion. It has been the greatest pleasure to debate with him, in spite of his steadfast opinion that I am always in the wrong. I admire his eloquence and his wonderful command of the English language. If, with all his ability, he is unable to find a logical and consistent defense of the New Deal, certainly it is not his fault but that of the New Deal itself.

Forward America. But which way is forward? Surely we have been going forward during the last one hundred and fifty years towards a goal which the Pilgrims established in 1620 and which was carried on by the founders of our nation. That goal was increased individual freedom, with more material welfare to enjoy it. Surely we went forward in spite of this talk about financial feudalism. Men were more free in 1932, *before* the New Deal, than they were in any other country in the world. Their material welfare had steadily increased until the average workman had a standard of living three times as high as it was in 1820. The average New Dealer seems to think that because 1933 represented the bottom of a financial depression there was no democracy or prosperity in the United States before Franklin D. Roosevelt. Surely a majority of the people decided every four years what kind of government they wished, and surely the Congresses then as now voted the way they thought their constituents wanted them to vote.

It is the New Dealers who no longer wish to go forward along our well-marked path. They started along that path in 1933 for a few years, but they have wandered farther and farther into the forest of Government regimentation until, in complete darkness, they are moving back in the direction of the Middle Ages. It is quite true, as Representative Smith implies, that they have moved in both directions at once. Some of their measures have sincerely tried to make our system work; others threaten to destroy America as we have known it.

Unlike Representative Smith, many of the New Dealers have no concern whatever for individual freedom. They are collectivists, like Marx and Lenin and Mussolini. They believe in planned economy; that the Government should regulate every detail of industrial and commercial and agricultural life. They are willing to sacrifice individual freedom in order supposedly to improve the conditions of the poor and increase their material welfare. But in this purpose the policy has completely failed. There are more than ten million people unemployed today, and a larger relief expense this year, ten years after the depression, than any in the history of the United States. Farm prices are lower than they have been for six years. Business men are discouraged and indignant. Deposits have piled up in the banks because rich and poor alike are afraid to put their time or money into private enterprise, because they fear that Government regulation will prevent success, and Government taxation will take whatever profit there might be. The New Deal policy is the only one which has ever plunged us into a second depression before we were out of the first. If any policy leads backward and not forward, it is the policy of spending billions of borrowed money and piling up a tremendous debt for future generations to pay. A policy which inevitably leads to bankruptcy and inflation of the currency will not only make the poor people poorer but it is likely to force a socialism which will utterly deprive them of individual freedom.

Representative Smith tonight states the philosophy which dictates this backward policy. He says, in effect, that the way to get less regimentation of our individual lives is to suffer more governmental regulation. He argues that we have substituted political regulation for economic regimentation, but he admits that a continuation of this policy leads to the corporate state of Mussolini. Think of it. The New Dealers, who know everything in the world about labor and securities and agriculture and every other man's business, excuse themselves from failure to prevent monopoly in industry because they have only had six years to find out about it. No, the New Deal policy is leading us rapidly backward today, and it is a faint hope that its direction can be turned by any monopoly committee of Congress.

It is the Republican party today which looks forward, and I am quite willing to accept Representative Smith's proposal that we start from 1932. Instead of throwing away all past experience and embarking on uncharted seas, we would keep the good things which the American system produced, encourage the principles which produced them, and correct the abuses which crept into it as they will creep into any system. Let us remember that conditions in the twenties in many ways were better than they ever have been since. Farm prices were more than twice what they are today. Unemployment practically did not exist. Men were eager to engage in new industries, expand old industries, and build up both production and employment. If we had the same national per capita income today as we had then, we would have ninety billion dollars instead of sixty-seven, and if we had this thirty-five per cent more income than we actually have today, we could put most of the unemployed men back to work. We must restore conditions in which thousands of men and women every year were willing to invest their time and money in building up the United States and the prosperity of the people of the United States.

We have heard a good deal about the depression of 1933 and the terrific condition left by the Republicans. But the depression of 1933 existed throughout the entire world, while the depression of 1937 was a special American depression, created by New Deal policies. Even the depression of 1933 was not solely a Republican affair. The biography of Carter Glass, which has just appeared, makes it very clear indeed that the bank crisis of 1933 was largely produced by the course of Franklin D. Roosevelt between the day of his election and the day of his inauguration. It is now perfectly clear that Roosevelt not only blocked the sound fiscal policies proposed by Hoover but that he refused to correct the impression, which really had such a sound basis, that he was contemplating a devaluation of the dollar.

Representative Smith says that Republicans wish the many well through the assured welfare of the few. Of course this is not true. No one has ever *assured* the welfare of any business enterprise until the New Dealers tried to do it under the N.R.A. It is said that two out of every three new businesses fail. It is not the assurance of success; it is the existence of conditions which make it likely that a man of exceptional ability or ingenuity, who is willing to work hard, shall have a chance to obtain exceptional rewards for himself or his family, a chance which shall not be destroyed by Government regulation and interference. This, says Representative Smith, is the " seepage " theory of welfare. As a matter of fact, the men who are put to work in new jobs by new enterprises get their living and their purchasing power many months and often many years before the men who start the enterprises receive their reward, if they do receive it.

We have tried the alternative theory of producing prosperity based on dishing out Government funds to great classes of people, and, while such action has been in part necessary, it has certainly failed completely to produce general prosperity, and has not even restored those men who receive it to the material welfare they enjoyed in the twenties.

What were the abuses to be corrected in the system of the twenties? There were too many people rich beyond their deserts. I thoroughly approve of the New Deal measures to prevent fraud and sharp practice through the sale of securities, which was one of the principal methods of acquiring undeserved wealth. There were undoubtedly some monopolies whose owners received profits greater than they deserved. I may say, however, that the monopolies before 1932 were nothing to the monopolies fostered and built up by the New Deal under the N.R.A. For a number of years the New Deal was dominated by the theory that all business should consist of Government-controlled monopolies. Undoubtedly the Government should keep competition free and open, so that men may not make profits which they do not deserve, but the existence of business monopoly has been exaggerated. In practically all of the articles which average people buy, there exist today, and existed in 1928, the most intense competition, notably in foodstuffs and clothing and automobiles.

The Republican party believes in a sincere effort to keep competition free and open, to the end that prices may be lowered and undeserved profits reduced. I might add that more anti-trust suits were filed under my father's administration than under any Democratic administration since that day. If wealth has been gained fairly, we believe that it can be reduced and is being reduced by income and inheritance taxation and that there still prevails largely in America the old tradition of the nineteenth century, "From shirt sleeves to shirt sleeves in three generations."

Another abuse of the system of the twenties was that the distribution of income was not sufficient for a decent living for the poorer groups. I might point out that this condition has always existed under every system and certainly exists in Russia under communism today. To increase the condition of the poor has been the earnest desire of every public-spirited statesman in either party. The question is not one of purpose; the question is what method will improve that condition. The Republican party thoroughly approves of old age pensions, unemployment insurance, relief when necessary, and subsidized housing, but all of these together have not improved the condition of the poor over what it was in the twenties. There are more underprivileged today than there were in the twenties. There are more people wholly unemployed, and many more earning a bare subsistence on relief. If we could restore the economic and business activity of 1928, we could add twenty-three billion to the national income, most of it to the relief classes. Relief and old age pensions together do not add more than four billion at a maximum.

Finally, in the twenties it is probable that the laboring groups and the farm groups were at a disadvantage in dealing with individual employers and individual buyers of farm products. The Wagner Act, to promote collective bargaining in the labor field, and the farm cooperative acts, to encourage collective bargaining on the part of the farmer, are sound measures, if properly administered, to see that oppression does not arise in the normal processes of bargaining and competition. But Representative Smith wholly fails to distinguish between measures designed to assist coöperative organization and measures proposing that the Government regulate agriculture and labor and industry. He confuses self-organization with governmental bureaucratic organizations. It is no slight confusion. It is the difference between freedom and slavery. In the Guffey coal act to regulate prices and wages in the coal industry, in the wage-hour act, except to the extent that it is a real minimum wage law, in the agricultural acts which practically fix the prices of agricultural products, in the administration of the Wagner Act, which goes far beyond the purpose of that act to tell employers how they shall run their business, in the power sought to make arbitrary changes in the value of the dollar and the currency to effect some individual's idea of what prices should be, we see being worked out a complete Government-controlled economy. In order to allow the farmer to organize, it is not necessary for the Government to pay out eight hundred and fifty million dollars in benefits, or lend money on cotton and wheat in excess of the value of cotton and wheat. These measures, like the N.R.A. and the A.A.A., lead backward. If we ever get to the point where the Government fixes the price of all basic commodities, we cannot stop short of complete regimentation. There is a fundamental distinction between measures intended to keep the course of competition and investment and individual incentive open and those measures intended to direct the activities of the men who engage in that competition and industry. Above all, we have the entire Government regulation process stimulated by the theory that Government spending can produce prosperity, a theory utterly disproved by our actual experience and by every sound economic principle.

The New Dealers today no longer go forward along the path which this country pursued for one hundred and fifty years. They admit it. They say that everything is changed; a new era has come, requiring new methods. I don't believe it. Americans are still American. They have the same basic ideals which they have had for hundreds of years. They are just as eager for individual freedom. They are just as anxious to be let alone by Government agents. They are just as anxious to run their own local affairs and their own schools. They don't like relief, and they know that a reasonable prosperity can do away with the necessity for relief. They know that thrift and ability and hard work ought to bring rewards today, as they did in the horse and buggy days, if it were not for Government interference. They know that only the Republican party can avert the disaster which will inevitably result from deficit spending, arbitrary price-fixing, excessive taxation, and Government regulation of everything and everybody.

APPENDIX

THE DECLARATION OF INDEPENDENCE *

IN CONGRESS JULY 4, 1776

THE UNANIMOUS DECLARATION of the THIRTEEN UNITED STATES OF AMERICA

WHEN, in the Course of human events, it becomes necessary for one people to dissolve the political bands which have connected them with another, and to assume among the powers of the earth, the separate and equal station to which the Laws of Nature and of Nature's God entitle them, a decent respect to the opinions of mankind requires that they should declare the causes which impel them to the separation. — We hold these truths to be self-evident, that all men are created equal, that they are endowed by their Creator with certain unalienable rights, that among these are Life, Liberty, and

* Since The Declaration of Independence is a primary source of those beliefs and ideals on which " the American way of life " is based, it seems appropriate to reprint it here as a major document in the American way of life.

the pursuit of Happiness. — That to secure these rights, Governments are instituted among Men, deriving their just powers from the consent of the governed, — That whenever any Form of Government becomes destructive of these ends, it is the Right of the People to alter or to abolish it, and to institute new Government, laying its foundation on such principles and organizing its powers in such form, as to them shall seem most likely to effect their Safety and Happiness. Prudence, indeed, will dictate that Governments long established should not be changed for light and transient causes; and accordingly all experience hath shewn, that mankind are more disposed to suffer, while evils are sufferable, than to right themselves by abolishing the forms to which they are accustomed. But when a long train of abuses and usurpations, pursuing invariably the same Object evinces a design to reduce them under absolute Despotism, it is their right, it is their duty, to throw off such Government, and to provide new Guards for their future security. — Such has been the patient sufferance of these Colonies; and such is now the necessity which constrains them to alter their former Systems of Government. The history of the present King of Great Britain is a history of repeated injuries and usurpations, all having in direct object the establishment of an absolute Tyranny over these States. To prove this, let Facts be submitted to a candid world. — He has refused his Assent to Laws, the most wholesome and necessary for the public good. — He has forbidden his Governors to pass Laws of immediate and pressing importance, unless suspended in their operation till his Assent should be obtained; and when so suspended, he has utterly neglected to attend to them. — He has refused to pass other Laws for the accommodation of large districts of people, unless those people would relinquish the right of representation in the Legislature, a right inestimable to them and formidable to tyrants only. — He has called together legislative bodies at places unusual, uncomfortable, and distant from the depository of their public Records, for the sole purpose of fatiguing them into compliance with his measures. — He has dissolved Representative Houses repeatedly, for opposing with manly firmness his invasions on the rights of the people. — He has refused for a long time, after such dissolutions, to cause others to be elected; whereby the Legislative powers, incapable of Annihilation, have returned to the People at large for their exercise; the State remaining, in the mean time exposed to all the dangers of invasions from without and convulsions within. — He has endeavored to prevent the population of these States; for that purpose obstructing the Laws for Naturalization of Foreigners, refusing to pass others to encourage their migration hither, and raising the conditions of new Appropriations of Lands. — He has obstructed the Administration of Justice, by refusing his Assent to Laws for establishing Judiciary powers. — He has made Judges dependent on his Will alone, for the tenure of their offices, and the amount and payment of their salaries. — He has erected a multitude of New Offices, and sent hither swarms of officers to harass our people, and eat out their substance. — He has kept among us, in times of peace, Standing Armies, without the Consent of our Legislatures. — He has affected to render the Military independent of and superior to the Civil power. — He has combined with others to subject us to a jurisdiction foreign to our constitution, and unacknowledged by our laws; giving his Assent to their Acts of pretended Legislation: — For quartering large bodies of armed troops among us: — For protecting them by a mock Trial, from punishment for any Murders which they should commit on the Inhabitants of these States: — For cutting off our Trade with all parts of the world: — For imposing Taxes on us without our Consent: — For depriving us in many cases, of the benefits of Trial by Jury: For transporting us beyond Seas to be tried for pretended offenses: — For abolishing the free System of English Laws in a neighboring Province, establishing therein an Arbitrary government, and enlarging its Boundaries so as to render it at once an example and fit instrument for introducing the same absolute rule into these Colonies: — For taking away our charters, abolishing our most valuable Laws, and altering fundamentally the Forms of our Governments: — For suspending our own Legislatures, and declaring themselves invested with power to legislate for us in all cases whatsoever. — He has abdicated Government here, by declaring us out of his Protection and waging War against us. He has plundered our seas, ravaged our Coasts, burnt our towns, and destroyed the lives of our people. — He is at this time transporting large armies of foreign Mercenaries to complete the works of death, desolation, and tyranny, already begun with circumstances of Cruelty & perfidy scarcely paralleled in the most barbarous ages, and totally unworthy the Head of a civilized nation. — He has constrained our fellow Citizens, taken Captive on the high Seas to bear Arms against their Country, to become the executioners of their friends and Brethren, or to fall themselves by their Hands. He has excited domestic insurrections amongst us, and has endeavored to bring on the inhabitants of our frontiers, the merciless Indian Savages, whose known rule of warfare, is an undistinguished destruction of all ages, sexes, and conditions. In every stage of these Oppressions We have Petitioned for Redress in the most humble terms: Our repeated Petitions have been answered only by repeated injury. A Prince, whose character is thus marked by every act which may define a Tyrant, is unfit to be the ruler of a free people.

Nor have We been wanting in attentions to our Brittish brethren. We have warned them from time to time of attempts by their legislature to extend an unwarrantable jurisdiction over us. We have reminded them of the circumstances of our emigration and settlement here. We have appealed to their native justice and magnanimity, and we have conjured them by the ties of our common kindred to disavow these usurpations, which, would inevitably interrupt our connections and correspondence. They, too, have been deaf to the voice of justice and of consanguinity. We must, therefore, acquiesce in the necessity which denounces our Separation, and hold them, as we hold the rest of mankind, Enemies in War; in Peace, Friends.

WE, THEREFORE, the Representatives of the UNITED STATES OF AMERICA, in General Congress, Assembled, appealing to the Supreme Judge of the world for the rectitude of our intentions, do, in the Name and by the Authority of the good People of these Colonies, solemnly publish and declare, That these United Colonies are, and of Right ought to be, FREE AND INDEPENDENT STATES; that they are Absolved from all Allegiance to the British Crown, and that all political connection between them and the State of Great Britain, is and ought to be totally dissolved; and that as Free and Independent States they have full Power to levy War, conclude Peace, contract Alliances, establish Commerce, and to do all other Acts and Things which Independent States may of right do. — And for the support of this Declaration, with a firm reliance on the protection of divine Providence, we mutually pledge to each other our Lives, our Fortunes, and our sacred Honor.

THE CONSTITUTION OF THE UNITED STATES

We the People of the United States, in Order to form a more perfect Union, establish Justice, insure domestic Tranquility, provide for the common defence, promote the general Welfare, and secure the Blessings of Liberty to ourselves and our Posterity, do ordain and establish this Constitution for the United States of America.

Article. I.

Section. 1. All legislative Powers herein granted shall be vested in a Congress of the United States, which shall consist of a Senate and House of Representatives.

Section. 2. The House of Representatives shall be composed of Members chosen every second Year by the People of the several States, and the Electors in each State shall have ∧ Qualifications requisite for Electors of the most numerous Branch of the State Legislature.

No Person shall be a Representative who shall not have attained to the Age of twenty five Years, and been seven Years a Citizen of the United States, and who shall not, when elected, be an Inhabitant of that State in which he shall be chosen.

Representatives and direct Taxes shall be apportioned among the several States which may be included within this Union, according to their respective Numbers, which shall be determined by adding to the whole Number of free Persons, including those bound to Service for a Term of Years, and excluding Indians not taxed, three fifths of all other Persons. The actual Enumeration shall be made within three Years after the first Meeting of the Congress of the United States, and within every subsequent Term of ten Years, in such Manner as they shall by Law direct. The Number of Representatives shall not exceed one for every thirty Thousand, but each State shall have at Least one Representative; and until such enumeration shall be made, the State of New Hampshire shall be entitled to chuse three, Massachusetts eight, Rhode-Island and Providence Plantations one, Connecticut five, New-York six, New Jersey four, Pennsylvania eight, Delaware one, Maryland six, Virginia ten, North Carolina five, South Carolina five, and Georgia three.

When vacancies happen in the Representation from any State, the Executive Authority thereof shall issue Writs of Election to fill such Vacancies.

The House of Representatives shall chuse their Speaker and other Officers; and shall have the sole Power of Impeachment.

Section. 3. The Senate of the United States shall be composed of two Senators from each State, chosen by the Legislature thereof, for six Years; and each Senator shall have one Vote.

Immediately after they shall be assembled in Consequence of the first Election, they shall be divided as equally as may be into three Classes. The Seats of the Senators of the first Class shall be vacated at the Expiration of the second Year, of the second Class at the Expiration of the fourth Year, and of the third Class at the Expiration of the sixth Year, so that one third may be chosen every second Year; and if Vacancies happen by Resignation, or otherwise, during the Recess of the Legislature of any State, the Executive thereof may make temporary Appointments until the next Meeting of the Legislature, which shall then fill such Vacancies.

No Person shall be a Senator who shall not have attained to the Age of thirty Years, and been nine Years a Citizen of the United States, and who shall not, when elected, be an Inhabitant of that State for which he shall be chosen.

The Vice President of the United States shall be President of the Senate, but shall have no Vote, unless they be equally divided.

The Senate shall chuse their other Officers, and also a President pro tempore, in the Absence of the Vice President, or when he shall exercise the Office of President of the United States.

The Senate shall have the sole Power to try all Impeachments. When sitting for that Purpose, they shall be on Oath or Affirmation. When the President of the United States ∧ the Chief Justice shall preside: And no Person
^{is tried,}
shall be convicted without the Concurrence of two thirds of the Members present.

Judgment in Cases of Impeachment shall not extend further than to removal from Office, and disqualification to hold and enjoy any Office of honor, Trust or Profit under the United States: but the Party convicted shall nevertheless be liable and subject to Indictment, Trial, Judgment and Punishment, according to Law.

Section. 4. The Times, Places and Manner of holding Elections for Senators and Representatives, shall be prescribed in each State by the Legislature thereof; but the Congress may at any time by Law make or alter such Regulations, except as to the Places of chusing Senators.

The Congress shall assemble at least once in every Year, and such Meeting shall be on the first Monday in December, unless they shall by Law appoint a different Day.

Section. 5. Each House shall be the Judge of the Elections, Returns and Qualifications of its own Members, and a Majority of each shall constitute a Quorum to do Business; but a smaller Number may adjourn from day to day, and may be authorized to compel the Attendance of absent Members, in such Manner, and under such Penalties as each House may provide.

Each House may determine the Rules of its Proceedings, punish its Members for disorderly Behaviour, and, with the Concurrence of two thirds, expel a Member.

Each House shall keep a Journal of its Proceedings, and from time to time publish the same, excepting such Parts as may in their Judgment require Secrecy; and the Yeas and Nays of the Members of either House on any question shall, at the Desire of one fifth of those Present, be entered on the Journal.

Neither House, during the Session of Congress, shall, without the Consent of the other, adjourn for more than three days, nor to any other Place than that in which the two Houses shall be sitting.

Section. 6. The Senators and Representatives shall receive a Compensation for their Services, to be ascertained by Law, and paid out of the Treasury of the United States. They shall in all Cases, except Treason, Felony and Breach of the Peace, be privileged from Arrest during their Attendance at the Session of their respective Houses, and in going to and returning from the same; and for any Speech or Debate in either House, they shall not be questioned in any other Place.

No Senator or Representative shall, during the Time for which he was elected, be appointed to any civil Office under the Authority of the United States, which shall have been created, or the Emoluments whereof shall have been encreased during such time; and no Person holding any Office under the United States, shall be a Member of either House during his Continuance in Office.

Section. 7. All Bills for raising Revenue shall originate in the House of Representatives; but the Senate may propose or concur with Amendments as on other Bills.

Every Bill which shall have passed the House of Representatives and the Senate, shall, before it become a Law, be presented to the President of the United States; If he approve he shall sign it, but if not he shall return it, with his Objections to that House in which it shall have originated, who shall enter the Objections at large on their Journal, and proceed to reconsider it. If after such Reconsideration two thirds of that House shall agree to pass the Bill, it shall be sent, together with the Objections, to the other House, by which it shall likewise be reconsidered, and if approved by two thirds of that House, it shall become a Law. But in all such Cases the Votes of both Houses shall be determined by yeas and Nays, and the Names of the Persons voting for and against the Bill shall be entered on the Journal of each House respectively. If any Bill shall not be returned by the President within ten Days (Sundays excepted) after it shall have been presented to him, the Same shall be a Law, in like Manner as if he had signed it, unless the Congress by their Adjournment prevent its Return, in which Case it shall not be a Law.

Every Order, Resolution, or Vote to which the Concurrence of the Senate and House of Representatives may be necessary (except on a question of Adjournment) shall be presented to the President of the United States; and before the Same shall take Effect, shall be approved by him, or being disapproved by him, shall be repassed by two thirds of the Senate and House of Representatives, according to the Rules and Limitations prescribed in the Case of a Bill. Section. 8. The Congress shall have Power To lay and collect Taxes, Duties, Imposts and Excises, to pay the Debts and provide for the common Defence and general Welfare of the United States; but all Duties, Imposts and Excises shall be uniform throughout the United States;

To borrow Money on the credit of the United States;

To regulate Commerce with foreign Nations, and among the several States, and with the Indian Tribes;

To establish an uniform Rule of Naturalization, and uniform Laws on the subject of Bankruptcies throughout the United States;

To coin Money, regulate the Value thereof, and of foreign Coin, and fix the Standard of Weights and Measures;

To provide for the Punishment of counterfeiting the Securities and current Coin of the United States;

To establish Post Offices and post Roads;

To promote the Progress of Science and useful Arts, by securing for limited Times to Authors and Inventors the exclusive Right to their respective Writings and Discoveries;

To constitute Tribunals inferior to the supreme Court;

To define and punish Piracies and Felonies committed on the high Seas, and Offences against the Law of Nations;

To declare War, grant Letters of Marque and Reprisal, and make Rules concerning Captures on Land and Water;

To raise and support Armies, but no Appropriation of Money to that Use shall be for a longer Term than two Years;

To provide and maintain a Navy;

To make Rules for the Government and Regulation of the land and naval Forces;

To provide for calling forth the Militia to execute the Laws of the Union, suppress Insurrections and repel Invasions;

To provide for organizing, arming, and disciplining, the Militia, and for governing such Part of them as may be employed in the Service of the United States, reserving to the States respectively, the Appointment of the Officers, and the Authority of training the Militia according to the discipline prescribed by Congress;

To exercise exclusive Legislation in all Cases whatsoever, over such District (not exceeding ten Miles square) as may, by Cession of particular States, and the Acceptance of Congress, become the Seat of the Government of the United States, and to exercise like Authority over all Places purchased by the Consent of the Legislature of the State in which the Same shall be, for the Erection of Forts, Magazines, Arsenals, dock-Yards, and other needful Buildings; — And

To make all Laws which shall be necessary and proper for carrying into Execution the foregoing Powers, and all other Powers vested by this Constitution in the Government of the United States, or in any Department or Officer thereof.

Section. 9. The Migration or Importation of such Persons as any of the States now existing shall think proper to admit, shall not be prohibited by the Congress prior to the Year one thousand eight hundred and eight, but a Tax or duty may be imposed on such Importation, not exceeding ten dollars for each Person.

The Privilege of the Writ of Habeas Corpus shall not be suspended, unless when in Cases of Rebellion or Invasion the public Safety may require it.

No Bill of Attainder or ex post facto Law shall be passed.

No Capitation, or other direct, Tax shall be laid, unless in Proportion to the Census or Enumeration herein before directed to be taken.

No Tax or Duty shall be laid on Articles exported from any State.

No Preference shall be given by any Regulation of Commerce or Revenue to the Ports of one State over those of another: nor shall Vessels bound to, or from, one State, be obliged to enter, clear, or pay Duties in another.

No Money shall be drawn from the Treasury, but in Consequence of Appropriations made by Law; and a regular Statement and Account of the Receipts and Expenditures of all public Money shall be published from time to time.

No Title of Nobility shall be granted by the United States: And no Person holding any Office of Profit or Trust under them, shall, without the Consent of the Congress, accept of any present, Emolument, Office, or Title, of any kind whatever, from any King, Prince, or foreign State.

Section. 10. No State shall enter into any Treaty, Alliance, or Confederation; grant Letters of Marque and Reprisal; coin Money; emit Bills of Credit; make any Thing but gold and silver Coin a Tender in Payment of Debts; pass any Bill of Attainder, ex post facto Law, or Law impairing the Obligation of Contracts, or grant any Title of Nobility.

No State shall, without the Consent of th ∧ Congress, lay any Imposts or Duties on Imports or Exports, except what may be absolutely necessary for executing it's inspection Laws: and the net Produce of all Duties and Imposts, laid by any State on Imports or Exports, shall be for the Use of the Treasury of the United States; and all such Laws shall be subject to the Revision and Controul of ^{the} ∧ Congress.

No State shall, without the Consent of Congress, lay any Duty of Tonnage, keep Troops, or Ships of War in time of Peace, enter into any Agreement or Compact with another State, or with a foreign Power, or engage in War, unless actually invaded, or in such imminent Danger as will not admit of delay.

Article. II.

Section. 1. The executive Power shall be vested in a President of the United States of America. He shall hold his Office during the Term of four Years, and, together with the Vice President, chosen for the same Term, be elected, as follows

Each State shall appoint, in such Manner as the Legislature thereof may direct, a Number of Electors, equal to the whole Number of Senators and Representatives to which the State may be entitled in the Congress: but no Senator or Representative, or Person holding an Office of Trust or Profit under the United States, shall be appointed an Elector.

The Electors shall meet in their respective States, and vote by Ballot for two Persons, of whom one at least shall not be an Inhabitant of the same State with themselves. And they shall make a List of all the Persons voted for, and of the Number of Votes for each; which List they shall sign

283

and certify, and transmit sealed to the Seat of the Government of the United States, directed to the President of the Senate. The President of the Senate shall, in the Presence of the Senate and House of Representatives, open all the Certificates, and the Votes shall then be counted. The Person having the greatest Number of Votes shall be the President, if such Number be a Majority of the whole Number of Electors appointed; and if there be more than one who have such Majority, and have an equal Number of Votes, then the House of Representatives shall immediately chuse by Ballot one of them for President; and if no Person have a Majority, then from the five highest on the List the said House shall in like Manner chuse the President. But in chusing the President, the Votes shall be taken by States, the Representation from each State having one Vote; A quorum for this Purpose shall consist of a Member or Members from two thirds of the States, and a Majority of all the States shall be necessary to a Choice. In every Case, after the Choice of the President, the Person having the greatest Number of Votes of the Electors shall be the Vice President. But if there should remain two or more who have equal Votes, the Senate shall chuse from them by Ballot the Vice President.

The Congress may determine the Time of chusing the Electors, and the Day on which they shall give their Votes; which Day shall be the same throughout the United States.

No Person except a natural born Citizen, or a Citizen of the United States, at the time of the Adoption of this Constitution, shall be eligible to the Office of President; neither shall any Person be eligible to that Office who shall not have attained to the Age of thirty five Years, and been fourteen Years a Resident within the United States.

In Case of the Removal of the President from Office, or of his Death, Resignation, or Inability to discharge the Powers and Duties of the said Office, the Same shall devolve on the Vice President, and the Congress may by Law provide for the Case of Removal, Death, Resignation or Inability, both of the President and Vice President, declaring what Officer shall then act as President, and such Officer shall act accordingly, until the Disability be removed, or a President shall be elected.

The President shall, at stated Times, receive for his Services, a Compensation, which shall neither be encreased nor diminished during the Period for which he shall have been elected, and he shall not receive within that Period any other Emolument from the United States, or any of them.

Before he enter on the Execution of his Office, he shall take the following Oath or Affirmation: — " I do solemnly swear (or affirm) that I will faithfully execute the Office of President of the United States, and will to the best of my Ability, preserve, protect and defend the Constitution of the United States."

Section. 2. The President shall be Commander in Chief of the Army and Navy of the United States, and of the Militia of the several States, when called into the actual Service of the United States; he may require the Opinion, in writing, of the principal Officer in each of the executive Departments, upon any Subject relating to the Duties of their respective Offices, and he shall have Power to grant Reprieves and Pardons for Offences against the United States, except in Cases of Impeachment.

He shall have Power, by and with the Advice and Consent of the Senate, to make Treaties, provided two thirds of the Senators present concur; and he shall nominate, and by and with the Advice and Consent of the Senate, shall appoint Ambassadors, other public Ministers and Consuls, Judges of the supreme Court, and all other Officers of the United States, whose Appointments are not herein otherwise provided for, and which shall be established by Law: but the Congress may by Law vest the Appointment of such inferior Officers, as they think proper, in the President alone, in the Courts of Law, or in the Heads of Departments.

The President shall have Power to fill up all Vacancies that may happen during the Recess of the Senate, by granting Commissions which shall expire at the End of their next Session.

Section. 3. He shall from time to time give to the Congress Information of the State of the Union, and recommend to their Consideration such Measures as he shall judge necessary and expedient; he may, on extraordinary Occasions, convene both Houses, or either of them, and in Case of Disagreement between them, with Respect to the Time of Adjournment, he may adjourn them to such Time as he shall think proper; he shall receive Ambassadors and other public Ministers; he shall take Care that the Laws be faithfully executed, and shall Commission all the Officers of the United States.

Section. 4. The President, Vice President and all civil Officers of the United States, shall be removed from Office on Impeachment for, and Conviction of, Treason, Bribery, or other high Crimes and Misdemeanors.

Article III.

Section. 1. The judicial Power of the United States, shall be vested in one supreme Court, and in such inferior Courts as the Congress may from time to time ordain and establish. The Judges, both of the supreme and inferior Courts, shall hold their Offices during good Behaviour, and shall, at stated Times, receive for their Services, a Compensation, which shall not be diminished during their Continuance in Office.

Section. 2. The judicial Power shall extend to all Cases, in Law and Equity, arising under this Constitution, the Laws of the United States, and Treaties made, or which shall be made, under their Authority; — to all Cases affecting Ambassadors, other public Ministers and Consuls; — to all

Cases of admiralty and maritime Jurisdiction; — to Controversies to which the United States shall be a Party; — to Controversies between two or more States; — between a State and Citizens of another State; — between Citizens of different States, — between Citizens of the same State claiming Lands under Grants of different States, and between a State, or the Citizens thereof, and foreign States, Citizens or Subjects.

In all Cases affecting Ambassadors, other public Ministers and Consuls, and those in which a State shall be Party, the supreme Court shall have original Jurisdiction. In all the other Cases before mentioned, the supreme Court shall have appellate Jurisdiction, both as to Law and Fact, with such Exceptions and under such Regulations as the Congress shall make.

The Trial of all Crimes, except in Cases of Impeachment, shall be by Jury; and such Trial shall be held in the State where the said Crimes shall have been committed; but when not committed within any State, the Trial shall be at such Place or Places as the Congress may by Law have directed. Section. 3. Treason against the United States, shall consist only in levying War against them, or in adhering to their Enemies, giving them Aid and Comfort. No Person shall be convicted of Treason unless on the Testimony of two Witnesses to the same overt Act, or on Confession in open Court.

The Congress shall have Power to declare the Punishment of Treason, but no Attainder of Treason shall work Corruption of Blood, or Forfeiture except during the Life of the Person attainted.

Article. IV.

Section. 1. Full Faith and Credit shall be given in each State to the public Acts, Records, and judicial Proceedings of every other State. And the Congress may by general

Laws prescribe the Manner in which such Acts, Records and Proceedings shall be proved, and the Effect thereof.

Section. 2. The Citizens of each State shall be entitled to all Privileges and Immunities of Citizens in the several States.

A Person charged in any State with Treason, Felony, or other Crime, who shall flee from Justice, and be found in another State, shall on Demand of the executive Authority of the State from which he fled, be delivered up, to be removed to the State having Jurisdiction of the Crime.

No Person held to Service or Labour in one State, under the Laws thereof, escaping into another, shall, in Consequence of any Law or Regulation therein, be discharged from such Service or Labour, but shall be delivered up on Claim of the Party to whom such Service or Labour may be due.

Section. 3. New States may be admitted by the Congress into this Union; but no new State shall be formed or erected within the Jurisdiction of any other State; nor any State be formed by the Junction of two or more States, or Parts of States, without the Consent of the Legislatures of the States concerned as well as of the Congress.

The Congress shall have Power to dispose of and make all needful Rules and Regulations respecting the Territory or other Property belonging to the United States; and nothing in this Constitution shall be so construed as to Prejudice any Claims of the United States, or of any particular State.

Section. 4. The United States shall guarantee to every State in this Union a Republican Form of Government, and shall protect each of them against Invasion; and on Application of the Legislature, or of the Executive (when the Legislature cannot be convened) against domestic Violence.

Article. V.

The Congress, whenever two thirds of both Houses shall deem it necessary, shall propose Amendments to this Constitution, or, on the Application of the Legislatures of two thirds of the several States, shall call a Convention for proposing Amendments, which, in either Case, shall be valid to all Intents and Purposes, as Part of this Constitution, when ratified by the Legislatures of three fourths of the several States, or by Conventions in three fourths thereof, as the one or the other Mode of Ratification may be proposed by the Congress; Provided that no Amendment which may be made prior to the Year One thousand eight hundred and eight shall in any Manner affect the first and fourth Clauses in the Ninth Section of the first Article; and that no State, without its Consent, shall be deprived of it's equal Suffrage in the Senate.

Article. VI.

All Debts contracted and Engagements entered into, before the Adoption of this Constitution, shall be as valid against the United States under this Constitution, as under the Confederation.

This Constitution, and the Laws of the United States which shall be made in Pursuance thereof; and all Treaties made, or which shall be made, under the Authority of the United States, shall be the supreme Law of the Land; and the Judges in every State shall be bound thereby, any Thing in the Constitution or Laws of any State to the Contrary notwithstanding.

The Senators and Representatives before mentioned, and the Members of the several State Legislatures, and all executive and judicial Officers, both of the United States and of the several States, shall be bound by Oath or Affirmation, to support this Constitution; but no religious Test shall ever be required as a Qualification to any Office or public Trust under the United States.

Article. VII.

The Ratification of the Conventions of nine States, shall be sufficient for the Establishment of this Constitution between the States so ratifying the Same.

The Word, "the," being interlined between the seventh and eighth Lines of the first Page, The word " Thirty " being partly written on an Erazure in the fifteenth Line of the first Page, The Words " is tried " being interlined between the thirty second and thirty third Lines of the first Page and the Word " the " being interlined between the forty third and forty fourth Lines of the second Page.

Attest WILLIAM JACKSON Secretary

done in Convention by the Unanimous Consent of the States present the Seventeenth Day of September in the Year of our Lord one thousand seven hundred and Eighty seven and of the Independance of the United States of America the Twelfth. In witness whereof We have hereunto subscribed our Names,

G⁰: WASHINGTON — Presdᵗ
and deputy from Virginia

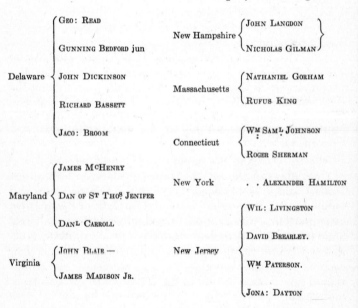

Delaware
{
GEO: READ

GUNNING BEDFORD jun

JOHN DICKINSON

RICHARD BASSETT

JACO: BROOM
}

Maryland
{
JAMES MᶜHENRY

DAN OF Sᵀ THOˢ JENIFER

DANᴸ CARROLL
}

Virginia
{
JOHN BLAIR —

JAMES MADISON JR.
}

New Hampshire
{
JOHN LANGDON

NICHOLAS GILMAN
}

Massachusetts
{
NATHANIEL GORHAM

RUFUS KING
}

Connecticut
{
WM SAMᴸ JOHNSON

ROGER SHERMAN
}

New York   . . ALEXANDER HAMILTON

New Jersey
{
WIL: LIVINGSTON

DAVID BREARLEY.

WM PATERSON.

JONA: DAYTON
}

290

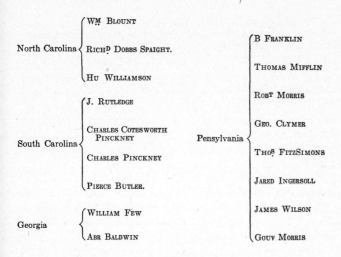

North Carolina
- Wᴹ Blount
- Richᴰ Dobbs Spaight.
- Hu Williamson

South Carolina
- J. Rutledge
- Charles Cotesworth Pinckney
- Charles Pinckney
- Pierce Butler.

Georgia
- William Few
- Abr Baldwin

Pensylvania
- B Franklin
- Thomas Mifflin
- Robᵀ Morris
- Geo. Clymer
- Thoˢ FitzSimons
- Jared Ingersoll
- James Wilson
- Gouv Morris

In Convention Monday, September 17th, 1787.
Present
The States of

New Hampshire, Massachusetts, Connecticut, Mr. Hamilton from New York, New Jersey, Pennsylvania, Delaware, Maryland, Virginia, North Carolina, South Carolina and Georgia.
Resolved,

That the preceeding Constitution be laid before the United States in Congress assembled, and that it is the Opinion of this Convention, that it should afterwards be submitted to a Convention of Delegates, chosen in each State by the People thereof, under the Recommendation of its Legislature, for their Assent and Ratification; and that each Convention assenting to, and ratifying the Same, should give Notice thereof to the United States in Congress assembled.

291

Resolved, That it is the Opinion of this Convention, that as soon as the Conventions of nine States shall have ratified this Constitution, the United States in Congress assembled should fix a Day on which Electors should be appointed by the States which shall have ratified the same, and a Day on which the Electors should assemble to vote for the President, and the Time and Place for commencing Proceedings under this Constitution. That after such Publication the Electors should be appointed, and the Senators and Representatives elected: That the Electors should meet on the Day fixed for the Election of the President, and should transmit their Votes certified, signed, sealed and directed, as the Constitution requires, to the Secretary of the United States in Congress assembled, that the Senators and Representatives should convene at the Time and Place assigned; that the Senators should appoint a President of the Senate, for the sole Purpose of receiving, opening and counting the Votes for President; and, that after he shall be chosen, the Congress, together with the President, should, without Delay, proceed to execute this Constitution.

By the Unanimous Order of the Convention.

G$^\circ$ WASHINGTON Presd^t

W. JACKSON Secretary.

IN CONVENTION, SEPTEMBER 17, 1787.

Sir,

We have now the honor to submit to the consideration of the United States in Congress assembled, that Constitution which has appeared to us the most adviseable.

The friends of our country have long seen and desired, that the power of making war, peace, and treaties, that of levying money and regulating commerce, and the correspondent executive and judicial authorities should be fully and effectually vested in the general government of the Union: But the impropriety of delegating such extensive trust to one body of men is evident — Hence results the necessity of a different organization.

It is obviously impracticable in the federal government of these states, to secure all rights of independent sovereignty to each, and yet provide for the interest and safety of all: Individuals entering into society, must give up a share of liberty to preserve the rest. The magnitude of the sacrifice must depend as well on situation and circumstance, as on the object to be obtained. It is at all times difficult to draw with precision the line between those rights which must be surrendered, and those which may be reserved; and on the present occasion this difficulty was encreased by a difference among the several states as to their situation, extent, habits, and particular interests.

In all our deliberations on this subject we kept steadily in our view, that which appears to us the greatest interest of every true American, the consolidation of our Union, in which is involved our prosperity, felicity, safety, perhaps our national existence. This important consideration, seriously and deeply impressed on our minds, led each state in the Convention to be less rigid on points of inferior magnitude, than might have been otherwise expected; and thus the Constitution, which we now present, is the result of a spirit of amity, and of that mutual deference and concession which the peculiarity of our political situation rendered indispensible.

That it will meet the full and entire approbation of every state is not perhaps to be expected; but each will doubtless consider, that had her interest been alone consulted, the consequences might have been particularly disagreeable or injurious to others; that it is liable to as few exceptions as could reasonably have been expected, we hope and believe; that it may promote the lasting welfare of that country so dear to us all, and secure her freedom and happiness, is our most ardent wish.

With great respect, We have the honor to be, Sir,
Your Excellency's
most obedient and humble servants,

GEORGE WASHINGTON, *President.*

By unanimous Order of the Convention.
His Excellency the President of Congress.

IN CONGRESS

FRIDAY, SEPTEMBER 28, 1787.

Congress assembled present New hampshire Massachusetts Connecticut New York New Jersey Pennsylvania, Delaware Virginia North Carolina South Carolina and Georgia and from Maryland Mr. Ross.

Congress having received the report of the Convention lately assembled in Philadelphia.

Resolved Unanimously that the said Report with the resolutions and letter accompanying the same be transmitted to the several legislatures in Order to be submitted to a convention of Delegates chosen in each state by the people thereof in conformity to the resolves of the Convention made and provided in that case.

SATURDAY, SEPTEMBER 13, 1788

Congress assembled present New hampshire Massachusetts Connecticut New York New Jersey Pennsylvania Virginia North Carolina South Carolina and Georgia and from Rhode island Mr. Arnold and from Delaware Mr. Kearny. . . .

Whereas the Convention assembled in Philadelphia pursuant to the resolution of Congress of the 21st of Feby. 1787 did on the 17th of Sept in the same year report to the United States in Congress assembled a constitution for the people of the United States, Whereupon Congress on the 28 of the same Sept did resolve unanimously " That the said report with the resolutions and letter accompanying the same be transmitted to the several legislatures in order to be submitted to a convention of Delegates chosen in each state by the people thereof in conformity to the resolves of the convention made and provided in that case " And whereas the constitution so reported by the Convention and by Congress transmitted to the several legislatures has been ratified in the manner therein declared to be sufficient for the establishment of the same and such ratifications duly authenticated have been received by Congress and are filed in the Office of the Secretary therefore

Resolved That the first Wednesday in Jany next be the day for appointing Electors in the several states, which before the said day shall have ratified the said constitution; that the first Wednesday in feby. next be the day for the electors to assemble in their respective states and vote for a president; and that the first Wednesday in March next be the time and the present seat of Congress the place for commencing proceedings under the said constitution.

AMENDMENTS TO THE CONSTITUTION.

[AMENDMENT I]

Congress shall make no law respecting an establishment of religion, or prohibiting the free exercise thereof; or abridging the freedom of speech, or of the press; or the right of the people peaceably to assemble, and to petition the Government for a redress of grievances.

[AMENDMENT II]

A well regulated Militia, being necessary to the security of a free State, the right of the people to keep and bear Arms, shall not be infringed.

[AMENDMENT III]

No Soldier shall, in time of peace be quartered in any house, without the consent of the Owner, nor in time of war, but in a manner to be prescribed by law.

[AMENDMENT IV]

The right of the people to be secure in their persons, houses, papers, and effects, against unreasonable searches and seizures, shall not be violated, and no Warrants shall issue, but upon probable cause, supported by Oath or affirmation, and particularly describing the place to be searched, and the persons or things to be seized.

[AMENDMENT V]

No person shall be held to answer for a capital, or otherwise infamous crime, unless on a presentment or indictment of a Grand Jury, except in cases arising in the land or naval forces, or in the Militia, when in actual service in time of War or public danger; nor shall any person be subject for the same offence to be twice put in jeopardy of life or limb, nor shall be compelled in any criminal case to be a witness against himself, nor be deprived of life, liberty, or property, without due process of law; nor shall private property be taken for public use, without just compensation.

[AMENDMENT VI]

In all criminal prosecutions, the accused shall enjoy the right to a speedy and public trial, by an impartial jury of the State and district wherein the crime shall have been committed, which district shall have been previously ascertained by law, and to be informed of the nature and cause of the accusation; to be confronted with the witnesses against him; to have compulsory process for obtaining Witnesses in his favor, and to have the Assistance of Counsel for his defence.

[AMENDMENT VII]

In Suits at common law, where the value in controversy shall exceed twenty dollars, the right of trial by jury shall be preserved, and no fact tried by a jury, shall be otherwise re-examined in any Court of the United States, than according to the rules of the common law.

[AMENDMENT VIII]

Excessive bail shall not be required, nor excessive fines imposed, nor cruel and unusual punishments inflicted.

[AMENDMENT IX]

The enumeration in the Constitution, of certain rights, shall not be construed to deny or disparage others retained by the people.

[AMENDMENT X]

The powers not delegated to the United States by the Constitution, nor prohibited by it to the States, are reserved to the States respectively, or to the people.

[AMENDMENT XI]

The Judicial power of the United States shall not be construed to extend to any suit in law or equity, commenced or prosecuted against one of the United States by Citizens of another State, or by Citizens or Subjects of any Foreign State.

[AMENDMENT XII]

The Electors shall meet in their respective states, and vote by ballot for President and Vice-President, one of whom, at least, shall not be an inhabitant of the same state with themselves; they shall name in their ballots the person voted for as President, and in distinct ballots the person voted for as Vice-President, and they shall make distinct lists of all persons voted for as President, and of all persons voted for as Vice-President, and of the number of votes for each, which lists they shall sign and certify, and transmit sealed to the seat of the government of the United States, directed to the President of the Senate; — The President of the Senate shall, in the presence of the Senate and House of Representatives, open all the certificates and the votes shall then be counted; — The person having the greatest number of votes for President, shall be the President, if such number be a majority of the whole number of Electors appointed; and if no person have such majority, then from the persons having the highest numbers not exceeding three on the list of those voted for as President, the House of Representatives shall choose immediately, by ballot, the President. But in choosing the President, the votes shall be taken by states, the representation from each state having one vote; a quorum for this purpose shall consist of a member or members from two-thirds of the states, and a majority of all the states shall be necessary to a choice. And if the House of Representatives shall not choose a President whenever the right of choice shall devolve upon them, before the fourth day of March next following, then the Vice-President shall act as President, as in the case of the death or other constitutional disability of the President. — The person having the greatest number of votes as Vice-President, shall be the Vice-President, if such number be a majority of the whole number of Electors appointed, and if no person have a majority, then from the two highest numbers on the list, the Senate shall choose the Vice-President; a quorum for the purpose shall consist of two-thirds of the whole number of Senators, and a majority of the whole number shall be necessary to a choice. But no person constitutionally ineligible to the office of President shall be eligible to that of Vice-President of the United States.

[AMENDMENT] XIII

Section 1. Neither slavery nor involuntary servitude, except as a punishment for crime whereof the party shall have been duly convicted, shall exist within the United States, or any place subject to their jurisdiction. Section 2. Congress shall have power to enforce this article by appropriate legislation.

[AMENDMENT] XIV

Section 1. All persons born or naturalized in the United States, and subject to the jurisdiction thereof, are citizens of the United States and of the State wherein they reside. No State shall make or enforce any law which shall abridge the privileges or immunities of citizens of the United States; nor shall any State deprive any person of life, liberty, or property, without due process of law; nor deny to any person within its jurisdiction the equal protection of the laws.

Section 2. Representatives shall be apportioned among the several States according to their respective numbers, counting the whole number of persons in each State, excluding Indians not taxed. But when the right to vote at any election for the choice of electors for President and Vice President of the United States, Representatives in Congress, the Executive and Judicial officers of a State, or the members of the Legislature thereof, is denied to any of the male inhabitants of such State, being twenty-one years of age, and citizens of the United States, or in any way abridged, except for participation in rebellion, or other crime, the basis of representation therein shall be reduced in the proportion which the number of such male citizens shall bear to the whole number of male citizens twenty-one years of age in such State.

Section 3. No person shall be a Senator or Representative in Congress, or elector of President and Vice President, or hold any office, civil or military, under the United States, or under any State, who, having previously taken an oath, as a member of Congress, or as an officer of the United States, or as a member of any State legislature, or as an executive or judicial officer of any State, to support the Constitution of the United States, shall have engaged in insurrection or rebellion against the same, or given aid or comfort to the enemies thereof. But Congress may by a vote of two-thirds of each House, remove such disability.

Section 4. The validity of the public debt of the United States, authorized by law, including debts incurred for payment of pensions and bounties for services in suppressing insurrection or rebellion, shall not be questioned. But neither the United States nor any State shall assume or pay any debt or obligation incurred in aid of insurrection or rebellion against the United States, or any claim for the loss or emancipation of any slave; but all such debts, obligations and claims shall be held illegal and void.

Section 5. The Congress shall have power to enforce, by appropriate legislation, the provisions of this article.

[AMENDMENT] XV

Section 1. The right of citizens of the United States to vote shall not be denied or abridged by the United States or by any State on account of race, color, or previous condition of servitude. ——

Section 2. The Congress shall have power to enforce this article by appropriate legislation. ——

[AMENDMENT] XVI

The Congress shall have power to lay and collect taxes on incomes, from whatever source derived, without apportionment among the several States, and without regard to any census or enumeration.

[AMENDMENT] XVII

The Senate of the United States shall be composed of two Senators from each State, elected by the people thereof, for six years; and each Senator shall have one vote. The electors in each State shall have the qualifications requisite for electors of the most numerous branch of the State legislatures.

When vacancies happen in the representation of any State in the Senate, the executive authority of such State shall issue writs of election to fill such vacancies: *Provided,* That the legislature of any State may empower the executive thereof to make temporary appointments until the people fill the vacancies by election as the legislature may direct.

This amendment shall not be so construed as to affect the election or term of any Senator chosen before it becomes valid as part of the Constitution.

[AMENDMENT XVIII]

SECTION 1. After one year from the ratification of this article the manufacture, sale, or transportation of intoxicating liquors within, the importation thereof into, or the exportation thereof from the United States and all territory subject

301

THE CONSTITUTION OF THE UNITED STATES

to the jurisdiction thereof for beverage purposes is hereby prohibited.

SEC. 2. The Congress and the several States shall have concurrent power to enforce this article by appropriate legislation.

SEC. 3. This article shall be inoperative unless it shall have been ratified as an amendment to the Constitution by the legislatures of the several States, as provided in the Constitution, within seven years from the date of the submission hereof to the States by the Congress.

[AMENDMENT XIX]

The right of citizens of the United States to vote shall not be denied or abridged by the United States or by any State on account of sex.

Congress shall have power to enforce this article by appropriate legislation.

[AMENDMENT XX]

SECTION 1. The terms of the President and Vice President shall end at noon on the 20th day of January, and the terms of Senators and Representatives at noon on the 3d day of January, of the years in which such terms would have ended if this article had not been ratified; and the terms of their successors shall then begin.

SEC. 2. The Congress shall assemble at least once in every year, and such meeting shall begin at noon on the 3d day of January, unless they shall by law appoint a different day.

SEC. 3. If, at the time fixed for the beginning of the term of the President, the President elect shall have died, the Vice President elect shall become President. If a President shall not have been chosen before the time fixed for the beginning of his term, or if the President elect shall have failed to qualify, then the Vice President elect shall act as President

302

until a President shall have qualified; and the Congress may by law provide for the case wherein neither a President elect nor a Vice President elect shall have qualified, declaring who shall then act as President, or the manner in which one who is to act shall be selected, and such person shall act accordingly until a President or Vice President shall have qualified.

SEC. 4. The Congress may by law provide for the case of the death of any of the persons from whom the House of Representatives may choose a President whenever the right of choice shall have devolved upon them, and for the case of the death of any of the persons from whom the Senate may choose a Vice President whenever the right of choice shall have devolved upon them.

SEC. 5. Sections 1 and 2 shall take effect on the 15th day of October following the ratification of this article.

SEC. 6. This article shall be inoperative unless it shall have been ratified as an amendment to the Constitution by the legislatures of three-fourths of the several States within seven years from the date of its submission.

[AMENDMENT XXI]

SECTION 1. The eighteenth article of amendment to the Constitution of the United States is hereby repealed.

SEC. 2. The transportation or importation into any State, Territory, or possession of the United States for delivery or use therein of intoxicating liquors, in violation of the laws thereof, is hereby prohibited.

SEC. 3. This article shall be inoperative unless it shall have been ratified as an amendment to the Constitution by conventions in the several States, as provided in the Constitution, within seven years from the date of the submission hereof to the States by the Congress.

AN ADDRESS BY THE SPEAKER OF
THE HOUSE OF REPRESENTATIVES*

WILLIAM B. BANKHEAD

I FEEL very deeply my great good fortune in being the Speaker of the House today, because of that position I am the one privileged to welcome you to this Hall on this memorable occasion.

A mere century and a half is relatively a short span in the history of a nation, but when that period is the limit of the official life of the most powerful nation on earth, it assumes a vastly more comprehensive significance.

One hundred and fifty years ago this day there assembled in the city of New York the First Congress of the United States of America under its newly adopted Constitution. The mere statement of that incident carries only a reflection of the years that have passed, but in terms of what that occasion meant there has been no more arresting episode in the history of modern civilization. The proprieties of this occasion forbid even a casual review on my part of the historical background of the event we are convened to celebrate.

The student of the records of civilization always remembers a few outstanding things that have marked the progress of man from the dawn of organized society on through the tortuous and halting centuries in his search for a decent and stable formula of government that would combine into a compact of action the peace and security of peoples.

The Ten Commandments, the Sermon on the Mount, St. Paul at Rome, the voyages of Columbus, the Napoleonic

---

* Delivered before both Houses of Congress, March 4, 1939, on the occasion of the 150th anniversary of the first Congress, and reprinted from the *Congressional Record*.

304

wars, Magna Carta, the Declaration of Independence, the establishment of our Constitution illustrate a few of the milestones that mark the pilgrimage of men on the journey from chaos to stability.

Today we may find the temper to forget advances in the realms of religion, science, discovery, warfare, and the cultural arts and fix our contemplation on government, and particularly our own Government.

There has been no period within the recollection of this generation more full of signs and portents than this present hour of the necessity of reappraising the soundness and desirability of our democratic form of government, and if it yet maintains the confidence and support of our people, and of other great nations of the world, as I believe to be the case, then it is our solemn duty to take every needful step and to assume every required obligation to preserve for our posterity the form and essence of a justly balanced and wisely conceived government for a free people. This obligation does not bear upon us as of selfish national concern for our own people alone, although that should always be our primary interest, but in addition thereto, it carries a profound moral obligation to our neighbors across the seas and in the Western Hemisphere, who have honored the prudence and wisdom of our founders by adopting in substance the theory of government that God has not yet created any one man wise enough or benevolent enough to fix and enforce his individual pattern to govern the hearts and minds and conscience and property and lives of every citizen under his jurisdiction. Democracy asserts the inalienable right of the people themselves, through orderly processes and under the restraints to contrive out of their collective judgment, through their legally chosen representatives, the means and measures by which they are to be prospered and protected in the age-old search for security and happiness.

That doctrine the people themselves long ago engrained

and chiseled into the structure of our National Constitution. It is yet the sanctuary of our freedom, and the sheet anchor of all our liberties, possessing upon this great anniversary the affection and reverence of our citizens. There are evidences of certain sinister influences and minorities now seeking to sap and mine the pillars of this temple of freedom. We may have been too generous in our hospitality to them. We may have been too tolerant of some of their recent manifestations of subversive treachery. We have sought with rather grim patience to respect the guaranty of freedom of speech; but it may be only fair to admonish all such groups that they take counsel of their prudence lest by going one step too far, it will be too late to escape the wrath and indignation of all real Americans.

After such fragmentary observations of our situation and attitude the time and occasion draw our attention back to our fundamental law which authorizes this legislative assembly. We are still officially celebrating the sesquicentennial of the ratification of the Constitution. Our reverence and devotion to that document is augmented by the passing of the years. Its wisdom and philosophy have been tested by the whirlwinds of party passions, fratricidal warfare, and grave economic convulsions. The inspiration of its construction and the tenacity of its existence have fully justified the praise bestowed upon it by Mr. Gladstone, which we should never tire of remembering, in these words:

> As the British Constitution is the most subtle organism which has proceeded from the womb and long gestation of progressive history, so the American Constitution is, so far as I can see, the most wonderful work ever struck off at a given time by the brain and purpose of man.

This anniversary conjures up in a parade of reverie and retrospection many solemn and yet comforting memories. Including the membership of the First Congress and up to the present session of the Seventy-sixth Congress 8,659 different individuals have served in the House and Senate. Eight hundred and sixty-two have served as Senators; 8,106 have served as Representatives; 450 have served in both Houses; 141 have served as Territorial Delegates and Commissioners.

What an intriguing pageant of brain and talent, of individuality and mannerism, of humor and pathos, of provincialism and scholarship! What a thrill of interest and admiration would we of this Congress obtain if we could see and hear many of those stalwarts of the long ago who so enthralled the admiration of their partisans and captivated the idolatry of the masses! What a stimulation of the intellect to peruse the older records of debate between the master minds of other but unforgotten days.

For 138 years such Representatives and Senators have come into these Chambers, played their parts in the drama of representative government, made their contributions of service to their country's progress and development, and then are seen no more — either "beckoned by the pallid messenger with the inverted torch to depart" or returned to the walks of private life from whence they came. They served their day and generation.

To my brethren in both branches of Congress this should be embraced as an occasion of rededication to the best interests of our Republic. Despite the limitations of our judgments and intellects — because, forsooth at no time nor under any administration, have we infallibly measured up to the full needs of the hour — nevertheless, we are the emissaries of our constituencies and the symbols of representative government. May we this day find the grace to renew the prayer of Daniel Webster, deposited in the cornerstone of this wing of the Capitol on July 4, 1851:

> If, therefore, it shall be hereafter the will of God that this structure shall fall from its base, that its foundation be upturned, and

this deposit brought to the eyes of men, be it then known that on this day the Union of the United States of America stands firm, that their Constitution still exists unimpaired and with all its original usefulness and glory; growing every day stronger and stronger in the affections of the great body of the American people and attracting more and more the admiration of the world. And all here assembled, whether belonging to public life or to private life, with hearts devoutly thankful to Almighty God for the preservation of the liberty and happiness of the country, unite in sincere and fervent prayers that this deposit, and the walls and arches, the domes and towers, the columns and entablatures, now to be erected over it, may endure forever!

God save the United States of America!

OUR CHIEF MAGISTRATE
AND HIS POWERS *

WILLIAM HOWARD TAFT

THERE is little danger to the public weal from the tyranny or reckless character of a President who is not sustained by the people. The absence of popular support will certainly in the course of two years withdraw from him the sympathetic action of at least one House of Congress, and by the control that that House has over appropriations, the Executive arm can be paralyzed, unless he resorts to a coup d'état, which means impeachment, conviction and deposition. The only danger in the action of the Executive under the present limitations and lack of limitation of his powers is when his popularity is such that he can be sure of the support of the elector-

---

* This is an excerpt from *Our Chief Magistrate and His Powers*, by William Howard Taft (New York: Columbia University Press; 1916).

ate and therefore of Congress, and when the majority in the legislative halls respond with alacrity and sycophancy to his will. This condition cannot probably be long continued. We have had Presidents who felt the public pulse with accuracy, who played their parts upon the political stage with histrionic genius and commanded the people almost as if they were an army and the President their Commander-in-Chief. Yet in all these cases, the good sense of the people has ultimately prevailed and no danger has been done to our political structure and the reign of law has continued. In such times when the Executive power seems to be all prevailing, there have always been men in this free and intelligent people of ours, who apparently courting political humiliation and disaster have registered protest against this undue Executive domination and this use of the Executive power and popular support to perpetuate itself.

The cry of Executive domination is often entirely unjustified, as when the President's commanding influence only grows out of a proper cohesion of a party and its recognition of the necessity for political leadership; but the fact that Executive domination is regarded as a useful ground for attack upon a successful administration, even when there is no ground for it, is itself proof of the dependence we may properly place upon the sanity and clear perceptions of the people in avoiding its baneful effects when there is real danger. Even if a vicious precedent is set by the Executive, and injustice done, it does not have the same bad effect that an improper precedent of a court may have, for one President does not consider himself bound by the policies or constitutional views of his predecessors.

The Constitution does give the President wide discretion and great power, and it ought to do so. It calls from him activity and energy to see that within his proper sphere he does what his great responsibilities and opportunities require. He is no figurehead, and it is entirely proper that an energetic and active clearsighted people, who, when they have work to do, wish it done well, should be willing to rely upon their judgment in selecting their Chief Agent, and having selected him, should entrust to him all the power needed to carry out their governmental purpose, great as it may be.

$\approx$

MARBURY VS. MADISON *

OPINION BY CHIEF JUSTICE MARSHALL
1803

THE QUESTION, whether an act, repugnant to the constitution, can become the law of the land, is a question deeply interesting to the United States; but, happily, not of an intricacy proportioned to its interest. It seems only necessary to recognize certain principles, supposed to have been long and well established, to decide it.

That the people have an original right to establish, for their future government, such principles, as, in their opinion, shall most conduce to their own happiness is the basis on which the whole American fabric has been erected. The exercise of this original right is a very great exertion; nor can it, nor ought it, to be frequently repeated. The principles, therefore, so established, are deemed fundamental. And as the authority from which they proceed is supreme, and can seldom act, they are designed to be permanent.

This original and supreme will organizes the government,

* This is an excerpt from the decision in the case of Marbury vs. Madison, reported in 1 Cranch 137, 175.

and assigns to different departments their respective powers. It may either stop here, or establish certain limits not to be transcended by those departments.

The government of the United States is of the latter description. The powers of the legislature are defined and limited; and that those limits may not be mistaken, or forgotten, the constitution is written. To what purpose are powers limited, and to what purpose is that limitation committed to writing, if these limits may, at any time, be passed by those intended to be restrained? The distinction between a government with limited and unlimited powers is abolished, if those limits do not confine the persons on whom they are imposed, and if acts prohibited and acts allowed, are of equal obligation. It is a proposition too plain to be contested, that the constitution controls any legislative act repugnant to it; or, that the legislature may alter the constitution by an ordinary act.

Between these alternatives there is no middle ground. The constitution is either a superior paramount law, unchangeable by ordinary means, or it is on a level with ordinary legislative acts, and, like other acts, is alterable when the legislature shall please to alter it.

If the former part of the alternative be true, then a legislative act contrary to the constitution is not law; if the latter part be true, then written constitutions are absurd attempts, on the part of the people, to limit a power in its own nature illimitable.

Certainly all those who have framed written constitutions contemplate them as forming the fundamental and paramount law of the nation, and, consequently, the theory of every such government must be, that an act of the legislature, repugnant to the constitution, is void.

This theory is essentially attached to a written constitution, and is, consequently, to be considered, by this court, as one of the fundamental principles of our society. It is not therefore to be lost sight of in the further consideration of this subject.

If an act of the legislature, repugnant to the constitution, is void, does it, notwithstanding its invalidity, bind the courts, and oblige them to give it effect? Or, in other words, though it be not law, does it constitute a rule as operative as if it was a law? This would be to overthrow in fact what was established in theory; and would seem, at first view, an absurdity too gross to be insisted on. It shall, however, receive a more attentive consideration.

It is emphatically the province and duty of the judicial department to say what the law is. Those who apply the rule to particular cases, must of necessity expound and interpret that rule. If two laws conflict with each other, the courts must decide on the operation of each.

So if a law be in opposition to the constitution; if both the law and the constitution apply to a particular case, so that the court must either decide that case conformably to the law, disregarding the constitution; or conformably to the constitution, disregarding the law; the court must determine which of these conflicting rules governs the case. This is of the very essence of judicial duty.

If, then, the courts are to regard the constitution, and the constitution is superior to any ordinary act of the legislature, the constitution, and not such ordinary act, must govern the case to which they both apply.

Those, then, who controvert the principle that the constitution is to be considered, in court, as a paramount law, are reduced to the necessity of maintaining that courts must close their eyes on the constitution, and see only the law.

This doctrine would subvert the very foundation of all written constitutions. It would declare that an act which, according to the principles and theory of our government, is entirely void, is yet, in practice, completely obligatory. It would declare that if the legislature shall do what is ex-

pressly forbidden, such act, notwithstanding the express prohibition, is in reality effectual. It would be giving to the
legislature a practical and real omnipotence, with the same
breath which professes to restrict their powers within narrow limits. It is prescribing limits, and declaring that those
limits may be passed at pleasure.

That it thus reduces to nothing what we have deemed the
greatest improvement on political institutions, a written constitution, would of itself be sufficient, in America, where
written constitutions have been viewed with so much reverence, for rejecting the construction. But the peculiar expres-
sions of the constitution of the United States furnish additional arguments in favour of its rejection.

The judicial power of the United States is extended to all
cases arising under the constitution.

Could it be the intention of those who gave this power, to
say that in using it the constitution should not be looked
into? That a case arising under the constitution should be
decided without examining the instrument under which it
arises?

This is too extravagant to be maintained.

In some cases, then, the constitution must be looked into
by the judges. And if they can open it at all, what part of it
are they forbidden to read or to obey?

There are many other parts of the constitution which
serve to illustrate this subject.

It is declared that " no tax or duty shall be laid on articles
exported from any state." Suppose a duty on the export of
cotton, of tobacco, or of flour; and a suit instituted to recover
it. Ought judgment to be rendered in such a case? ought the
judges to close their eyes on the constitution, and only see
the law?

The constitution declares " that no bill of attainder or ex
post facto law shall be passed."

If, however, such a bill should be passed, and a person

313

should be prosecuted under it; must the court condemn to death those victims whom the constitution endeavors to preserve?

" No person," says the constitution, " shall be convicted of treason unless on the testimony of two witnesses to the same overt act, or on confession in open court."

Here the language of the constitution is addressed especially to the courts. It prescribes, directly for them, a rule of evidence not to be departed from. If the legislature should change that rule, and declare one witness, or a confession out of court, sufficient for conviction, must the constitutional principle yield to the legislative act?

From these, and many other selections which might be made, it is apparent, that the framers of the constitution contemplated that instrument as a rule for the government of courts, as well as of the legislature.

Why otherwise does it direct the judges to take an oath to support it? This oath certainly applies in an especial manner, to their conduct in their official character. How immoral to impose it on them, if they were to be used as the instruments, and the knowing instruments, for violating what they swear to support!

The oath of office, too, imposed by the legislature, is completely demonstrative of the legislative opinion on this subject. It is in these words: " I do solemnly swear that I will administer justice without respect to persons, and do equal right to the poor and to the rich; and that I will faithfully and impartially discharge all the duties incumbent on me as ——, according to the best of my abilities and understanding agreeably to the constitution and laws of the United States."

Why does a judge swear to discharge his duties agreeably to the constitution of the United States, if that constitution forms no rule for his government? if it is closed upon him, and cannot be inspected by him?

If such be the real state of things, this is worse than solemn mockery. To prescribe, or to take this oath, becomes equally a crime.

It is also not entirely unworthy of observation, that in declaring what shall be the supreme law of the land, the constitution itself is first mentioned; and not the laws of the United States generally, but those only which shall be made in pursuance of the constitution, have that rank.

Thus, the particular phraseology of the constitution of the United States confirms and strengthens the principle, supposed to be essential to all written constitutions, that a law repugnant to the constitution is void; and that courts, as well as other departments, are bound by that instrument.

RESOLUTION OF THE LEGISLATURE OF KENTUCKY RELATIVE TO THE ALIEN AND SEDITION LAWS *

III. RESOLVED, That it is true as a general principle, and is also expressly declared by one of the amendments to the Constitution, that " the powers not delegated to the United States by the Constitution, nor prohibited by it to the States, are reserved to the States respectively, or to the people "; and that no power over the freedom of religion, freedom of

---

* This extract is from Virginia and Kentucky Resolutions, General Assembly House of Delegates.

speech, or freedom of the press being delegated to the United States by the Constitution, nor prohibited by it to the States, all lawful powers respecting the same did of right remain, and were reserved to the States, or to the people: That thus was manifested their determination to retain to themselves the right of judging how far the licentiousness of speech and of the press may be abridged without lessening their useful freedom, and how far those abuses which cannot be separated from their use, should be tolerated rather than the use be destroyed; and thus also they guarded against all abridgement by the United States of the freedom of religious opinions and exercises, and retained to themselves the right of protecting the same, as this State by a law passed on the general demand of its citizens, had already protected them from all human restraint or interference: And that in addition to this general principle and express declaration, another and more special provision has been made by one of the amendments to the Constitution which expressly declares, that " Congress shall make no law respecting an establishment of religion, or prohibiting the free exercise thereof, or abridging the freedom of speech, or of the press," thereby guarding in the same sentence, and under the same words, the freedom of religion, of speech and of the press, insomuch, that whatever violates either, throws down the sanctuary which covers the others, and that libels, falsehoods, and defamation, equally with heresy and false religion, are withheld from the cognizance of federal tribunals. That therefore the act of the Congress of the United States passed on the 14th day of July 1798, entitled " An Act in addition to the act for the punishment of certain crimes against the United States," which does abridge the freedom of the press, is not law, but is altogether void and of no effect.

IV. RESOLVED, That alien friends are under the jurisdiction and protection of the laws of the State wherein they are;

that no power over them has been delegated to the United States, nor prohibited to the individual States distinct from their power over citizens; and it being true as a general principle, and one of the amendments to the Constitution having also declared, that " The powers not delegated to the United States by the Constitution nor prohibited by it to the States are reserved to the States respectively or to the people," the act of the Congress of the United States passed on the 22nd day of June 1798 entitled " An act concerning aliens," which assumes power over alien friends not delegated by the Constitution, is not law, but is altogether void and of no force.

V. RESOLVED, That in addition to the general principle as well as the express declaration, that powers not delegated are reserved, another and more special provision inserted in the Constitution from abundant caution has declared, " That the migration or importation of such persons as any of the States now existing shall think proper to admit, shall not be prohibited by the Congress prior to the year 1808." That this commonwealth does admit the migration of alien friends described as the subject of the said act concerning aliens; that a provision against prohibiting their migration is a provision against all acts equivalent thereto, or it would be nugatory; that to remove them when migrated is equivalent to a prohibition of their migration, and is therefore contrary to the said provision of the Constitution, and void.

VI. RESOLVED, That the imprisonment of a person under the protection of the laws of this Commonwealth on his failure to obey the simple order of the President to depart out of the United States, as is undertaken by the said act entitled " an Act concerning Aliens," is contrary to the Constitution, one amendment to which has provided, that " no person shall be deprived of liberty without due process of law," and that another having provided " That in all criminal prosecutions, the accused shall enjoy the right to a public

317

trial by an impartial jury, to be informed of the nature and cause of the accusation, to be confronted with the witnesses against him, to have compulsory process for obtaining witnesses in his favor, and to have the assistance of counsel for his defence," the same act undertaking to authorize the President to remove a person out of the United States who is under the protection of the law, on his own suspicion, without accusation, without jury, without public trail, without confrontation of the witnesses against him, without having witnesses in his favor, without defence, without counsel, is contrary to these provisions also of the Constitution, is therefore not law, but utterly void and of no force.

That transferring the power of judging any person who is under the protection of the laws, from the Courts to the President of the United States, as is undertaken by the same act concerning aliens, is against the article of the Constitution which provides, that "The judicial power of the United States shall be vested in Courts, the Judges of which shall hold their offices during good behavior," and that the said act is void for that reason also; and it is further to be noted, that this transfer of judiciary power is to that magistrate of the General Government who already possesses all the Executive, and a qualified negative in all the Legislative powers.

VII. RESOLVED, That the construction applied by the General Government (as is evinced by sundry of their proceedings) to those parts of the Constitution of the United States which delegate to Congress a power to lay and collect taxes, duties, imposts, and excises; to pay the debts, and provide for the common defence, and general welfare of the United States, and to make all laws which shall be necessary and proper for carrying into execution the powers vested by the Constitution in the Government of the United States, or any department thereof, goes to the destruction of all the limits prescribed to their power by the Constitution — That words meant by that instrument to be subsidiary only to the execution of the limited powers, ought not to be so construed as themselves to give unlimited powers, nor a part so to be taken, as to destroy the whole residue of the instrument: That the proceedings of the General Government under color of these articles, will be a fit and necessary subject for revisal and correction, at a time of greater tranquillity, while those specified in the preceding resolutions call for immediate redress.

VIII. RESOLVED, That the preceding resolutions be transmitted to the Senators and Representatives in Congress from this Commonwealth who are hereby enjoined to present the same to their respective Houses, and to use their best endeavors to procure at the next session of Congress, a repeal of the aforesaid unconstitutional and obnoxious acts.

~~~~~~

UNEMPLOYMENT AND RELIEF[*]

EXCERPTS FROM THE REPORT OF THE SPECIAL COMMITTEE TO INVESTIGATE UNEMPLOYMENT AND RELIEF

IN the expenditure of public funds to relieve the hardships of unemployment, the committee feels that reliance must be had on the following: (1) unemployment compensation; (2) public assistance; (3) public work.

All three of these programs have already been inaugu-

---

[*] This material consists of excerpts from the Senate Majority Report (Pursuant to S. Res. 36, 75th Cong.) of the Special Committee to Investigate Unemployment and Relief, filed January 14, 1939.

rated in the United States. The committee has examined the current operation of them and recommends certain amendments to the end that they may be of maximum effectiveness.

Unemployment compensation is designed to provide for workers during periods of sudden or temporary unemployment. Public assistance should have the effect of providing security and support for old people, children, and handicapped persons. Public work should provide employment and a means of livelihood for unemployed workers at times when and as long as private industry cannot use their service. . . .

The increased unemployment compensation benefits urged as the first line of defense would greatly reduce the number of unemployed seeking relief or work on account of temporary lay-offs.

A program of public work should be provided for the unemployed not covered by unemployment compensation or whose unemployment benefits are exhausted and for whom private employment is not available.

A work program, however, should not be expected to suddenly expand in order to take care of a great increase in unemployment caused by an unexpected recession in business. Unemployment compensation should be the source of financial help to the worker who loses his job because of a falling off in general business. At the appropriate time the Federal work program can be increased so as to provide additional work.

Each year the Budget, in the light of existing conditions, can set forth the amount of money it is deemed advisable to allot to public work in cooperation with the States and local governments. The allotments should be based upon the population of the States as determined by the census, and upon the number of unemployed in the various States as ascertained by the Unemployment Census of 1937 until such time as the Employment Service is able to currently supply such information.

For those projects which are known as Federal projects the entire cost would naturally be paid from Federal funds.

On all other projects, which would be prosecuted in co-operation with the States, cities, and counties or other public bodies, it is essential that some formula be devised so that the cost of them shall be shared by the national and local governments on a uniform basis. The percentage of cost paid by local governments on projects of the Works Progress Administration is at present approximately 22 percent. The percentage of cost paid by local governments on projects of the Public Works Administration is 55 percent. It is recommended that in future the formula be that two-thirds of the total cost of projects in a State be borne by the Federal Government and one-third by the local government; provided that in States where the average per capita income is less than the average per capita income in the entire United States the local contribution to projects in those States shall be proportionately reduced. This does not mean that the same percentage of the cost of each project should be paid by local governments. To require a sharing of cost on each project would make for too great rigidity. It is sufficient if this percentage of cost-sharing prevail for the entire group of projects, aside from Federal projects, undertaken within a State, the percentage of cost to be paid by the local government for each project within the State to be determined by the State director.

We now have Public Works Administration and Works Progress Administration engaged in public works. Regardless of what may be the intention of those in charge of administration, there will always be competition between the representatives of the two organizations for the most desirable projects. Public Works Administration offers a grant of 45 percent and requires a contribution of 55 percent in cash or obligations of the local government. Works Progress Administration asks of sponsors an average contribution of 22 percent instead of 55 percent.

The two agencies are engaged in construction of public buildings of the same character. The local governments which often assert that they cannot make a contribution of 22 percent or its equivalent for Works Progress Administration projects, have within the past few months contracted to put up 55 percent for Public Works Administration projects, for which the last Congress appropriated one and a half billion dollars, and are clamoring for a billion dollars more of Federal funds on the basis of 55–45.

We should have one public-work program, administered preferably by a Department of Public Work. If this is not practicable, then by a Division of Public Works in an existing department. The State or city that asks Federal officials to approve a project, expressing its willingness to contribute 55 percent of a project, could not well declare to the same officials its inability to make a contribution of 33⅓ percent in cash or the equivalent in materials for another project. When local officials can go to two different departments to secure approval of projects, they can have two different stories. When they must go to one department, there can be but one story.

As long as we regarded unemployment as an emergency problem we could excuse the continuance of emergency agencies. There is now a necessity for a coordinated program. We cannot continue to permit the unemployed worker to apply for unemployment compensation only to learn after some weeks that the amount to which he is entitled is $2.79 per week; then have him apply for public work only to be informed that he is eligible for unemployment benefits and therefore may not have a job; and thereby force him to go to the relief office of the city or State for direct relief.

322

There should be one office where unemployment benefits will be granted and where the Employment Service will aid a man to secure private employment. There should also be a Department of Public Work providing a work program based upon current advices as to unemployment throughout the Nation. Through the same office, workers for whom private employment is not available should be assigned to a job on a work program conducted by a Department of Public Work. By the merging of organizations engaged in the same work, great savings can be effected in administration costs.

Projects conducted by the Department of Public Works should be of a public nature. They may be let to contract or conducted on force account depending upon the character of the project.

The Civilian Conservation Corps and the National Youth Administration are temporary organizations designed to give work opportunities and training to unemployed young men and boys of working age. It seems to the committee that the work of these two agencies should be coordinated and placed under the direction of the Department of Public Work. This seems appropriate in view of the fact that the youth in both agencies are either engaged in public work or receiving training designed to prepare them for private employment.

The directing head of the Federal Public Work Program should be appointed by the President and confirmed by the Senate for a definite term and his duties should be defined by law. His principal subordinates should also be so appointed and confirmed. Thus the identity and tenure of all officials who shape the policy of the program within the limits of legal authority will be fixed by the President and the Senate according to the accepted constitutional mandate.

All other administrative and supervisory personnel

should be chosen from lists prepared by the Civil Service Commission.

In those sections of the country affected at times by drought of such serious character as to destroy hope of earning an income upon which to live, and where there is necessarily a limited number of work projects upon which men can be employed without leaving the communities in which they reside, provision should be made for adequate relief through the Farm Security Administration in loans or in loans and grants to relieve the hardships of unemployment until the worker again has an opportunity to earn an income. . . .

The committee renews the recommendation made in its former report that benefit payments, which under the contributory old-age insurance system begin in 1942, be commenced in 1940. The funds will be available. The payment of benefits would mean that older workers would be retired from the labor market to make way for younger workers awaiting jobs. . . .

The majority of the members of the Committee on Unemployment and Relief have not believed an investigation into so-called political activity of the Works Progress Administration was within the scope or purpose of the resolution authorizing the committee.

The committee has studiously refrained from entering into any investigation or discussion of irregularities in the Works Progress Administration, nor has it sought to examine into any charge of misuse of relief funds.

The committee has believed its purpose concerned the broad, general questions of unemployment and reemployment as the major study. Relief has been accepted as something which flows from unemployment, it being the pain rather than the disease itself. Nevertheless, in view of current discussions, the committee believes it should make some recommendations concerning political activity in the administration of relief. . . .

| JAMES F. BYRNES, | CARL A. HATCH, |
| BENNETT C. CLARK, | LYNN J. FRAZIER. |

I concur in the entire report, with the exception of the provision as to a formula for the distribution of public-work funds, on which question I withhold my determination for the present.

JAMES E. MURRAY.

THE SOCIAL SECURITY ACT IN
OPERATION *

On April 19, 1935, the House of Representatives passed the Doughton Bill, or H. R. 7260, by a non-partisan majority of 372 to 33. Two months later the Senate passed the same bill by as overwhelming a vote, 77 to 6. After a series of conferences on amendments inserted by both houses, the bill was accepted in its final form on August 8 and 9. On August 14, 1935, it was signed by the President and became law as the Social Security Act. . . .

Meanwhile, most European countries and some of the

* This material is from the first chapter of *The Social Security Act in Operation*, by Birchard E. Wyatt, Ph.D., and William H. Wandel, Ph.D., in collaboration with William L. Schurz, Ph.D., copyright, 1937, by the Graphic Arts Press, Inc.

South American republics already had in operation comprehensive programs of social insurance. In fact, that of Germany dated from 1889. France had had an old-age insurance law since 1911. . . .

It required the industrial cataclysm of the early thirties to give the necessary impetus to the movement in the United States. . . .

Not even in relatively prosperous times is the average worker able to accumulate enough to assure himself and his wife of subsistence in their old age. As a rule, he can look forward only to dependency, in one form or another, either upon his children or upon charity. A man at 65 can expect about 12 more years of life; a woman, 15 more years. To provide a monthly income of $25 for these remaining years, a man must have saved about $3,300, a woman about $3,600. Only a minority have built up even so small a reserve against the unproductive years. . . .

As with old age, so with childhood. Through loss of parental support by death, disability, or desertion of the family breadwinner, or from other circumstances, juvenile dependency had become a major social problem. The costs to society in material and moral values of such a condition were very high. . . .

Though unemployment had always been with us, even in the best of times, it had never assumed such proportions as it did in the early thirties. In the relatively prosperous years from 1922 to 1929 an average of 8 percent of all industrial workers were jobless. At the lowest the number never fell under 1,500,000. By the depth of the depression it had probably risen to between 15,000,000 and 16,000,000. Approximately one-third of all normally gainful workers were unemployed in 1933. In Michigan nearly half were without work and in Pennsylvania over 40 percent. The situation was beyond any of the halting techniques ordinarily resorted to in the past and clearly demanded against its future recurrence some more permanent protection than was afforded by payment of relief. . . .

In spite of its manifest incompleteness, the Social Security Act provides a well-rounded framework for a national program of social insurance. It makes no pretensions to completeness or finality, and assumes that subsequent amendment will be inevitable and necessary as experience demonstrates its inadequacies or permits a broadened scope. However, it constitutes a sound foundation for dealing with problems too urgent to await legal perfection. Meanwhile, it assumes that the future may be trusted to take care of such administrative difficulties as are certain to arise in the course of its operation. For the time being a working plan was made ready for use. . . .

While provision is made in the Social Security Act against three of the major misfortunes of life — juvenile and old-age dependency, and unemployment — certain other features common to foreign social insurance systems are omitted. Thus, in the general field of physical disability, except for the assistance provisions made for the needy blind, the approach is toward prevention or therapy. . . .

Among the major issues which remain for future determination are (1) extension of the coverage of the Federal old-age benefits program to some of the classes at present excluded; (2) the inclusion of health and invalidity insurance; (3) the soundness of the old-age benefits plan, and of the Old-Age Reserve Account as a fiscal device; (4) the most suitable scales of assistance grants and benefit payments; and (5) the proper adjustment of the elaborate Federal-State relationships involved in the program. These are controversial matters which can be resolved only by Congressional action. Among the larger administrative problems which have already developed are (1) the most satisfactory methods for the collection of the Federal taxes required under the old-age benefits and unemployment compensation plans; (2) the practicability of the wage-records system used by the Bureau of Old-Age Insurance; and (3) the proper degree of administrative decentralization of the three operating Bureaus.

~~~~~~

EXCERPTS FROM "UNION LABOR AND THE ENLIGHTENED EMPLOYER"

SAMUEL GOMPERS
JUNE, 1921

The Struggle for Rights

IF EMPLOYERS, investors and the various kinds of retainers and aspirants for place and power who make up what is known as the employing world are determined to restrict or destroy rights which the working people consider essential then it must be clear that the organizations of the working people will form the line of opposition to the employers.

The line has been so formed. The struggle today is for workshop rights, for the extension of workshop democracy, for the development of a workshop program that shall be in keeping with the democratic principles that form the basis of our political organization.

Even when the enemies of labor have sought to use the political machinery for the limitation of rights of workers, the struggle is essentially a workshop struggle, for all of the restrictive and coercive legislation against which labor protests is calculated to converge on the workshop, affecting what there transpires.

The trade union objects to much that employers are doing and trying to do today, not because American labor has any dogmatic opposition to employers per se, but because labor believes thoroughly that there is a better way, not only for labor, but for all and it believes that better way is that proposed by the labor movement.

There is no mystery about what labor proposes. There is nothing involved or devious about it. Labor, being at all times close to the elementals of life, thinks from point to point, in direct line. Labor does not have its being in the realms of " deals " and " schemes " and " shrewd " moves. It takes raw materials and makes finished products. It uses tools to gain definite results. It is seldom possible to misunderstand labor. The pursuits of men have more than a little to do with their manner of expression.

There was an excellent illustration of this thought in the president's first industrial conference. The labor delegation submitted its program. It stated a definite principle in plain language. The employers spent days trying to " compromise " by means of getting language that would look like what labor had said but that would mean what the employers wanted it to mean. They were hunting for a collection of words that would take the color of whatever book they might later find themselves in, binding the employers to nothing, or everything, as the case might be.

Organization the First Essential

The trade union movement believes that organization of workers is the first essential to progress and freedom in the modern world. Workers must be able to organize freely because individually the workman today has no voice with which to call attention to grievances and no power or agency through which to secure redress.

The second essential is the right of workers to act in their organized capacity — to negotiate as organized bodies, to be represented by representatives of their own choosing, to enter into agreements and to withhold service and patronage.

The exercise of these rights in modern industry is nothing more than the application of the constitutional bill of rights to the conditions of our time.

The right to speak and write freely, the right to assemble in peace and to petition government for the redress of wrongs, the right to be represented by counsel and above all, the right to life, liberty and the pursuit of happiness — these are the guarantees upon which the labor movement stakes its right to existence.

Against these the more brutal employers frequently invoke the right to bear arms, which right they then proceed to exercise by proxy.

Having set forth the essential rights of the workers in industry, it is proper to explain labor's purposes as an organized participant in industry. It is the contention of some that labor seeks only its own satisfaction and makes no contribution in return. This is wholly untrue.

Labor believes that the agreement between workers and employers, negotiated in conference, based upon experience and operating to secure justice, is the most important contract in all human relations today. It is reciprocal instead of one-sided. It gives the largest possible measure of justice to the workers and it gives a guarantee of stability and cooperation to industry. Only when there is an agreement, freely entered into by the workers, writing into definite terms their obligations and their rights, can there be the highest free contributions of human labor energy to industry. The agreement is the channel through which labor pours into industry its greatest effort, its most intelligent effort, its constructive thought. But more than that, it is the document through which complete revolution is wrought in the principle of conduct in industry. From the moment in which workers and employer negotiate and agree upon terms, hours, conditions and wages, the principle of autocratic domination gives way to the principle of democratic operation. That is the vital point in the whole question of labor relations and it is precisely that point that arbitrary and reactionary employers fear to pass. King John before them struggled over the same principle. King George the First struggled over the same principle. The late Czar and the ex-Kaiser did likewise. Every great force that has stood against this principle has, in the great hour of decision, been compelled to give away.

THE MONROE DOCTRINE

EXCERPTS FROM THE SEVENTH ANNUAL MESSAGE OF PRESIDENT JAMES MONROE, DECEMBER 2, 1823

. . . In the discussions to which this interest has given rise and in the arrangements by which they may terminate the occasion has been judged proper for asserting, as a principle in which the rights and interests of the United States are involved, that the American continents, by the free and independent condition which they have assumed and maintain, are henceforth not to be considered as subjects for future colonization by any European powers.

. . . In the wars of the European powers in matters relating to themselves we have never taken any part, nor does it comport with our policy so to do. It is only when our rights are invaded or seriously menaced that we resent injuries or make preparation for our defense. With the movements in this hemisphere we are of necessity more immediately connected, and by causes which must be obvious to all enlightened and impartial observers. . . . We owe it, therefore, to candor and to the amicable relations existing between the United States and those powers to declare that we should consider any attempt on their part to extend their system to any portion of this hemisphere as dangerous to our peace and safety. With the existing colonies or dependencies of any European power we have not interfered and shall not interfere. But with the Governments who have declared their independence and maintained it, and whose independence we have, on great consideration and on just principles, acknowledged, we could not view any interposition for the purpose of oppressing them, or controlling in any other manner their destiny, by any European power in any other light than as the manifestation of an unfriendly disposition toward the United States. . . .

. . . Our policy in regard to Europe, which was adopted at an early stage of the wars which have so long agitated that quarter of the globe, nevertheless remains the same, which is, not to interfere in the internal concerns of any of its powers; to consider the government de facto as the legitimate government for us; to cultivate friendly relations with it, and to preserve those relations by a frank, firm, and manly policy, meeting in all instances the just claims of every power, submitting to injuries from none. . . .

EXCERPT FROM GEORGE WASHING-
TON'S FAREWELL ADDRESS

SEPTEMBER 17, 1796

OBSERVE good faith and justice toward all nations. Cultivate peace and harmony with all. Religion and morality enjoin this conduct. And can it be that good policy does not equally enjoin it? It will be worthy of a free, enlightened, and at no distant period a great nation to give to mankind the magnanimous and too novel example of a people always guided by an exalted justice and benevolence. Who can doubt that in the course of time and things the fruits of such a plan would richly repay any temporary advantages which might be lost by a steady adherence to it? Can it be that Providence has not connected the permanent felicity of a nation with its virtue? The experiment, at least, is recommended by every sentiment which ennobles human nature. Alas! is it rendered impossible by its vices?

In the execution of such a plan nothing is more essential than that permanent, inveterate antipathies against particular nations and passionate attachments for others should be excluded, and that in place of them just and amicable feelings toward all should be cultivated. The nation which indulges toward another an habitual hatred or an habitual fondness is in some degree a slave. It is a slave to its animosity or to its affection, either of which is sufficient to lead it astray from its duty and its interest. Antipathy in one nation against another disposes each more readily to offer insult and injury, to lay hold of slight causes of umbrage, and to be haughty and intractable when accidental or trifling occasions of dispute occur.

Hence frequent collisions, obstinate, envenomed, and

333

bloody contests. The nation prompted by ill will and resentment sometimes impels to war the government contrary to the best calculations of policy. The government
sometimes participates in the national propensity, and
adopts through passion what reason would reject. At other
times it makes the animosity of the nation subservient to
projects of hostility, instigated by pride, ambition, and other
sinister and pernicious motives. The peace often, sometimes perhaps the liberty, of nations has been the victim.

So, likewise, a passionate attachment of one nation for
another produces a variety of evils. Sympathy for the favorite nation, facilitating the illusion of an imaginary common
interest in cases where no real common interest exists, and
infusing into one the enmities of the other, betrays the
former into a participation in the quarrels and wars of the
latter without adequate inducement or justification. It leads
also to concessions to the favorite nation of privileges denied to others, which is apt doubly to injure the nation
making the concessions by unnecessarily parting with what
ought to have been retained, and by exciting jealousy, ill
will, and a disposition to retaliate in the parties from whom
equal privileges are withheld; and it gives to ambitious,
corrupted, or deluded citizens (who devote themselves to
the favorite nation) facility to betray or sacrifice the interests of their own country without odium, sometimes even
with popularity, gilding with the appearances of a virtuous
sense of obligation, a commendable deference for public
opinion, or a laudable zeal for public good the base or fool-
ish compliances of ambition, corruption, or infatuation.

As avenues to foreign influence in innumerable ways,
such attachments are particularly alarming to the truly
enlightened and independent patriot. How many opportunities do they afford to tamper with domestic factions, to
practice the arts of seduction, to mislead public opinion, to
influence or awe the public councils! Such an attachment of

a small or weak toward a great and powerful nation dooms the former to be the satellite of the latter. Against the insidious wiles of foreign influence (I conjure you to believe me, fellow-citizens) the jealousy of a free people ought to be constantly awake, since history and experience prove that foreign influence is one of the most baneful foes of republican government. But that jealousy, to be useful, must be impartial, else it becomes the instrument of the very influence to be avoided, instead of a defense against it. Excessive partiality for one foreign nation and excessive dislike of another cause those whom they actuate to see danger only on one side, and serve to veil and even second the arts of influence on the other. Real patriots who may resist the intrigues of the favorite are liable to become suspected and odious, while its tools and dupes usurp the applause and confidence of the people to surrender their interests.

The great rule of conduct for us in regard to foreign nations is, in extending our commercial relations to have with them as little political connection as possible. So far as we have already formed engagements let them be fulfilled with perfect good faith. Here let us stop.

Europe has a set of primary interests which to us have none or a very remote relation. Hence she must be engaged in frequent controversies, the causes of which are essentially foreign to our concerns. Hence, therefore, it must be unwise in us to implicate ourselves by artificial ties in the ordinary vicissitudes of her politics or the ordinary combinations and collisions of her friendships or enmities.

Our detached and distant situation invites and enables us to pursue a different course. If we remain one people, under an efficient government, the period is not far off when we may defy material injury from external annoyance; when we may take such an attitude as will cause the neutrality we may at any time resolve upon to be scrupulously respected; when belligerent nations, under the impossibility of making acquisitions upon us, will not lightly hazard the giving us provocation; when we may choose peace or war, as our interest, guided by justice, shall counsel.

Why forego the advantages of so peculiar a situation? Why quit our own to stand upon foreign ground? Why, by interweaving our destiny with that of any part of Europe, entangle our peace and prosperity in the toils of European ambition, rivalship, interest, humor, or caprice?

It is our true policy to steer clear of permanent alliances with any portion of the foreign world, so far, I mean, as we are now at liberty to do it; for let me not be understood as capable of patronizing infidelity to existing engagements. I hold the maxim no less applicable to public than to private affairs that honesty is always the best policy. I repeat, therefore, let those engagements be observed in their genuine sense. But in my opinion it is unnecessary and would be unwise to extend them.

Taking care always to keep ourselves by suitable establishments on a respectable defensive posture, we may safely trust to temporary alliances for extraordinary emergencies.

Harmony, liberal intercourse with all nations are recommended by policy, humanity, and interest. But even our commercial policy should hold an equal and impartial hand, neither seeking nor granting exclusive favors or preferences; consulting the natural course of things; diffusing and diversifying by gentle means the streams of commerce, but forcing nothing; establishing with powers so disposed, in order to give trade a stable course, to define the rights of our merchants, and to enable the Government to support them, conventional rules of intercourse, the best that present circumstances and mutual opinion will permit, but temporary and liable to be from time to time abandoned or varied as experience and circumstances shall dictate; constantly keeping in view that it is folly in one nation to look for disinterested favors from another; that it must pay with a portion of its independence for whatever it may accept under that character; that by such acceptance it may place itself in the condition of having given equivalents for nominal favors, and yet of being reproached with ingratitude for not giving more. There can be no greater error than to expect or calculate upon real favors from nation to nation. It is an illusion which experience must cure, which a just pride ought to discard.

ADDRESS BY THE CHIEF JUSTICE OF THE UNITED STATES*

CHARLES EVANS HUGHES

MARCH 4, 1939

MR. PRESIDENT, Mr. Vice President, Mr. Speaker, Members of the Senate and House of Representatives, members of the Diplomatic Corps, ladies and gentlemen:

I thank Senator Barkley from the depths of my heart for his very generous words.

Gentlemen of the Senate and House of Representatives, the most significant fact in connection with this anniversary is that after 150 years, notwithstanding expansion of territory, enormous increase in population, and profound economic changes, despite direct attack and subversive influ-

---

* Delivered before both Houses of Congress, March 4th, 1939, on the occasion of the 150th anniversary of the first Congress, and reprinted from the *Congressional Record*.

ences, there is every indication that the vastly preponderant sentiment of the American people is that our form of government shall be preserved.

We come from our distinct departments of governmental activity to testify to our unity of aim in maintaining that form of government in accordance with our common pledge. We are here not as masters but as servants, not to glory in power but to attest our loyalty to the commands and restrictions laid down by our sovereign, the people of the United States, in whose name and by whose will we exercise our brief authority. If as such representatives we have, as Benjamin Franklin said, "no more durable preeminence than the different grains in an hour glass," we serve our hour by unremitting devotion to the principles which have given our Government both stability and capacity for orderly progress in a world of turmoil and revolutionary upheavals. Gratifying as is the record of achievement, it would be extreme folly to engage in mere laudation or to surrender to the enticing delusions of a thoughtless optimism. Forms of government, however well contrived, cannot assure their own permanence. If we owe to the wisdom and restraint of the fathers a system of government which has thus far stood the test, we all recognize that it is only by wisdom and restraint in our own day that we can make that system last. If today we find ground for confidence that our institutions which have made for liberty and strength will be maintained, it will not be due to abundance of physical resources or to productive capacity, but because these are at the command of a people who still cherish the principles which underlie our system and because of the general appreciation of what is essentially sound in our governmental structure.

With respect to the influences which shape public opinion, we live in a new world. Never have these influences operated more directly, or with such variety of facile instruments, or with such overwhelming force. We have mass production in opinion as well as in goods. The grasp of tradition and of sectional prejudgment is loosened. Postulates of the past must show cause. Our institutions will not be preserved by veneration of what is old, if that is simply expressed in the formal ritual of a shrine. The American people are eager and responsive. They listen attentively to a vast multitude of appeals and, with this receptivity, it is only upon their sound judgment that we can base our hope for a wise conservatism with continued progress and appropriate adaptation to new needs.

We shall do well on this anniversary if the thought of the people is directed to the essentials of our democracy. Here in this body we find the living exponents of the principle of representative government — not government by direct mass action but by representation which means leadership as well as responsiveness and accountability.

Here the ground swells of autocracy, destructive of parliamentary independence, have not yet upset or even disturbed the authority and responsibility of the essential legislative branch of democratic institutions. We have a National Government equipped with vast powers which have proved to be adequate to the development of a great nation, and at the same time maintaining the balance between centralized authority and local autonomy. It has been said that to preserve that balance, if we did not have States we should have to create them. In our 48 States we have the separate sources of power necessary to protect local interests and thus also to preserve the central authority, in the vast variety of our concerns, from breaking down under its own weight. Our States, each with her historic background and supported by the loyal sentiment of her citizens, afford opportunity for the essential activity of political units, the advantages of which no artificial territorial arrangement could secure. If our checks and balances sometimes prevent the speedy action which is thought desirable, they also assure in the long run a more deliberate judgment. And what the people really want, they generally get. With the ultimate power of change through amendment in their hands they are always able to obtain whatever a preponderant and abiding sentiment demands.

We not only praise individual liberty but our constitutional system has the unique distinction of insuring it. Our guaranties of fair trials, of due process in the protection of life, liberty, and property — which stands between the citizen and arbitrary power — of religious freedom, of free speech, free press and free assembly, are the safeguards which have been erected against the abuses threatened by gusts of passion and prejudice which in misguided zeal would destroy the basic interests of democracy. We protect the fundamental right of minorities, in order to save democratic government from destroying itself by the excesses of its own power. The firmest ground for confidence in the future is that more than ever we realize that, while democracy must have its organization and controls, its vital breath is individual liberty.

I am happy to be here as the representative of the tribunal which is charged with the duty of maintaining, through the decision of controversies, these constitutional guaranties. We are a separate but not an independent arm of government. You, not we, have the purse and the sword. You, not we, determine the establishment and the jurisdiction of the lower Federal courts and the bounds of the appellate jurisdiction of the Supreme Court. The Congress first assembled on March 4, 1789, and on September 24, 1789, as its twentieth enactment, passed the Judiciary Act — to establish the judicial courts of the United States — a statute which is a monument of wisdom, one of the most satisfactory acts in the long history of notable congressional legislation. It may be said to take rank in our annals as next in importance to the Constitution itself.

In thus providing the judicial establishment, and in equipping and sustaining it, you have made possible the effective functioning of the department of government which is designed to safeguard with judicial impartiality and independence the interests of liberty. But in the great enterprise of making democracy workable we are all partners. One member of our body politic cannot say to another: "I have no need of thee." We work in successful cooperation by being true, each department to its own functions, and all to the spirit which pervades our institutions, exalting the processes of reason, seeking through the very limitations of power the security of life, liberty, and the pursuant of happiness, and promotion of the wise use of power, and finding the ultimate the promise of continued stability and a rational progress in the good sense of the American people.

THE FEDERALIST No. 1

(ALEXANDER HAMILTON)

To the People of the State of New York:

After an unequivocal experience of the inefficiency of the subsisting federal government, you are called upon to deliberate on a new Constitution for the United States of America. The subject speaks its own importance; comprehending in its consequences nothing less than the existence of the UNION, the safety and welfare of the parts of which it is composed, the fate of an empire in many respects the most interesting in the world. It has been frequently remarked that it seems to have been reserved to the people of this country, by their conduct and example, to decide the important question, whether societies of men are really capable or not of establishing good government from reflection and choice, or whether they are forever destined to depend for their political constitutions on accident and force. If there be any truth in the remark, the crisis at which we are arrived may with propriety be regarded as the era in which that decision is to be made; and a wrong election of the part we shall act may, in this view, deserve to be considered as the general misfortune of mankind.

This idea will add the inducements of philanthropy to those of patriotism, to heighten the solicitude which all considerate and good men must feel for the event. Happy will it be if our choice should be directed by a judicious estimate of our true interest, unperplexed and unbiased by considerations not connected with the public good. But this is a thing more ardently to be wished than seriously to be expected. The plan offered to our deliberations affects too many particular interests, innovates upon too many local institutions, not to involve in its discussion a variety of objects foreign to its merits, and of views, passions and prejudices little favorable to the discovery of truth.

Among the most formidable of the obstacles which the new Constitution will have to encounter may readily be distinguished the obvious interest of a certain class of men in every State to resist all changes which may hazard a diminution of the power, emolument, and consequence of the offices they hold under the State establishments; and the perverted ambition of another class of men, who will either hope to aggrandize themselves by the confusion of their country, or will flatter themselves with fairer prospects of elevation from the subdivision of the empire into several partial confederacies than from its union under one government.

It is not, however, my design to dwell upon observations of this nature. I am well aware that it would be disingenuous to resolve indiscriminately the opposition of any set of men (merely because their situations might subject them to suspicion) into interested or ambitious views. Candor will oblige us to admit that even such men may be actuated by upright intentions; and it cannot be doubted that much of the opposition which has made its appearance, or may hereafter make its appearance, will spring from sources, blameless at least, if not respectable — the honest errors of minds led astray by preconceived jealousies and fears. So numerous indeed and so powerful are the causes which serve to give a false bias to the judgement, that we, upon many occasions, see wise and good men on the wrong as well as on the right side of questions of the first magnitude to society. This circumstance, if duly attended to, would furnish a lesson of moderation to those who are ever so much persuaded of their being in the right in any controversy. And a further reason for caution, in this respect, might be drawn from the reflection that we are not always sure that those who advocate the truth are influenced by purer principles than their antagonists. Ambition, avarice, personal animosity, party opposition, and many other motives not more laudable than these, are apt to operate as well upon those who support as those who oppose the right side of a question. Were there not even inducements to moderation, nothing could be more ill-judged than that intolerant spirit which has, at all times, characterized political parties. For in politics, as in religion, it is equally absurd to aim at making proselytes by fire and sword. Heresies in either can rarely be cured by persecution.

And yet, however just these sentiments will be allowed to be, we have already sufficient indications that it will happen in this as in all former cases of great national discussion. A torrent of angry and malignant passions will be let loose. To

343

judge from the conduct of the opposite parties, we shall be led to conclude that they will mutually hope to evince the justness of their opinions, and to increase the number of their converts by the loudness of their declamations and the bitterness of their invectives. An enlightened zeal for the energy and efficiency of government will be stigmatized as the offspring of a temper fond of despotic power and hostile to the principles of liberty. An over-scrupulous jealousy of danger to the rights of the people, which is more commonly the fault of the head than of the heart, will be represented as mere pretence and artifice, the stale bait for popularity at the expense of the public good. It will be forgotten, on the one hand, that jealousy is the usual concomitant of love, and that the noble enthusiasm of liberty is apt to be infected with a spirit of narrow and illiberal distrust. On the other hand, it will be equally forgotten that the vigor of government is essential to the security of liberty; that, in the contemplation of a sound and well-informed judgement, their interest can never be separated; and that a dangerous ambition more often lurks behind the specious mask of zeal for the rights of the people than under the forbidding appearance of zeal for the firmness and efficiency of government. History will teach us that the former has been found a much more certain road to the introduction of despotism than the latter, and that of those men who have overturned the liberties of republics the greatest number have begun their career by paying an obsequious court to the people; commencing demagogues, and ending tyrants.

In the course of the preceding observations, I have had an eye, my fellow-citizens, to putting you upon your guard against all attempts, from whatever quarter, to influence your decision in a matter of the utmost moment to your welfare, by any impressions other than those which may result from the evidence of truth. You will, no doubt, at the same time, have collected from the general scope of them, that they proceed from a source not unfriendly to the new Constitution. Yes, my countrymen, I own to you that, after having given it an attentive consideration, I am clearly of opinion it is your interest to adopt it. I am convinced that this is the safest course for your liberty, your dignity, and your happiness. I affect not reserves which I do not feel. I will not amuse you with an appearance of deliberation when I have decided. I frankly acknowledge to you my convictions, and I will freely lay before you the reasons on which they are founded. The consciousness of good intentions disdains ambiguity. I shall not, however, multiply professions on this head. My motives must remain in the depository of my own breast. My arguments will be open to all, and may be judged of by all. They shall at least be offered in a spirit which will not disgrace the cause of truth.

I propose, in a series of papers, to discuss the following interesting particulars: — *The Utility of the UNION to your political prosperity — The insufficiency of the present Confederation to preserve that Union — The necessity of a government at least equally energetic with the one proposed, to the attainment of this object — The conformity of the proposed Constitution to the true principles of republican government — Its analogy to your own State constitution* — and lastly, *The additional security which its adoption will afford to the preservation of that species of government, to liberty, and to property.*

In the progress of this discussion I shall endeavor to give a satisfactory answer to all the objections which shall have made their appearance, that may seem to have any claim to your attention.

It may perhaps be thought superfluous to offer arguments to prove the utility of the UNION, a point, no doubt, deeply engraved on the hearts of the great body of the people in every State, and one, which it may be imagined, has no adversaries. But the fact is, that we already hear it whispered in the private circles of those who oppose the new Constitution, that the thirteen States are of too great extent for any general system, and that we must of necessity resort to separate confederacies of distinct portions of the whole. This doctrine will, in all probability, be gradually propagated, till it has votaries enough to countenance an open avowal of it. For nothing can be more evident, to those who are able to take an enlarged view of the subject, than the alternative of an adoption of the new Constitution or a dismemberment of the Union. It will therefore be of use to begin by examining the advantages of that Union, the certain evils, and the probable dangers, to which every State will be exposed from its dissolution. This shall accordingly constitute the subject of my next address.

PUBLIUS

INDEX

INDEX

iv

A NOTE ON THE TYPE

This book is set in Caledonia, a new Linotype face designed by W. A. Dwiggins. Caledonia belongs to the family of printing types called " modern face " by printers — a term used to mark the change in style of type-letters that occurred about 1800. Caledonia is in the general neighborhood of Scotch Modern in design, but is more freely drawn than that letter.

The book was composed, printed and bound by The Plimpton Press, Norwood, Massachusetts. The paper was made by S. D. Warren Company, Boston. The typography and binding are after designs by W. A. Dwiggins.